Early Adopter VoiceXML

Eve Astrid Andersson
Stephen Breitenbach
Tyler Burd
Nirmal Chidambaram
Paul Houle
Daniel Newsome
Xiaofei Tang
Xiaolan Zhu

Wrox Press Ltd. ®

Early Adopter VoiceXML

Published by Wrox Press Ltd,
Arden House, 1102 Warwick Road, Acocks Green,
Birmingham, B27 6BH, UK
Printed in the United States
ISBN 1-861005-62-8

Trademark Acknowledgements

Wrox has endeavored to provide trademark information about all the companies and products mentioned in this book by the appropriate use of capitals. However, Wrox cannot guarantee the accuracy of this information.

Credits

Authors
Eve Astrid Andersson
Stephen Breitenbach
Tyler Burd
Nirmal Chidambaram
Paul Houle
Daniel Newsome
Xiaofei Tang
Xiaolan Zhu

Technical Reviewers
Terry Allen
William Hatcher
Kamran Kordi
Robert (Bob) Laberge
Otto Leung
Faisal Nazir
Ian Stokes-Rees
Xiaofei Tang
Dmitry E. Voytenko
Srdjan Vujosevic

Category Managers
Dave Galloway
Sonia Mullineux

Technical Architect
Amanda Kay

Technical Editors
Richard Deeson
Simon Mackie
Nick Manning
Chris Mills

Author Agent
Trish Weir

Project Manager
Beckie Stones

Production Manager
Simon Hardware

Production Co-ordinator
Emma Eato

Figures
Natalie O'Donnell

Indexing
Bill Johncocks

Cover
Chris Morris

Proofreader
Chris Smith

About the Authors

Eve Astrid Andersson

Eve Andersson is co-founder of the ArsDigita Corporation, and has been building Web services since 1994 and VoiceXML services since February 2001. She wrote much of the code for the ArsDigita Community System, an open source toolkit for building Internet applications. Eve holds engineering degrees from Caltech and U.C. Berkeley, and can recite the first few hundred digits of pi from memory, although she confesses that she knows fewer than 100 digits of *e*! Eve lives in Cambridge, Massachusetts, with Internet pioneers Philip Greenspun and Alex Samoyed. Her personal web site is to be found at http://eveander.com.

Stephen Breitenbach

Stephen Breitenbach, a software engineer working for the Indicast Corporation, is an alumnus of Penn State's Electrical Engineering program and a member of the IEEE. An accomplished programmer, Steve utilizes the Perl language as a foundation for his numerous projects and writings. A resident of beautiful San Diego in California, he enjoys scuba diving, body boarding, exploring the back country in his Jeep, reading, and simply "kicking-back" as a means to get away from the daily digital existence we all now have.

'Special thanks for my success are due to Lalaine and my parents, Rita and Steve, for all the loving guidance, inspiration, and support they have provided over the years. Also, thanks go to Jim and the team at Indicast for their understanding and help in making the time to write. Finally, I'd like to send my thanks to the staff of Wrox Press for this opportunity to share my knowledge and experience with others.'

Tyler Burd

Tyler Burd began coding at the age of 13, teaching himself C++ with a CodeWarrior compiler that he purchased by saving his allowance and lawn-mowing revenue. Now, with ten years professional experience in the industry behind him, he now finds himself the co-founder and CIO of Pop Fizz Media, a jack-of-all-trades design and development firm in Denver, CO. While away from the keyboard, Tyler enjoys sailing, as well as dancing and performing with 23 Skidoo!, Denver's premier performance and instructional dance troupe. At work, Tyler develops in languages such as C++, Java, Visual Basic, Delphi, PHP, and ASP (to name a few), in addition to carrying out his executive responsibilities.

'I would like to dedicate my contribution to this book to Brianna Barsell, whose mere presence in the world motivated me to stay in and write, and whose knowledge of the IT sphere is matched only by her keen wit. Thanks for everything, Brie!'

Nirmal Chidambaram

Nirmal Chidambaram is currently working for the Ivega Corporation, where he designs and develops distributed applications for Ivega's clients in the financial world. He first started programming when he had just left school. As his fascination for computers grew, he continued studies related to any computer topic, even though his engineering major was in a Mechanical branch. He still fondly remembers the feeling of excitement and awe when he first set eyes on Windows 1.0, and the thrill of running his first 16-bit Windows program. Nirmal's expertise ranges from topics such as Distributed Object Computing, to Graphics programming using OpenGL. Nowadays, his main area of interest lies in SOAP and Web Services.

'To Soja, my sweetheart.'

Paul Houle

Originally trained as a theoretical physicist, Paul Houle now works as an Internet Consultant, advising clients from all around the globe. A partisan of free software and the open source ethos, Paul enjoys rural life in Brooktondale, NY, where he spends quality time with his two cats and two horses, or riding his mountain bike in the nearby state forest. Paul may be contacted at paul@honeylocust.com.

Daniel Newsome

Daniel Newsome is the co-founder and President of Denver-based design and development firm Pop Fizz Media where he works alongside Tyler Burd. The average day finds him marketing, meeting with clients, overseeing a team of designers and developers, as well as programming Lingo, ColdFusion, Java, or PHP.

Xiaofei Tang

Xiaofei – or Jeff – Tang has been in the software development business for over 12 years. His many roles have included Principal Software Engineer, Senior Software Engineer, and Software Consultant, working both with start-ups and Fortune 500 companies. He has got to grips with VoiceXML, Nuance, and Speechworks technologies while designing and developing voice-enabled applications. He has also helped in the design and development of a wide range of enterprise applications, including clinical information systems, document imaging programs, web-based computer telephony applications, multimedia Internet applications, and enterprise order management systems. He also has experience and skills in natural language processing, machine translation, and artificial intelligence. Currently his overriding professional goal is to build more intelligent and useful voice systems that help make the world a better place – and not only because he would be richer in it! He would be glad to hear your thoughts and opinions on the book or related subjects, via e-mail at jtang@openland.com.

Xiaolan Zhu

Xiaolan – also known as Jessica – Zhu is a Senior Software Engineer leading the voice group at Yopa, Inc., a San Jose, California, company developing leading-edge voice and wireless business solutions. Before joining Yopa, she worked as a software architect at Tellngo where she designed and developed voice applications using Nuance, VoiceXML, and Java technologies. Prior to that, she worked as Senior Software Engineer and Lead Software Architect at Digitial Archaeology and Profusion, developing web and Internet meta-search engine applications. Xiaolan has two Ph.D. degrees, one in Computer Science, the other in Cognitive Psychology. She likes to live peacefully somewhere in-between the twin worlds of reality and ideas – but she enjoys both!

```
<?xml version="1.0"?>
<vxml version="1.0">
<form id="foo">
<block>
<prompt>
Hi. My name is Bob
</prompt>
</block>
</form>
</vxml>
```

Table of Contents

<?xml version="1.0"?>
<vxml version="1.0">
<form id="foo">
<block>
<prompt>
Hi. My name is Bob
</prompt>
</block>
</form>
</vxml>

Introduction

A few years ago, if you were asked to describe the Web, you would probably have thought of a browser displaying information on a PC screen, with clickable hyperlinks and static images. More recently, with the advent of WAP and I-Mode phones and an array of other mobile devices, this picture has become less clear cut, with the interface requiring tailoring for a particular user's device. However, the common thread with all these interactions is that they are primarily visual.

Now, a new way of interacting with Internet applications has been introduced. VoiceXML provides a mechanism by which the world's billion-plus telephones can be connected via speech to applications on the Web; be they old black candlestick phones, new mobile phones, or even PC telephony interfaces.

According to Datacomm Research (http://www.datacommresearch.com/voicepr.html), two billion people will be using Internet voice portals or voice-enabled web sites by 2005, with more Internet access via phones than via PCs. A Kelsey Group report in March 2001 (http://www.kelseygroup.com) concluded that spending and revenue for the Voice Web and associated applications could exceed $40 billion by 2005. There is little doubt that this market has enormous potential, and great rewards are awaiting the arrival of the first killer Voice-apps.

Who is this Book for?

This book is for those developers with some experience of the Web who want to get ahead of their peers by exploring this emerging technology, to prepare for the VoiceXML explosion that is set to shake the Internet to its foundations.

While the initial chapters on VoiceXML and grammars assume little more than a basic XML knowledge, later chapters use XSLT, ASP, JSP, PHP, and Java alongside VoiceXML. Knowledge of one or more of these technologies would be helpful, but explanatory notes are provided, along with further web references should they be required.

What does the Book Cover?

The first chapter gives an overview of the current VoiceXML situation: including where it's come from and where it's going. Then, in Chapter 2, we take you on a tour of the software currently available for the development, testing, and deployment of voice services.

In the next section, you will start getting deeper into the theory and syntax of VoiceXML, beginning by looking at two of the grammar formats that can be used when building applications. Chapters 4 and 5 turn the focus towards the building blocks of VoiceXML: the forms and elements that go together to define a dialog that leads the user through an application. Chapter 6 consolidates and builds on this foundation by detailing the issues involved in the design of voice services that give the user the best possible experience.

The following Chapters 7, 8, and 9 give you a feel of what can be achieved with VoiceXML, by examining three situations where VoiceXML can be used and integrated with other technologies. These take a case-study approach to walk through the process of voice-enabling a web site, voice-enabling e-mail, and creating multiple interfaces to a single set of data.

Chapter 10 describes the powerful features that can be exposed by extending the core VoiceXML functionality with the use of plug-in components written in traditional languages. In particular, we discuss Nuance's Java-based SpeechObjects, which can permit more complex and sophisticated dialogs.

Finally, we look towards the future. In this ever-changing arena, in Chapter 11 we take a glimpse of where this technology may go, both in the short term with the release of standards, and in the longer term that extends as far as the limits of our imaginations.

What do I Need to Use this Book?

To write VoiceXML applications you will need nothing more extravagant than a plain old text editor such as Windows Notepad. However, due to the XML format of the language, you may prefer to use a more elaborate XML editor such as XML Spy, available for a 30-day evaluation from http://www.xmlspy.com/.

There are several options for testing your applications. Possibly the most straightforward approach is to use the online tools provided by the major voice portals, for which you will need access to the Internet and a standard telephone for making test calls. Alternatively, you may prefer to download software to your system that can then be used to develop and test VoiceXML applications locally. These options are described in more detail in Chapter 2.

In the chapter covering SpeechObjects, software from Nuance may be needed. Where to get this software and how to use it is described in the text, but all downloads are currently free once registration is complete.

In fact, the only part of this book where money may need to change hands is where out-bound telephone alerts are discussed in Chapter 9. The voice portals prefer to keep this service for paying clients, as it is potentially open to malicious use.

Finally, you will just need the time to read and digest the ideas we discuss, coupled with a sprinkling of imagination to take this nascent technology to its limits.

Conventions

To help you get the most from the text and keep track of what's happening, a number of conventions are used throughout the book.

Code examples that you have not come across before are generally highlighted like this:

```
<?xml version="1.0"?>
<vxml version="1.0">
<form>
  <field>
    <prompt> This is a prompt that will be read out </prompt>
  </field>
</form>
</vxml>
```

If the example is repeated again, for example, if it is updated with some new code lines, the sections you have seen before will no longer be highlighted:

```
  <field>
    <prompt> This is a prompt that will be read out </prompt>
    <prompt> This is another prompt that will be read out </prompt>
  </field>
```

As for styles in the text:

- Important terms, when first introduced, are highlighted as follows: **important words**.
- Filenames, and code within the text appear as: `root.vxml`.
- Text in user interfaces, and URLs, are shown in this style: File/Save As...
- Keys that you may be required to press are indicated in italic, like so: *Ctrl*, *Alt*, *Ctrl-z*, *F12*.

In addition:

> **These boxes hold important, not-to-be forgotten information, which is directly relevant to the surrounding text.**

While this background style is used for asides to the current discussion.

Customer Support

If you encounter any difficulties while working through the book, Wrox provides three main ways of seeking support. You can:

- Check for book errata
- Enroll in the peer-to-peer forums at http://p2p.wrox.com
- E-mail technical support a query or feedback on our books in general

Errata and Code Download

Errata and code from the book are posted at the Wrox web site for easy access. Simply navigate to the main page for this book using the following URL:

http://www.wrox.com/Books/Book_Details.asp?ISBN=1861005628

Look for the links for Book Errata and Download Code on the above page. If you're one of those readers who likes to type in code yourself, you can use our files to check the results you should be getting – they should be your first stop if you're getting an unexpected error in your code. If you're one of those readers who don't like typing, then downloading the source code from our web site is a must!

P2P Lists

You can enroll in our peer-to-peer discussion forums at http://p2p.wrox.com where you can put your questions to the authors, reviewers, and fellow industry professionals. For this book, we suggest that you go to the "XML" category, which includes the following lists:

- **voice_xml**
  Discussion of VoiceXML
- **xml**
  Discussion of any and all XML-related topics
- **xslt**
  Discussion and programming help for XSLT transformations

You may choose to join the mailing lists, so you can receive messages either as and when they arrive, or compiled into a daily digest. If you don't have the time or inclination to receive these lists, you can search the online archives by specific subject area or keyword.

Since these lists are moderated, mails can be edited or moved by the moderator into the correct place, so you can be confident of finding good, accurate information quickly. Junk and spam mail are deleted, and your own e-mail address is protected by the unique Lyris system from marauding web-bots that can automatically collect newsgroup mailing list addresses.

E-mail Support

If you wish to point out new errata to post on the web site, or directly query an expert who knows the book in detail, then e-mail support@wrox.com. Your e-mail will need to include the following information:

- The name of the book, the last four digits of the book's ISBN, and the page number of the problem in the Subject field.
- Your name, contact information and description of the problem in the body of the message.

Tell Us What You Think

The authors and the Wrox team have worked hard to make this book a pleasure to read as well as being useful and educational. We are always keen to hear what you liked best and what improvements you think are possible, and appreciate feedback on our efforts, taking both criticism and praise on board for future editorial projects. When necessary, we'll forward comments and queries to the authors concerned. If you've anything to say, just let us know by returning the reply card in the back of the book, or by sending an e-mail to feedback@wrox.com.

```
<?xml version="1.0"?>
<vxml version="1.0">
<form id="foo">
<block>
<prompt>
Hi. My name is Bob
</prompt>
</block>
</form>
</vxml>
```

1

Introduction to Voice Technologies

Imagine a world where you could design applications that have nothing to do with a mouse or a keyboard – instead, all interactions with computers happen just like interactions between people: through speech. VoiceXML is a giant leap in this direction. Just as HTML is a markup language for describing text, VoiceXML is a markup language to describe dialogs between humans and computers, via any device that has sound input and output, such as a standard phone. Though these capabilities, often called IVR (Interactive Voice Response), have been available for some time, and we are already accustomed to them in our normal lives from phone services like telephone banking and customer hotlines, it has traditionally required a great deal of specialized knowledge and equipment to develop and deploy such products. With VoiceXML, creating those kinds of applications becomes radically simpler, and within reach of any developer.

It seems like everyone these days is talking about XML and all the benefits it offers. Platform independence, unlimited extensibility, widespread adoption, and more; it all seems too good to be true! While no technology can solve all of our problems, XML goes a long way to make programs easier to integrate with other programs, and allows a method of interaction between vendors that isn't platform specific. Combine that with the startling advances in computing power and the accompanying drop in price that's been seen over the last decade, throw some innovative telephony/speech technology into the mix, and you have VoiceXML. We're on the verge of a crucial convergence between telecommunications and the web, and this language, promising voice interfaces with much the same power as traditional web browsers, is set to play a vital role.

This chapter sets out to outline exactly what VoiceXML is, how it works, what it does well, and also what it does not quite so well, including future enhancements that may address such failings. We'll also consider some of the real-world situations where voice applications could be deployed, to give you a glimpse of the exciting potential offered by VoiceXML.

Voice Technology History

Several large corporations have been working towards the integration of telephony and Internet technologies for many years. This objective led to the creation of a whole family of markup languages, such as VoxML, SpeechML, and PhoneML. VoiceXML 1.0 is the golden child of this family, created when AT&T, Motorola, IBM, and Lucent Technologies got together to form the VoiceXML forum (http://www.voicexml.org), an independent organization. In devising the language, they drew on the best features of all its predecessors, and submitted the specification as a Note to the World Wide Web Consortium (W3C) in May 2000.

IVR is not new, and dates from at least the 1960s. Suburban Trust Co., a bank in Washington, DC USA, was one of the early trail-blazers, rolling out a system built on an IBM 7770 "Audio Response Unit" that allowed the bank's customers to check their balance by telephone. Despite the long history, IVR has typically been the domain of a very specialized group of developers, but with the advent of increasingly powerful servers and more highly-tuned speech recognition algorithms, that is now about to change. There are well over one billion phones in the world, and the major technology corporations are not blind to the enormous potential they have as a platform for electronic commerce. VoiceXML opens up this platform to the average developer, obviating the need for expensive hardware and esoteric development languages.

VoiceXML as an XML-Based Language

Whenever the IT community turns its mind to the matter of creating a new standard to facilitate a particular aspect of the computing world, the first thing people will think of is XML. Over the space of just a few years, almost every vendor is utilizing, supporting, or extending XML in one way or another. While no technology is perfect, it has gone from a relatively obscure language, originally evolved from IBM's Web SGML, to becoming the cornerstone of many standardized enterprise infrastructures. Over the coming years, we shall see the establishment of more XML dialects that will smooth over the gaps between disparate data systems and hardware, and make data trading between any two companies far more simple than it is now. The upshot for developers is that we will be better able to concentrate on solving the true business issues at stake, rather than being caught up in awkward compatibility issues.

So what are the key advantages of using XML?

- While there are specialized IDEs for XML and VoiceXML in particular, any text editor can easily manipulate the source code.
- Similarly, XSLT tools can be leveraged for uses such as transforming XML data to working VoiceXML pages. See Chapter 7 for a detailed example.
- As it is built on existing web infrastructure, the technology to deploy it is already in place.
- Applications are easy to read, and use consistent encoding across platforms.

The Voice Architecture

We will be looking in more detail at the architecture to employ when developing, testing, and deploying your voice applications in the following chapter. However, here we'll take a brief look at the constituent parts of a voice system.

The key component of any system built on VoiceXML is known as the **voice browser**. This is the software that renders the VoiceXML markup as a sequence of two-way dialogs between the system and the user. It consists of a core VoiceXML interpreter, integrated with software components for **Text To Speech** (TTS) and audio file output, and for speech recording and recognition (namely, **Automatic Speech Recognition** – or ASR – functionality). The voice browser is commonly referred to as the **client**, since it is here that the code is interpreted and "displayed".

Any one of the billion-plus home and mobile phones in existence around the world today can be used to dial up to the voice browser (the phone interface needed is not shown here). You may have one phone number for each VoiceXML application, or a single phone number with extension numbers or a menu system to reach the independent applications.

Finally, there is the web server where the application pages are found, whether it consists of plain VoiceXML files, ASP, JSP, or PHP to dynamically create VoiceXML pages, or a mixture of the two. This server can be the same server used by a company for its regular web content. You'll see several examples of the dynamic creation of VoiceXML documents in Chapters 7 through 9.

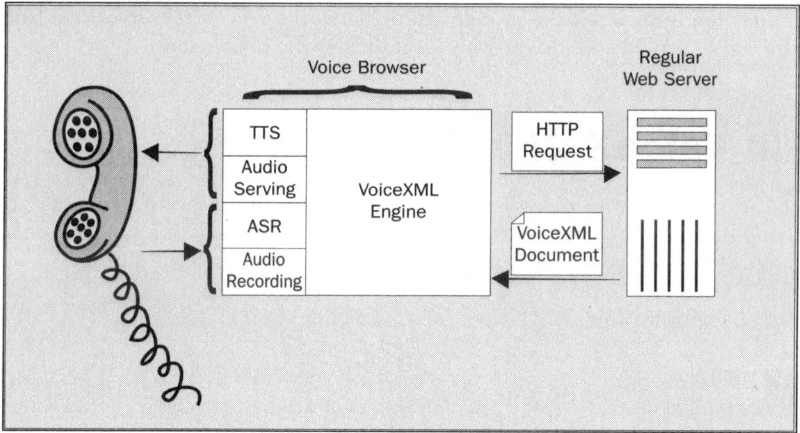

The process of interacting with a voice application mirrors traditional web browsing, as shown by the following table:

Visual Web Model	Voice Web Model
The user requests a page by opening their browser, and typing in a URL.	The user dials in to a particular phone number and/or extension.
The browser makes an HTTP Request to a server for that HTML page.	The voice browser sends an HTTP Request for the VoiceXML document to a server determined from the dialed number.
The browser consumes the HTML to create a visual page that responds to user input through the keyboard or mouse.	The voice browser renders the VoiceXML as a sequential dialog, consisting of prompts using either text-to-speech or pre-recorded audio. Input is available through speech or touch-tone key presses.

Since the code is processed "client-side" on the voice browser, any user on any phone can dial into your application: there is no need to tailor content for different phones, a big hurdle when developing mobile applications for iMode, WAP, or XHTML. Anything from the simplest of phones to complex PBX systems can be used equally well with VoiceXML.

Note that at this time you do still need to take into consideration developing applications for different voice browsers (whose implementations of the VoiceXML specification differ, and which implement their own proprietary elements). However, unlike WAP and iMode, you can still reach every telephony device by developing your application for a specific voice browser that any phone can then dial up.

At the current time, the voice browser is most likely to be an integral part of the service used to deploy the application, whether that is a voice gateway, an application service provider (ASP) voice portal, or software hosted on your own servers. (See Chapter 2 for more on these deployment options.) In the future, however, it is possible that equipment will become available with VoiceXML browsers built-in. Such equipment would probably include mobile telephones, but other specialized devices may also emerge. For example, there are already cars being built in the US that incorporate VoiceXML browsers. On pressing a button on the dashboard, a connection is made via the mobile phone network to a central server that feeds VoiceXML documents to the car, to provide the driver with location-specific information.

Thinking in VoiceXML

Web sites are conceptually a way of laying out data spatially: a number of items may be presented on-screen at the same time. A voice application, however, does not have this spatial dimension. Instead, it must use time: progression through the application follows a sequence of dialogs one after the other.

Let's take a look at a simple VoiceXML document, `color.vxml`.

```
<?xml version="1.0"?>
<vxml version="1.0">
  <menu>
    <prompt>Which is your favorite color of the following <enumerate/></prompt>
    <choice next="blue.vxml"> blue </choice>
    <choice next="green.vxml"> green </choice>
    <choice next="yellow.vxml"> yellow </choice>
    <choice next="purple.vxml"> purple </choice>
    <help>
      Please choose one of <enumerate/> as your favorite color.
    </help>
    <noinput>
      Come on, there must be one you prefer
    </noinput>
    <nomatch>
      Please speak clearly and try again. Remember your choices are <enumerate/>
    </nomatch>
  </menu>
</vxml>
```

If this was stored on the web server in the diagram above, and the user dialed into the particular number at the voice browser connected to this document, the following conversation could take place between the user and the system:

System:	"What is your favorite color? blue, green, yellow, purple."
User:	"Help."
System:	"Please choose one of blue, green, yellow, purple as your favorite color."
User:	*Says nothing*
System:	"Come on, there must be one you prefer."
User:	"Orange."
System:	"Please speak clearly and try again. Remember your choices are blue, green, yellow, purple."
User:	"Purple."
System:	*Transfers to the VoiceXML document* `purple.vxml`

Of course, this is a fairly trivial example, but you can see how dialogs need to be tightly designed to lead users to respond appropriately, and allow for short user sessions by providing intuitive and clear interfaces.

So how does all this work? We'll be taking an in-depth look at the syntax of VoiceXML in Chapters 4 and 5, but let's take a sneak preview now.

Dialog Flow and Control

The principal building blocks of most VoiceXML applications are the `<form>` and `<menu>` elements, the basic containers for a dialog of some kind. Each of these can contain a variety of other elements, specifying prompts to play to the user, particular words the system should expect the user to say, and actions to take when certain conditions are fulfilled. The VoiceXML specification outlines a fairly rigorous procedure called the FIA (Form Interpretation Algorithm) for the interpretation of a dialog, and to govern transitions to other dialogs. We'll see this in some detail in Chapter 4.

There are two basic models for dialogs within a VoiceXML application – **directed** and **mixed initiative**. Directed dialogs are the simplest, and consist of a dialog containing a number of elements that are entered in sequence, each requesting one piece of information at a time. Mixed initiative dialogs, on the other hand, attempt to implement a more natural conversational pattern, asking a complex question initially, which invites the user to provide several information items in a single reply. The idea is that such dialogs more closely match real human speech patterns, and can thus make an application appear friendlier. You will see more on these in Chapter 5.

Speech Recognition

Automatic Speech Recognition, ASR, provides much of the magic that powers VoiceXML. Although the technology behind speech recognition has progressed rapidly in the past few years, it would be a truly monumental task to design software to recognize arbitrary human speech, with all the possible variation of tone, nuances, and accent, without some assistance. In VoiceXML, this assistance comes from the use of the **grammar**.

A grammar is a way of specifying the utterances that the user may make at one particular point in a dialog. If the speech recognizer identifies user input as correctly matching one of these expected utterances, the engine allocates the value given in the grammar to this field. In practice, ASR engines, on hearing a spoken response, will assign a score to each word in the appropriate grammar indicating the level of confidence for that particular word. Most current engines don't allow us to know these confidence scores, but such functionality is likely in the future, allowing more reliable applications to be built.

There are various ways of specifying a grammar. It can be written as a separate file, or included within the VoiceXML document inside a `<grammar>` element. However, the syntax for the grammar itself is not specified by the VoiceXML 1.0 specification, leaving different speech recognition engines to support different grammar formats, of which the two most common are investigated in Chapter 3.

One other way of specifying a grammar is implicitly through the `<choice>` elements inside a `<menu>` element, as in the previous example. In that case, the expected utterances are given as "blue", "yellow", "purple", and "green", words that can also be spoken by the voice browser using TTS and the `<enumerate>` element. In simple cases, this is probably as good an approach as any, but in more complex situations, developing specific grammars is likely to be preferable.

DTMF Recognition

Dual Tone Multi Frequency, DTMF, is the name of the standard set of tones produced by the keys on a telephone handset. They provide a ready and convenient method of user input other than voice, and one that VoiceXML allows through the creation of DTMF grammars using `<dtmf>`, or the `dtmf` attribute of certain elements. Again, this will be covered in Chapter 3.

Responding to the User

There are two halves to any interactive dialog: namely speaking and listening. We have seen how the voice browser deals with incoming speech, so let's now turn our attention to the outgoing speech mechanisms of VoiceXML.

TTS Playback

Text-to-speech (TTS) synthesis is the term used to describe the electronic transformation of simple text into a corresponding speech waveform. Modern algorithms achieve a remarkably good result considering the difficulties in working out the correct pronunciation of a word by examining the spelling alone.

However, the quality of the automated voice still leaves much to be desired in some situations, so TTS is best reserved for applications based on dynamic content, where it can be invaluable in allowing the listener to hear arbitrary text, such as an e-mail, or a dynamic element such as a balance or status report. Wherever possible, pre-recorded messages should be used for prompts and other fixed announcements when an application is made available for public access, but in the development phases, TTS offers a rapid means of assembling prototypes. Occasionally, network problems can delay the downloading of pre-recorded audio files. In VoiceXML, an alternative TTS message can be given to use in place of the pre-recorded audio when fetching the file exceeds the specified timeout period.

Pre-Recorded Audio Playback

TTS engines currently sound impersonal at best, and have particular difficulty with words with unusual pronunciations, so it is best where possible to use pre-recorded audio for fixed prompts and messages. The following code sample shows how the `<audio>` element is used to play an audio file to the user. While VoiceXML 1.0 doesn't specify what format you have to use for pre-recorded audio files, `.wav` and `.vox` are generally supported.

```
<?xml version="1.0"?>
<vxml version="1.0">
  <form>
    <block>
      <audio src="http://www.ezspend.com/audio/goodbye.wav"
        fetchtimeout="750ms">
        Thank-you for shopping with EZ-Spend! Goodbye!
      </audio>
    </block>
  </form>
</vxml>
```

The message that appears inside the `<audio>` tags will be spoken by TTS if the audio file quoted in the `src` attribute takes over 750 milliseconds to fetch.

VoiceXML: Practical Uses

For years, the movies have been portraying extravagant interactions between humans and computers, and we computer professionals have always laughed at their naivety, knowing that such a thing could never really be a possibility. 2001: A Space Odyssey (with HAL), James Bond, Star Trek – there are just too many technical hurdles for speech recognition to become a reality in the near future, or so it seemed. Now it has become just another possible interface to our data, letting users interact with computers in a way more similar to how we interact with one another. It seems like a lot of fun, and indeed there are many applications that would benefit from a voice or even **multi-modal** (where screen typed input and voice operate simultaneously) interface.

There is also a great need to access database information from phones, for example banking information, weather, and stock prices, and though it is possible to do this with existing equipment, from a cost perspective, VoiceXML provides outstanding value. A company desiring to launch a traditional IVR service would have to invest in both costly hardware and developers with specialized skills for that platform. Furthermore, someone besides the developer would typically be required to design the flow. With VoiceXML, application service providers can be used to supply the hardware to host applications, much in the same manner as many traditional web sites are hosted. In addition, because the XML format quite naturally fits the flow of dialogs, it is possible to design the transitions of a voice application in much the same way as you would for a traditional HTML site.

v-commerce

With the capabilities of the Web now accessible by an interface as common as the phone, the possibility of buying anything from anywhere is now realistic. VoiceXML architecture handles commerce through the same tried and true methods as the Internet:

- Since `.vxml` pages can be served from a traditional web server, it's easy to make on-the-fly changes that integrate with your existing infrastructure, such as special offers, inventory control, and so on.
- Since SSL (Secure Sockets Layer) can be used between the voice browser and the web server, VoiceXML transactions can be made highly secure, and do not require any human intervention.
- Each page acts as a standalone module that can be tested and debugged easily.

Call Centers

According to some estimates, the average call-center seat costs over $70K per annum to staff, maintain and equip. Each call has an estimated cost of anywhere from $2 to $5. An automated call powered by VoiceXML can cost as little as from $0.10 to $0.32: a convincing case for investing in VoiceXML.

Enterprise Applications

Some of the most widely useful of applications for VoiceXML are basic messaging tasks such as e-mail and paging, and just such a voice-enabled e-mail system is developed in Chapter 9.

Other key enterprise applications could be provided with similar VoiceXML front-ends allowing people to readily access important data from just about any source – anywhere that a standard phone is available.

Value-Added Services

Services such as weather, horoscopes, news, stocks, could be deployed over higher rate phone lines, or using normal lines funded by advertising. This opens up an entirely new revenue source for information providers. Some companies have even launched ad-supported portals where developers can test out their VoiceXML applications on a real server before launching to the public.

Alternatively, these types of service can be provided as extras by banks and so on, to increase customer loyalty and satisfaction.

Accessibility

The Internet has gone from the domain of scientists and academics to a rich graphic and multimedia device in over 40% of North American homes. Though the overall worldwide trend is one of growth, the fact remains that many people still do not have access to its benefits, for lack of equipment, lack of knowledge, or in some cases physical inability to use a computer. VoiceXML offers the possibility for everyone to use a natural procedure for computer interactions. For the visually impaired, VoiceXML has great potential, making the phone a possible solution for many day-to-day needs.

Advantages and Disadvantages

VoiceXML is likely to be appealing even to users of current phones with WAP browsers, in that voice input is much easier than keypad input for many people and situations. On top of this are the potential benefits that a hands-free VoiceXML interface brings to a wide range of messaging and enterprise applications: you can see why it is causing so many ripples in the world of mobile applications. In the future, convergence of VoiceXML and WAP is likely, as the two technologies would complement each other very well. Chapter 11, *The Future*, examines the factors of such convergence in more detail.

Other advantages of VoiceXML that make it particularly useful in many situations have already been covered, so now I will turn to the disadvantages that make it of more limited utility in others.

While there are many technologies concerned with speech recognition as a means of automated dictation, translation, and so on, VoiceXML is not one of them. Sure, there are elements of these technologies present, but VoiceXML limits dialogs to enable voice interaction with arbitrary members of the public. It is a language that lends itself readily to the design of customer service systems, data retrieval applications, and v-commerce portals. Generic voice to text conversion, such as dictation or translation, currently requires some degree of training of the speech recognition engine in order to reliably recognize the speech pattern of a given user and is not a task suited to VoiceXML.

Other limitations of the language include:

- People with heavy accents, speech impediments, or who use very informal speech will often experience problems.
- The delay in TTS and ASR can sometimes be lengthy, especially if networks are running close to capacity.
- Using speech technologies in a noisy environment or over poor cellular connections can be problematic, since these environments make it harder for the ASR engine to recognize speech. However, VoiceXML applications can be made to adapt to noisy situations by restricting allowed input to key-presses only.

Of course, advances in ASR engines, telephony hardware, and processor speeds, coupled with increasing consumer demand, are likely to see these problems resolved soon.

The Future

Although there is already a plethora of companies offering VoiceXML services, and many VoiceXML applications have already been deployed, voice technologies are still far from mature and are consequently evolving very quickly.

The VoiceXML 2.0 Specification

The specification for VoiceXML is controlled by an industry consortium of approximately 300 companies, invited members, and a general advisory committee. Additionally, any developer can register for support-level membership and submit suggestions about the specification. The end result is a better product for everyone. The interest of this consortium includes the marketing of, education in, and adherence to the VoiceXML language. More information on this process can be found at:

http://www.w3.org/Consortium/Process-20010208/

Technologies evolve, usually for the better, though sometimes the tradeoff is added complexity. With a technology as young as VoiceXML, there are almost no limitations to where it could go and there have been hundreds of suggestions for additions and modifications to the specification. While not everything can be incorporated, the W3C will release the VoiceXML 2.0 working draft in the near future. Many other voice technology specifications have been provided, though also still at an early stage. For example, a non-proprietary XML grammar format is now at Working Draft stage. A further discussion of these issues can be found in Chapter 11.

It's not likely to be long before improved speech recognition allows voice engines to build text replies from user dictation, and there is already a proposed element, `<transcribe>`, for such a feature. It is unlikely to appear in VoiceXML 2.0 however, except perhaps as an optional extension for contexts where technology already allows it.

The Far Future

As Chapter 11 discusses, the future of the web is likely to see the coming together of various disparate technologies to provide a more complete and seamless user experience. There are so many possible combinations of technologies that it's impossible to conceive them all. Perhaps we'll have package drop-off boxes that notify us with a phone call when an overnight letter has been deposited, or perhaps we'll be able to tell our phones to call us at a particular time with a particular message. Personal assistants, commerce, messaging, and information applications have potential limited only by the imaginations of developers.

DSP (Digital Signal Processing), a technology that takes analog data such as voice and turns it into digital signals, interpretable by a computer, is a foundation technology that has come a long way in the last few years due to strong research and development efforts by companies like Texas Instruments. They also play a large part in 3G cellular technologies, the next generation of mobile phones that will feature better screens, high bandwidth connections, and an exciting array of add-ons and peripherals. If 3G technology gets off the ground over the next couple of years, the phone could become the most widely used means of accessing data, taking over from the desktop computer. With such a future ahead, VoiceXML may well come to play an important role in the lives of all IT professionals.

```
<?xml version="1.0"?>
<vxml version="1.0">
<form id="foo">
<block>
<prompt>
Hi. My name is Bob
</prompt>
</block>
</form>
</vxml>
```

2

Getting Started with VoiceXML

This chapter is all about the tools available for developing and deploying voice applications.

First, we'll take a look at some development environments, many of which are online. These not only provide a convenient way to make VoiceXML documents accessible by telephone, but also have many very useful online tools to expedite authoring and debugging of applications. If we prefer not to develop applications online, then standalone, end-to-end voice application development toolkits are available that simulate a telephone interface. The best ones support Text-to-Speech (TTS) and speech recognition (ASR) to allow you to test applications using your desktop's sound output and a microphone.

When your application is ready for production, you have several options: you can outsource hosting entirely, outsource just the telephony components while hosting the application logic yourself, or operate everything – all software and hardware – in-house. Later in the chapter, we will examine these deployment options.

Development Environments

Today's popular voice development environments all offer a suite of tools to make VoiceXML development and debugging easier. Most of the tools are web-based, but some are downloadable for use offline. Once you sign up for a developer account, most or all of these tools are provided for free. The useful facilities typically provided include:

- Syntax checkers
- Real-time debuggers
- Logs of past incoming phone calls
- Simulators
- Extensive documentation
- Libraries of audio clips, grammars, and code samples

Each online environment (or **voice gateway**) has its pros and cons. For example, you might find the TTS "voice" of one service superior for your purposes to others, or you might choose a product because it may conform best to the VoiceXML specification – or alternatively, you may want to take advantage of a particular platform's own non-standard extensions to VoiceXML, that are potentially very useful for your application. Be wary of becoming overly dependant on a particular service's product however, as it may present problems should a need to switch platforms arise in the future. Regardless of which voice platform you choose for development, you will find that the tools that they offer are invaluable for rapidly developing and debugging voice applications.

In case you choose, instead, to run an offline voice software development kit on your desktop machine, we shall also look at a couple of the better packages. Voice software development kits provide end-to-end development environments, including editing, validation, and interpretation of VoiceXML applications. They offer speech recognition, TTS synthesis, and DTMF (touch tone) simulation. You run the software on your local computer and simulate a telephone environment using a microphone and soundcard.

A standalone development kit has a couple of advantages over a voice gateway:

- You don't need a telephone or even an Internet connection to create your application.
- You're assured a higher level of privacy because your code does not need to be on a publicly accessible server.

There are also a couple drawbacks of this approach:

- Since the telephone interface is simulated, you won't have a completely accurate feel for the user experience.
- Your development environment will more than likely be built on a different browser engine from the production environment, so you'll have to do additional testing before you deploy.

Voice Gateways

Voice gateways are a great way of creating and deploying telephone applications. They consist of a voice browser, as described in Chapter 1, together with the telephone and Internet capabilities to run a VoiceXML application: from hosting the phone number to access it, to requesting the application code from whichever server it is on. In the early days of the 1990s, companies wishing to offer an Automated Speech Recognition (ASR) service would have to run their own telephony hardware and software. This can be complicated and expensive, and requires lots of expertise to do well. Running telephony equipment may still make sense for some large companies with the resources available, but typically it's more cost-effective to apply resources to developing application logic instead. VoiceXML provides a layer of abstraction that makes it efficient to outsource the telephony work to a voice gateway.

The most well known gateways are BeVocal, HeyAnita, Tellme, VoiceGenie, and Voxeo. All offer free developer accounts. If you decide to leave the tricky telephony stuff to one of these gateways, all you have to do is run a web server to serve your voice application. Any web server will do; generally the best approach is to extend your existing HTML server to produce VoiceXML documents as well. When you sign up for a developer account at a gateway, they will give you a phone number or extension that allows you to access applications by setting your developer account to point to the URL of your VoiceXML application. For simple applications, it is not even necessary to have your own web-server, as most hosting services allow you a certain amount of space on their servers for your own files.

If you are making dynamic voice applications or wish to incorporate content from a database, the technical issues are no different from those for creating traditional dynamic or database-driven web applications. The major change, of course, is that your scripts need to output VoiceXML content as opposed to HTML.

This means that it's relatively straightforward to make your voice application interface with existing web applications, as covered step-by-step in Chapter 8. Most data on your visual web site can be served to users over the telephone via VoiceXML, and you can probably even reuse some of your web application logic. However, since the amount of information a user is prepared to listen to at one time is far less than is generally found on a visual web page, you will probably need to re-architect the presentation of data to your voice users.

The next few sections will give you an idea of what to expect from a voice gateway development environment. Note that the voice application market is evolving rapidly, and all of the gateways are liable to add new capabilities to their environment; some may even begin to charge for their services. The following overviews are designed to give you a starting point for evaluating a service's offerings.

Sign Up for a Developer Account!

Go ahead and sign up for a developer account with one (or more) of the gateways. There are no bad choices, so just pick one. Here are the URLs:

- BeVocal: http://cafe.bevocal.com/
- HeyAnita: http://freespeech.heyanita.com/
- Tellme: http://studio.tellme.com/
- VoiceGenie: http://developer.voicegenie.com/
- Voxeo: http://community.voxeo.com/

Note: all gateways use JavaScript on their web sites, therefore it is recommended that you use a somewhat modern browser, for example Netscape or Internet Explorer 4 or higher, to access their online development environments.

VoiceXML Interpretation

Most platforms allow you to create a static voice application that can be executed even if you don't have a web server running. BeVocal, HeyAnita, and Tellme provide web-based forms allowing you to type in some VoiceXML, have the syntax checked automatically, and then call up a phone number and hear how it sounds. BeVocal and HeyAnita will also let you upload files from your desktop machine onto their servers and test them. These are excellent ways to experiment with new syntax or hear how a dialog in your application progresses.

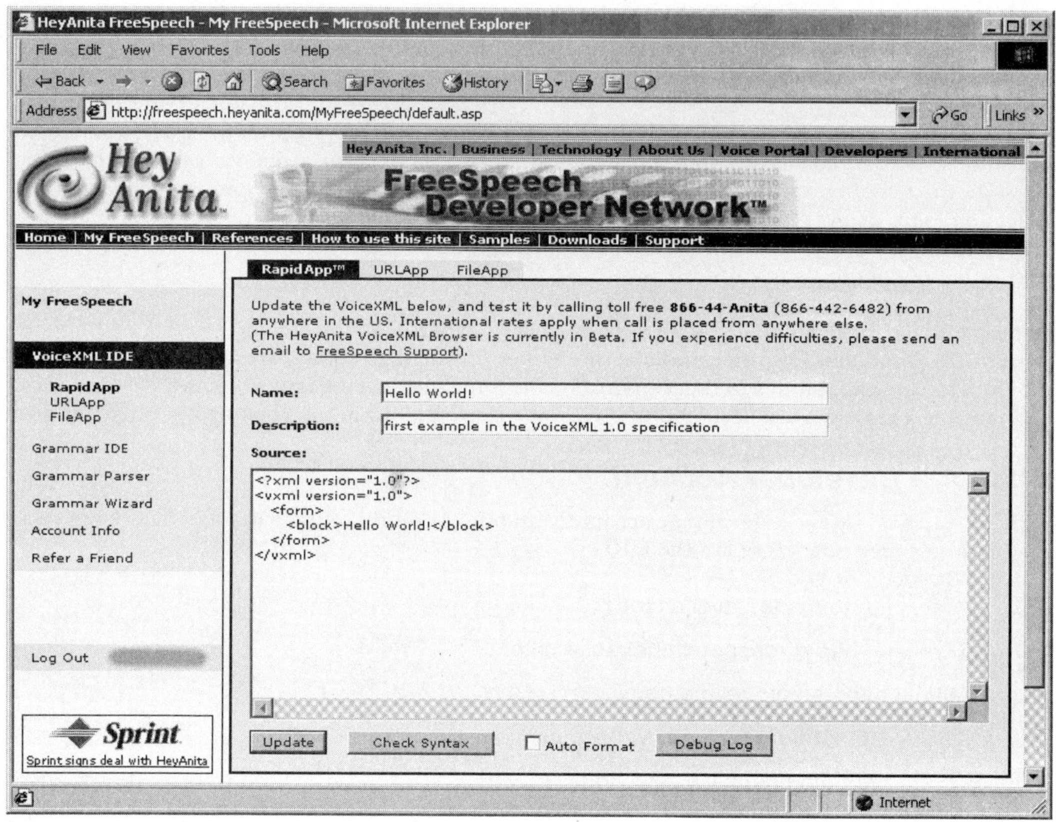

In the above screenshot, you can see HeyAnita RapidApp, which is a web-based form that you can use to quickly test your VoiceXML code. RapidApp includes a VoiceXML validator to uncover syntax errors. You can also call up a toll-free number to hear and interact with your running code. If you open up the debug log window, you can view the dialog flow and any parameter values.

If you run your application on your own server or, for that matter, on a free server like GeoCities, you just need to specify the URL of your application's starting document using the appropriate form on the gateway's site, so that that document can be fetched and executed when people access your application.

Debuggers

BeVocal, HeyAnita, Tellme, and Voxeo all have online debuggers that can trace execution of an application in real-time. You can follow live calls as they progress, and watch the status of variables, events, errors, and debugging statements. VoiceGenie provides a debugger called GenieTracer that you can download and run on a Windows machine. BeVocal and VoiceGenie also provide logs of all past calls so that you can analyze usage later. This can be particularly useful when testing an application to see how easy it is to use – see Chapter 6.

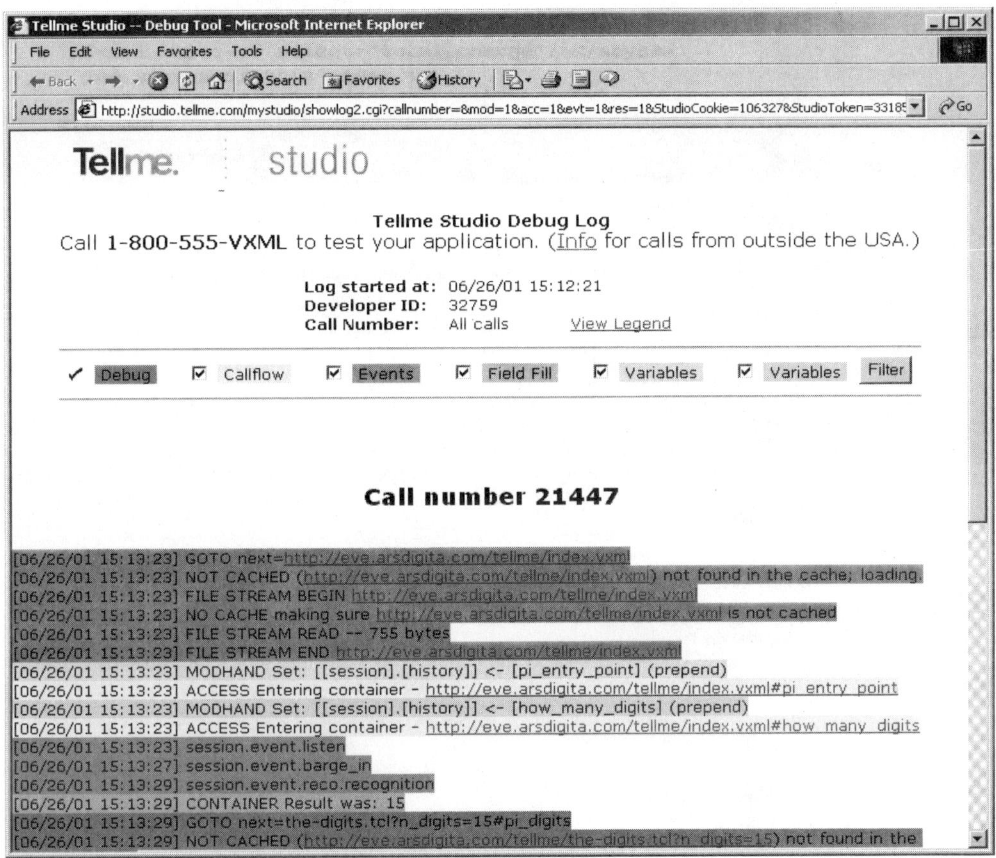

Tellme's Debug Log (shown above) displays information about telephone calls as they progress in real time. You can use it to view as much or as little information about a call as you wish. It can show you the variable values, form field values, events, call flow, and debugging statements, or you can apply a filter to view only the information that is interesting to you.

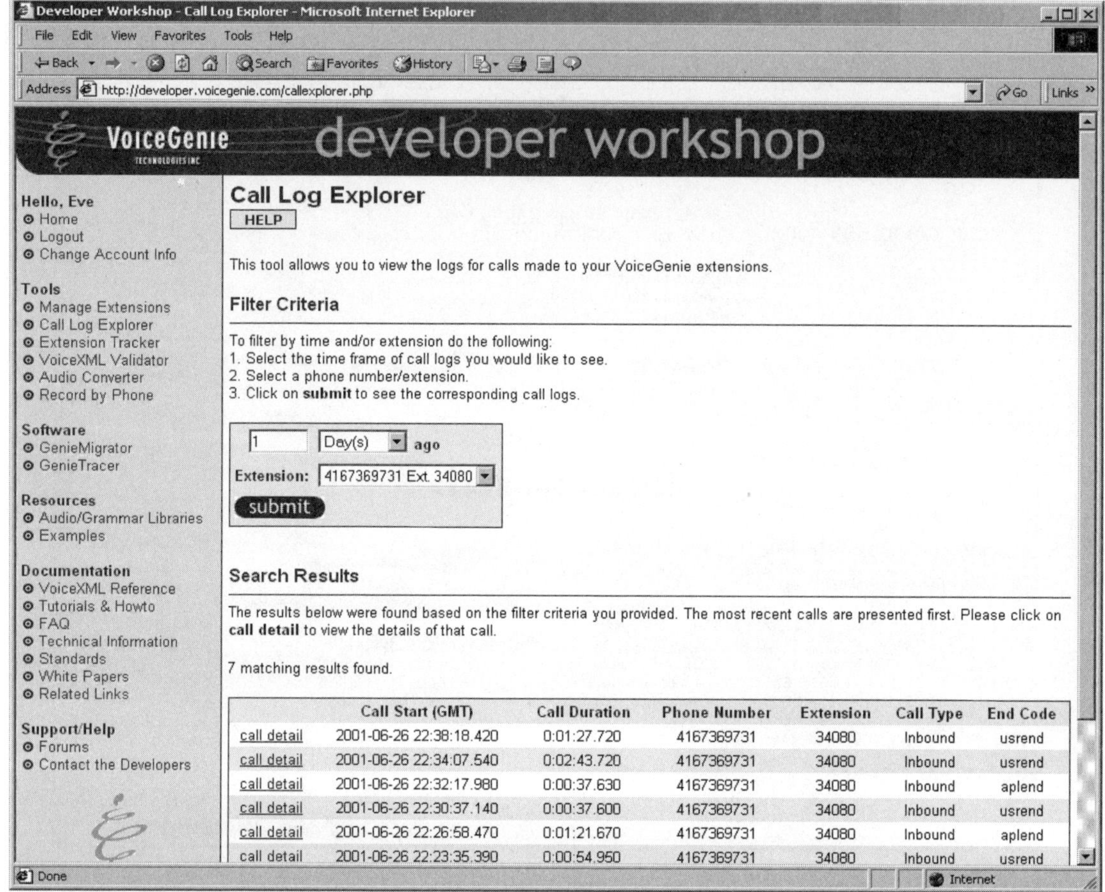

VoiceGenie's Call Log Explorer (shown above) lists all the calls that your application has received during a specified time period. For each call, you can see: the telephone number and extension that the user dialled, the start time, the call duration, the caller's telephone number (when available), and the cause for termination of the call (for example, if the user hung up or the application finished running).

Simulators

BeVocal and Tellme both provide web-based simulators so that you can test your application without a telephone. No speech is involved; both inputs and outputs are typed. It's a fast, inexpensive way to do some first-pass debugging, although it won't give you such a good feel for the user experience or warn you of any speech recognition or pronunciation problems that may arise during actual use.

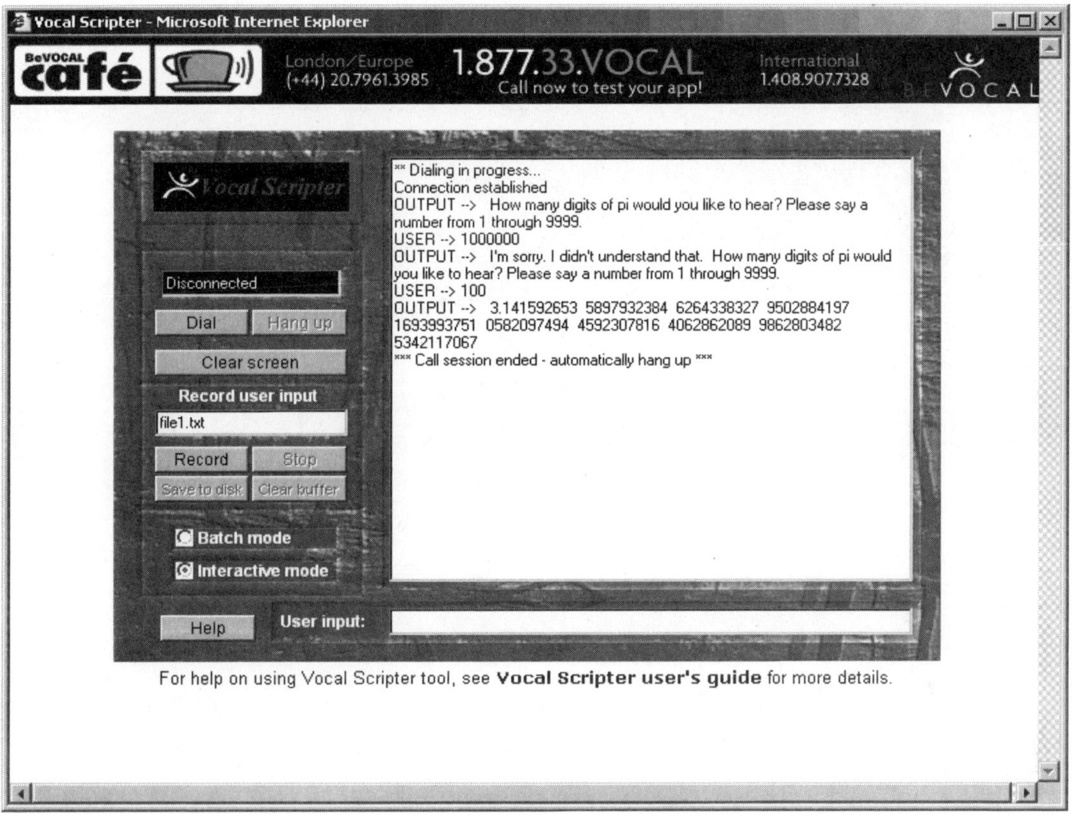

BeVocal's Java-based simulator, the VocalScripter, runs in a browser window. When you click Dial, it will access your application, write out any words that would be spoken by your application, and accept typed input from you. You can run it in "interactive mode" where you type responses in real time as you are prompted, or you can record a series of responses and run it in "batch mode" to save yourself some effort when testing iteratively.

Authoring Tools

HeyAnita provides a toolkit for developing, validating, and testing applications on your desktop computer. Called the FreeSpeech Developer Toolkit, it includes tools for setting up a microphone and testing/tuning grammars without the need for a speech recognition engine or other special hardware.

Voxeo offers a desktop editor called Voxeo Designer, which provides a graphical means of editing VoiceXML applications. It's quite fun to use – you can drag and drop dialog components, and when you're through, out pops a VoiceXML document. Even if you use some other editor for development, you can import your finished code and Voxeo Designer will create a beautiful flowchart of your application.

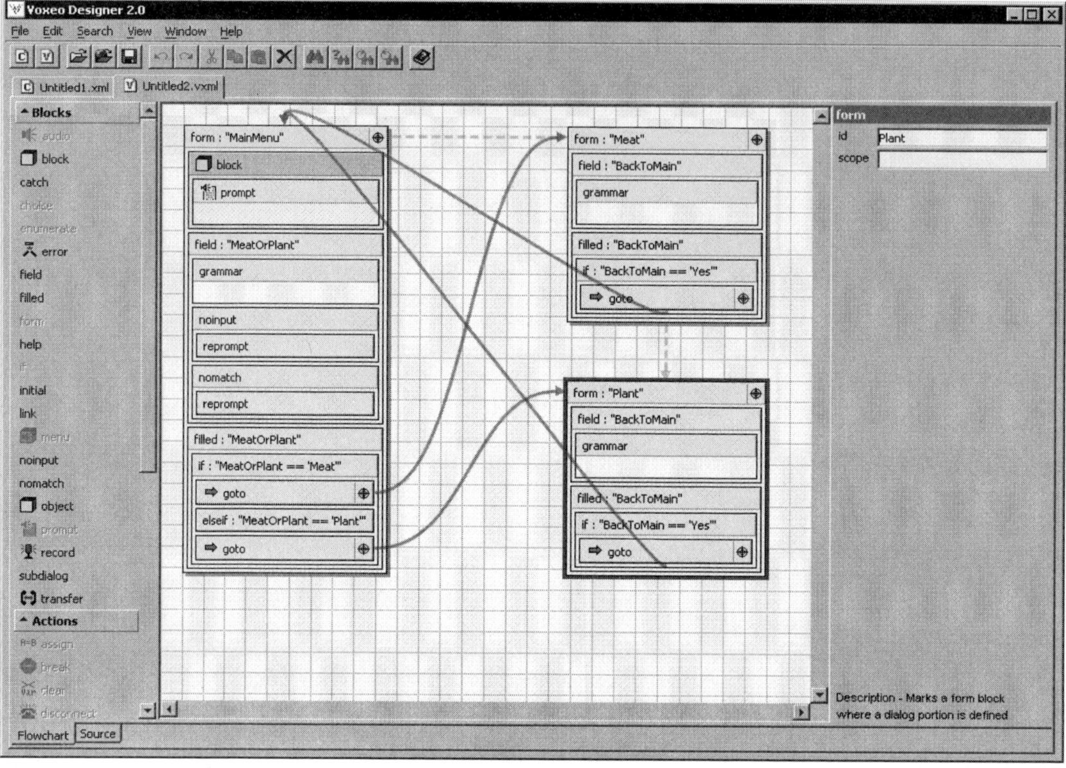

The above flowchart, produced by Voxeo Designer, depicts the call flow within one VoiceXML document. It was created automatically by typing VoiceXML code into a text editor window (not shown). The reverse is also possible: you can create flowcharts by dragging and dropping VoiceXML elements from the left-hand side of the screen and Voxeo Designer will automatically create the corresponding VoiceXML document.

Libraries

Several gateways provide developers with libraries of useful grammars, audio files, and code. They are great, especially the grammars, because they can save so much time.

Tellme has the most extensive libraries, with extraordinarily useful and flexible grammars. For example, the `TELLME_DATE` grammar recognizes spoken phrases such as:

- "July 2nd, 2001"
- "next Saturday"
- "Thanksgiving"
- "next week"
- "tomorrow" & "yesterday"
- "three days from now"

and turns them into parsable dates. Tellme also has grammars for cities/states/ZIP codes, numbers, dollar amounts, credit cards, and telephone numbers.

Tellme has a number of professional-sounding audio clips, for example, quiet background music to play during long pauses, and a range of auditory icons ("beeps" and "boops"), for purposes such as indicating that the application understood what the user said.

Tellme's code library is also impressive, with dozens of reusable code modules and examples, for example, the `Caller-Geography` object, which looks at the incoming phone number to determine the caller's city, state, ZIP code, and time zone.

BeVocal has code samples, an extensive audio library, including common phrases, numbers, currencies, dates, and some very useful grammar extensions for commercial applications, including airports, airlines, equities, streets, street numbers, and cities/states.

Voxeo distributes a few open source applications, such as the City Locator, and has an audio library containing greetings, dates and times, airport codes, and other professionally-recorded spoken text.

HeyAnita provides a number of grammars, including basic commands, list navigation, numbers, and dates, and a few code tutorial samples.

VoiceGenie provides a few reusable audio and grammar components and code samples, as well.

Documentation

Each gateway's web site has plenty of online documentation. BeVocal and Tellme have especially extensive documentation, including tutorials, tag references, grammar references, and sample applications. Tellme and HeyAnita have documents outlining common VoiceXML errors. BeVocal has some interesting guides, such as *VoiceXML Performance* and *VoiceXML Porting.*

VoiceXML Compliance

VoiceXML compliance is important for portability, in the event that you choose to move to a different gateway later or run your own voice server software.

At the time of writing, there are subtle differences between different gateways' interpretations of the VoiceXML specification, and not all have implemented all of the tags in the VoiceXML 1.0 spec. BeVocal, HeyAnita, and VoiceGenie seem to conform most closely to the standard. Fortunately, all five gateways are moving in the direction of total compliance, and most are also active in VoiceXML standards committees. Compliance will become less and less of an issue.

Grammar Formats

A grammar defines what a user is allowed to say at various points when interacting with your VoiceXML application. Grammars can be specified in a variety of vendor-specific formats, as described in detail in Chapter 3. The VoiceXML 1.0 specification does not require any one particular grammar format, so each gateway has chosen which grammar(s) to support. BeVocal, Tellme, VoiceGenie, and Voxeo all support the Nuance GSL (Grammar Specification Language). VoiceGenie also supports the platform-independent ABNF (Augmented Backus-Naur Format) and AT&T Watson Grammars. BeVocal also supports the XML Grammar format. HeyAnita supports the XML Grammar format as well as JSGF (Java Speech Grammar Format) and BNF (Backus-Naur Format).

If you know you'll be deploying in an environment that accepts a particular format, try to develop with a gateway that uses the same format. It's not always easy to translate grammars from one format to another, and precision can be lost in the translation.

Note that the W3C is currently developing a platform-independent XML-based grammar format as part of the VoiceXML 2.0 specification. It is likely that all gateways will support this format in the near future.

Client-Side Scripting Languages

ECMAScript, a standardization of JavaScript, is the only client-side scripting language specified in the VoiceXML 1.0 specification (naturally you can use any server-side scripting language you like). All five gateways support ECMAScript. HeyAnita supports VBScript as well.

Text-to-Speech Quality

Text-to-speech (TTS) engines really do have their work cut out trying to pronounce words or names they've never encountered before, and all in all, they do an amazing job. Nonetheless, they are still somewhat imperfect and have a distinctly robotic sound. Tellme recommends that you use TTS for rapid development and then switch to pre-recorded audio clips when you're ready to go to production. However, there are times when you won't be able to use pre-recorded output, say if you are writing a dynamic VoiceXML interface for an existing database-backed application, as covered in Chapter 8. In that chapter, a technique for substituting unusual words with phonetic spellings is described, but you will still need to make sure the TTS engine of a platform produces output of acceptable quality.

Of the five gateways, four have female voices and one (Voxeo) has a male voice. All five voices are relatively annoying to listen to when they are reciting long passages of text. Ultimately, this is a matter of personal preference, but I found HeyAnita to be the most pleasant, with the best phrasing, pronunciation, and delivery. BeVocal and Tellme sound almost identical, probably because both systems are powered by the Lernout & Hauspie RealSpeak TTS engine. All five are quite understandable, however.

Automated Speech Recognition (ASR) Quality

Each of the gateways does an excellent job of speech recognition. CT Labs, an independent testing facility, tested BeVocal, HeyAnita, Tellme, and VoiceGenie in January, 2001. Testing each gateway with 600 pre-recorded voice inputs, CT Labs found that BeVocal had no recognition errors, HeyAnita had recognition errors 0 .002% of the time, Tellme had a 0 .03% error rate, and VoiceGenie had a 0 .12% error rate. BeVocal and VoiceGenie took significantly longer than HeyAnita and Tellme to recognize the input and play the resulting prompt: the user would have to wait roughly 1.7 seconds for BeVocal and VoiceGenie, as opposed to around 1.2 seconds for HeyAnita and Tellme.

I did some careful but non-scientific tests of my own in a quiet room using a grammar containing 50 first names of my colleagues (and their dogs!). Speaking clearly but not excessively slowly, I found the ASR quality of all five gateways to be virtually indistinguishable, with a recognition failure rate of around 5%. Noisy rooms are much, much worse. If you're communicating with a voice application and your neighbor coughs, the application is likely to try to interpret the cough and then say, "I'm sorry, I didn't understand you. Please repeat your response."

International Access

If you live outside the United States, you may still be able to access your applications through a gateway's toll-free US telephone number, but will be charged standard international rates for doing so.

BeVocal provides the most options for international access. In addition to its toll-free US phone number, it also has a London phone number and a non-toll-free US phone number, both of which can be accessed anywhere in the world.

Tellme, VoiceGenie, and Voxeo have non-toll-free US (or Canada) phone numbers for international access.

Using the BeVocal or Tellme online simulator, or an offline SDK, will also save long-distance fees when doing development outside of the United States.

Miscellaneous Features

BeVocal provides Speaker Verification, its own experimental extension to VoiceXML. Your application can ask a user to record some text, which is then used as their voice-print, and it will be able to verify their identity on subsequent visits to the application.

BeVocal also provides a port estimator (the number of ports corresponds to the number of telephone lines available to connect callers to your application). By entering the number of calls expected to be received by the service per hour, as well as the average duration of those calls, the port estimator shows us what percentage of our callers will receive busy (or engaged) signals based on the number of ports we choose to have. For example, if we expect to receive 50 calls/hour, each call lasting 3 minutes on average, we will need 9 ports in order to achieve an acceptably low number of busy signals.

As well as responding to users' calls, all five platforms are capable of making automated outgoing calls. Note however that only Voxeo makes this service available to non-paying developers. This feature is very exciting and opens up the possibility of building services like automated reminders or wake-up-calls. An example of this is included in Chapter 9 using the BeVocal platform.

HeyAnita and Tellme provide online grammar development environments, which can be used to generate, validate, and test phrases against grammars.

Tellme and VoiceGenie both let developers record sound files by telephone. This means that an application can be enhanced with sound clips without the need to buy a microphone or recording software.

VoiceGenie has an audio format converter. You can upload a file in any one of twenty seven formats, and it will be converted to Dialogic Vox format, the audio format that VoiceGenie supports for pre-recorded audio playback.

VoiceGenie provides a particularly interesting tool: GenieMigrator. If you feed it a VoiceXML document that runs on the Tellme platform, GenieMigrator will convert it to VoiceGenie-compliant VoiceXML. Let the gateway wars begin!

Our First VoiceXML Application

It's time to create our first VoiceXML application! You may have already spotted the ubiquitous "Hello World" application in one of the screenshots earlier, so we will skip that one and go on to something more interesting: a simple dialog to ask a question, listen for the response, and act accordingly.

```
<?xml version="1.0"?>
<vxml version="1.0">
  <menu id="HundredDollarQuestion">
    <prompt>Welcome to Who Wants To Be A Millionaire. Here is your first
      question, worth $100. Which of the following is not an animal?
      <enumerate/></prompt>
    <choice next="#IncorrectAnswer">
      Cow
    </choice>
    <choice next="#IncorrectAnswer">
      Pig
    </choice>
    <choice next="#CorrectAnswer">
```

```
        Cactus
      </choice>
      <choice next="#IncorrectAnswer">
        Goat
      </choice>
      <noinput>I am going to have to press you now. Which of the following living
        things is not an animal? <enumerate/></noinput>
    </menu>
    <form id="CorrectAnswer">
      <block>
        Congratulations, that is the correct answer.
        <disconnect/>
      </block>
    </form>
    <form id="IncorrectAnswer">
      <block>
        That is not the correct answer. Game over!
        <disconnect/>
      </block>
    </form>
  </vxml>
```

How this sounds:

System:	"Welcome to Who Wants To Be A Millionaire. Here is your first question, worth $100. Which of the following is not an animal? Cow, Pig, Cactus, Goat"
User:	"Pig"
System:	"That is not the correct answer. Game over!"

Or it could go like this:

System:	"Welcome to Who Wants To Be A Millionaire. Here is your first question, worth $100. Which of the following is not an animal? Cow, Pig, Cactus, Goat."
User:	*Silence*
System:	"I am going to have to press you now. Which of the following living things is not an animal? Cow, Pig, Cactus, Goat."
User:	"Cactus."
System:	"Congratulations, that is the correct answer."

Try this out in the development environment of your choice.

Note: one small modification is needed if you are using the Voxeo gateway. Please add the following tag above the `<vxml version="1.0">` tag:

```
<!DOCTYPE vxml PUBLIC '-//Nuance/DTD VoiceXML 1.0b//EN'
'http://community.voxeo.com/vxml/nuancevoicexml.dtd'>
```

The above tag specifies the Document Type Definition (DTD) that the VoiceXML document is validated against. Strictly speaking, all XML documents, including VoiceXML documents, ought to specify the DTD, but most gateways let you be lazy and leave it out. Even the examples in the VoiceXML 1.0 specification omit the DTD.

Standalone Voice Software Development Kits

The HeyAnita FreeSpeech Toolkit, described earlier, can be used as a standalone development kit, as can the following toolkits:

IBM WebSphere Voice Server SDK implements an extended subset of the VoiceXML 1.0 specification. It supports English (US and UK), German, and French, and uses the JSGF grammar format. The SDK runs on Windows NT Workstation or Server 4.0. You can download it free from http://www.ibm.com/software/speech/enterprise/ep_12.html.

The Nuance V-Builder supports 18 languages, including a few flavors of English, Dutch, Cantonese, and Swedish, to name a few. All VoiceXML tags are supported, as well as a few custom tags, and the Nuance GSL grammar format is used. V-Builder runs on Windows NT 4.0 SP5 or higher. It is also free, and available from the Nuance Developer Network at http://extranet.nuance.com/developer/.

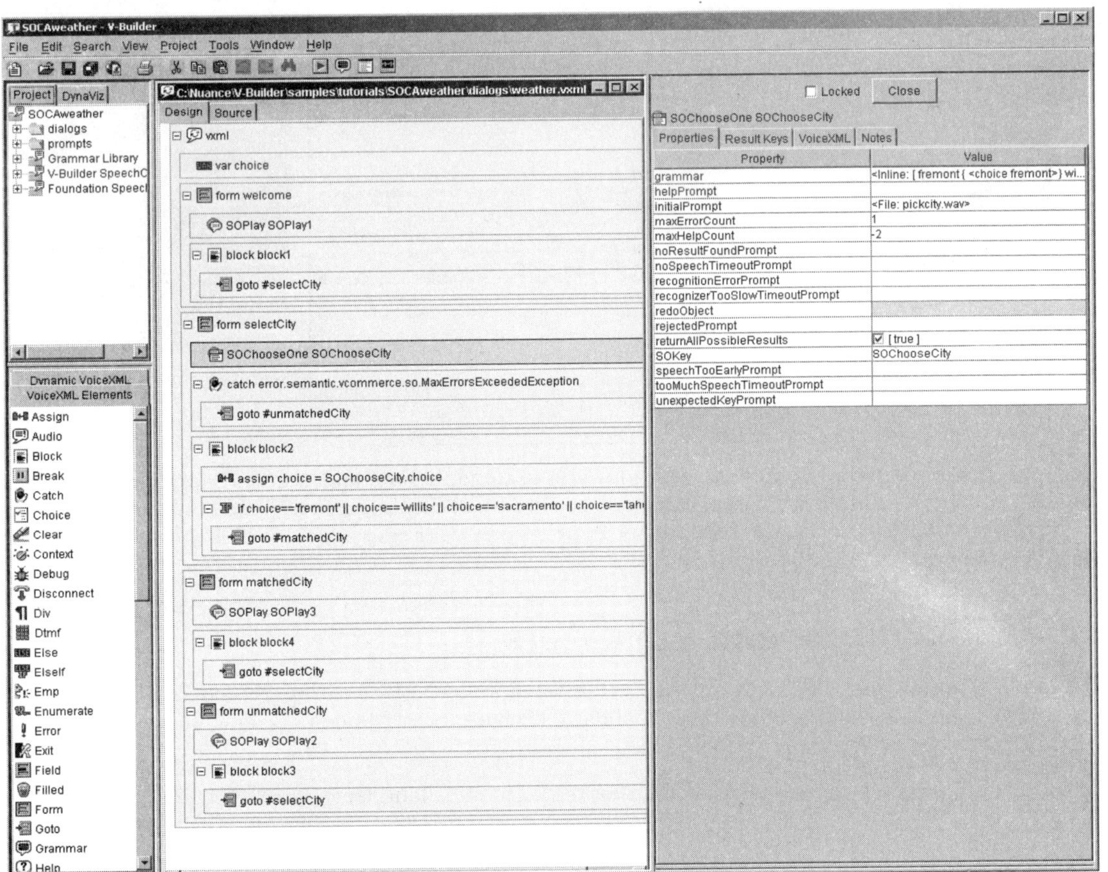

Nuance V-Builder (shown above) allows you to build, debug, and test voice applications. Here we see the graphical editing environment with Nuance's sample weather application open. Nuance provides quite a few sample applications to help get you started. (Image © Nuance Communications, used with permission.)

Motorola provides a Mobile ADK that allows you to simulate both VoiceXML applications and WAP applications. This developer kit implements a large subset of the VoiceXML 1.0 specification and supports the Nuance GSL grammar format. The Mobile ADK can be freely downloaded from http://developers.motorola.com/developers/wireless/downloads/madk_download.html. It runs on Windows 95, 98, 2000, and NT 4.0, and even includes built-in grammars, such as `boolean`, `data`, `digits`, `currency`, `number`, `phone`, and `time`.

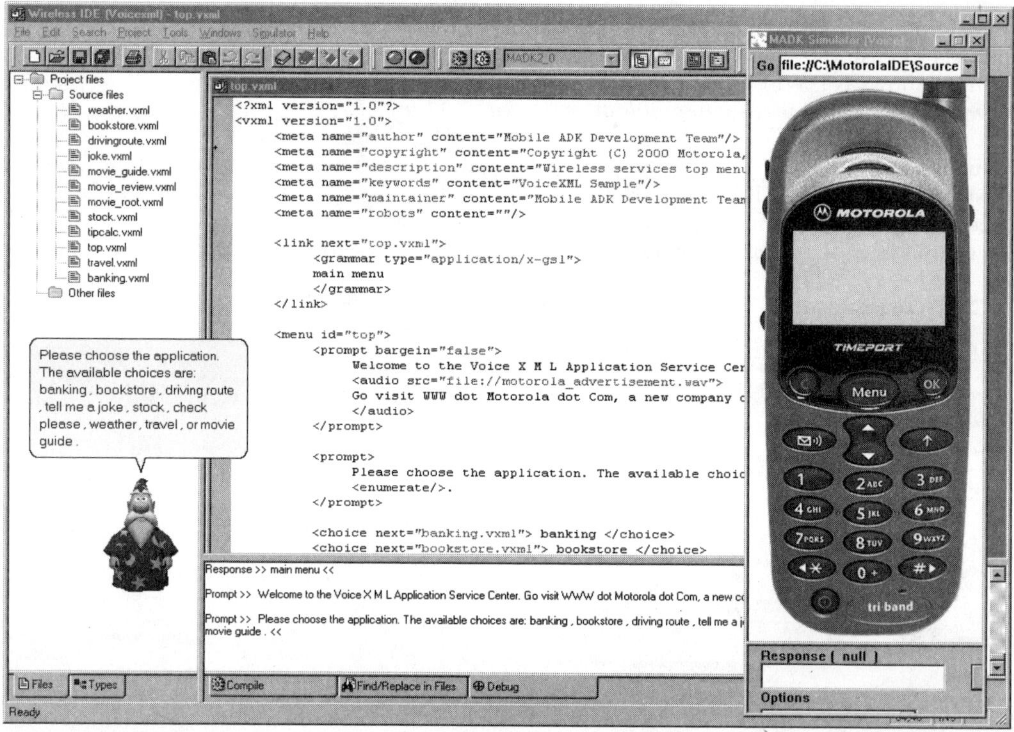

Motorola's Mobile ADK provides a means for you to build, debug, and test your application. Here we see the testing environment. Prompts are spoken aloud and displayed in a speech bubble emanating from the cute wizard (optional). You can speak or type in your responses, or click on the telephone keypad when DTMF input is required.

VoiceXML Editors and Validators

VoiceXML editors make it easier to write well-formed VoiceXML by properly indenting code, color-coding tags, and automating some tasks. Validators ensure that a VoiceXML document conforms to the specified Document Type Definition (DTD).

Voxeo Designer, mentioned earlier in the chapter, is an excellent, free VoiceXML editor.

IBM WebSphere Studio contains a VoiceXML editor that includes syntax checking. You can download a free Entry Edition from http://www.ibm.com/software/webservers/studio/download.html. A copy of the Professional Edition costs approximately $500.

If you use the Emacs text editor, you will be familiar with major modes and how useful they are. You're in luck: you can download an Emacs major mode for VoiceXML editing from the Tellme web site, at http://studio.tellme.com/downloads/code-emacsmode.html. VoiceXML tags are then highlighted in the editor, and you have access to certain special commands, such as C-c / to close the current tag. You can also validate your VoiceXML by typing C-c C-v. Note that the DTD given in the instructions is specific to the Tellme platform; thus, if you use the suggested DTD, the validator may reject some tags supported by the specification, or another gateway.

Deployment

We have seen a number of tools to use for application development. Now we'll briefly cover how to set up a production environment.

For low-volume, non-mission-critical applications, you may be able to continue to use your developer account with no additional cost. Tellme and BeVocal encourage this and even have free directory listings for their members' voice applications.

For high-volume sites, the three most common deployment models are:

- **Application Service Provider (ASP) model.** You outsource the entire application development and hosting.
- **Gateway model.** You remain in control of the application logic and leave the telephony work and VoiceXML interpretation to one of the gateways.
- **In-house model.** You run the telephony software/hardware yourself, as well as your application logic.

Application Service Provider (ASP) Model

With the ASP model, you either outsource the entire application development, hosting, and maintenance to another firm, or you may do the development yourself and hand over maintenance when you're done. The advantage is that you don't have to run any software or hardware yourself. The disadvantage is that you lose direct control over the application logic and possibly any sensitive customer data that the application must access.

Voxeo, BeVocal, and HeyAnita provide ASP services. Many web development firms will also develop and host your application for you, in partnership with a voice gateway.

You can expect to pay for the following:

- Professional services fees for application development and maintenance.
- Hosting fees.
- Telephone access fees, either per-minute for low-volume applications, or per-port for high, predicable-volume applications. A one-time setup fee may also be charged.
- Software license fees for voice browser, TTS, ASR, and certain other software components (for example, a pre-built component, such as an Address Book module).

Gateway Model

This is the most exciting model. Many companies and individuals run their own web servers or have access to their own domain on external web servers. But buying telephony equipment and paying the salaries of experts who know how to set up, maintain, and tune these systems can be prohibitively expensive. The clean interface that VoiceXML provides between the application logic and the telephony components means that you can do the interesting parts yourself and leave the tricky stuff to the experts.

Tellme so strongly believes in the gateway model that they do not offer ASP or in-house services or products. This is also Voxeo's preferred model because they find it to be the most cost-effective for their customers. BeVocal, HeyAnita, and VoiceGenie all offer gateway services, but they do offer other deployment models as well.

Once you've developed and tested the application logic, it can take a few weeks for the gateway to supply your application's telephone numbers and test the entire setup, before deployment is possible.

The costs are similar to the ASP model, except that you may save a little money by taking the development and hosting of your application in-house. You'll pay:

- Telephone access fees, either per-minute for low-volume applications, or per-port for high, predictable-volume applications. A one-time setup fee may also be charged.
- Software license fees for voice browser, TTS, ASR, and possibly other software components.
- Any costs associated with developing and hosting internally.

In-House Model

In this model, you run everything yourself at your own facilities. You will need the following software:

- Text-to-Speech software, such as AT&T Watson, Fonix TTS, Speechworks Speechify, or Lernout & Hauspie RealSpeak. License fees start from around $600 per port (each port can handle one caller at a time).
- Automated speech recognition software, such as Nuance, Speechworks, or AT&T Watson. License fees range from $200, to over $1,500, depending on the features needed.
- A voice server, such as IBM WebSphere Voice Server ($15,000, including IBM's own TTS and ASR software), Motorola Vx500, VoiceGenie VoiceXML Gateway, HeyAnita's FreeSpeech Gateway Server, BeVocal's platform, or Voxeo's platform.
- Any web server.
- Your application-specific software.
- Possibly pre-built software components, such as BeVocal's Driving Directions module.

You will also need to run the following hardware:

- Computer(s) to run your web server software and application.
- Computer(s) to run your voice server, ASR, and TTS software.

- Telephony interface card, such as Dialogic, NMS, Brooktrout, or Acculab, so that your voice server can talk to the PSTN (Public Switched Telephone Network), understand DTMF, and play back pre-recorded audio.
- Network interface card so that your application can talk to your voice server.

You will also need to arrange for your telephone company to supply:

- Telecom capacity, for example T1 lines coming into your facility.
- The telephone numbers that customers will use to reach your service.

Finally, you will need your own team of experts to set up, run, tune, and maintain all of the above.

This is no small feat. If you have an efficient team working in parallel to set up all required components, it will typically take no less than six months. Provisioning the telecom capacity alone takes a few months. Even after deployment, tuning the TTS/ASR software will be an ongoing process for many months as you learn how customers really interact with your software.

The upfront cost for all this will be a few hundred thousand dollars for a very small commercial deployment. The figure will typically approach around a million dollars for a more typical deployment, and can easily exceed the million-dollar mark in practice. And then there's the upkeep: maintenance, upgrades, and your team of experts will set you back hundreds of thousands of dollars every year.

Although this is an expensive and time-intensive deployment option, it may make sense to deploy in-house if you have a very high-volume application and you already have in-house voice expertise and telephony equipment. At this point, you begin to enjoy the same economies of scale that the gateways do, so it may become the most cost-effective option for you in the long run.

If you do decide to take this route, you can still develop and initially deploy your application using a gateway. That way, you'll be able to make sure your application is viable and acceptable to real users before investing resources in the infrastructure.

It's also worth considering the use of a gateway for overflow capacity if the application is likely to have "spikey" call volumes, so that extra equipment and software licenses don't need to be purchased just to accommodate temporary usage peaks.

Summary

We've seen some very useful development environments that provide authoring tools, debugging facilities, code/grammar/audio libraries, and other interesting and valuable features.

Voice gateways (see gateway summary overleaf) give us a development environment that closely mimics the production environment. Standalone toolkits on the other hand, provide a little more privacy, and relieve us of the need to use a telephone to test applications.

We've also reviewed our options for deployment. Small-scale applications can be deployed for free using a voice gateway. For large-scale applications, we can outsource all development and hosting, outsource just the telephony components to a voice gateway, or run the entire service in-house. The gateway option is the newest and most innovative. It has the potential to bring about significant cost savings – and higher quality – when developing voice applications, and promises to generate a new wave of voice services.

Gateways at a Glance

	Tellme	VoiceGenie	Voxeo	BeVocal	HeyAnita
Developer URL	http://studio.tellme.com	http://developer.voicegenie.com	http://community.voxeo.com	http://cafe.bevocal.com	http://freespeech.heyanita.com
VoiceXML Interpretation	web-based form, URL	URL	URL	web-based form, file upload, URL	web-based form, file upload, URL
Debuggers	real-time	call log, desktop app	real-time	real-time, call log	real-time
Simulator	web-based			web-based	
Desktop Authoring Tools			Voxeo Designer		FreeSpeech Developer Toolkit
Libraries	extensive audio, grammar, and code	audio, grammar, and code	audio (extensive) and code	extensive audio, grammar, and code	grammar and code
Documentation	extensive	some	some	extensive and interesting	some
VoiceXML Compliance	high	very high	high	very high	very high
Grammar Formats	GSL	GSL, ABNF, AT&T Watson	GSL	GSL, XML	XML, JSGF, BNF
Client-Side Scripting	ECMAScript	ECMAScript	ECMAScript	ECMAScript	ECMAScript and VBScript
Voice	female	female	male	female	female

	Tellme	VoiceGenie	Voxeo	BeVocal	HeyAnita
Access Telephone Numbers	toll-free US and non-toll-free US	non-toll-free Canada	toll-free US and non-toll-free US	toll-free US, non-toll-free US, UK	toll-free US
Miscellaneous Features	record audio files by phone, grammar development environment	record audio files by phone, audio converter, Genie Migrator	outgoing calls free to developers	speaker verification, port estimator	grammar development environment
Deployment Options	gateway	gateway, in-house	ASP, gateway, in-house	ASP, gateway, in-house	ASP, gateway, in-house

```
<?xml version="1.0"?>
<vxml version="1.0">
<form id="foo">
<block>
<prompt>
Hi. My name is Bob
</prompt>
</block>
</form>
</vxml>
```

3

VoiceXML Grammars

A fundamental aspect of on voice application is the quality of speech processing used on, something dependent not only on the capabilities of the servers used by the application, but also the effectiveness of the speech processing algorithms employed. Speech recognition is a technology that continues to evolve, and is currently at the point where recognition engines are capable of identifying words spoken by previously unknown users. However, in order to achieve this, the range of words that a user can say must be constrained by defining an appropriate grammar.

In this chapter we will discuss what a grammar is and the role that grammars play in VoiceXML applications. We will start with a general discussion of why and where grammars are needed before looking at specific details of the two main grammar formats – JSGF (Sun Microsystems's Java Speech Grammar Format) and Nuance GSL (Nuance Grammar Specification Language).

The Role of the Grammar

Where traditional forms of input are required by an application, the input can usually be constrained in some way, so that input from the user is limited to what makes sense in that context. For example, Windows applications accept input from a pointing device such as a mouse, and unavailable options in a drop-down list can be excluded or grayed out. Similarly, in a field that requests the user's age, the application can restrict allowed input to the number keys only. In this way, the program reduces the processing required for that field.

Grammars in VoiceXML provide a similar function, allowing the application designer to define a **grammar rule** – the set of allowed words for a particular input – thus facilitating the task of identifying the user utterance for that field. The term 'grammar' is really somewhat of a misnomer, as these elements are not in fact concerned with defining grammar, but rather with specifying the legal vocabulary for a given context. It's a way of providing a context for the speech engine; so, if for instance it picks up a user utterance that sounds like "ullo", it can use the grammar (that contains the words "hello" and "goodbye") to determine that this most closely matches "hello", rather than say, "hollow". This still allows for the situation where the user says "elephant" for example, such that the system can determine that this is not near enough to any of the allowed inputs specified in the grammar to constitute a confident match.

Let's consider the following example of a JSGF grammar for a food ordering application. Don't worry too much about the details of this notation, which will be covered in later sections of this chapter. The user can choose whether their particular hunger is for pizza, hamburgers, or donuts. The task of the recognition engine is now simplified when this grammar is active, as it only needs to listen out for the specified utterances. Any utterances that are not matched by the grammar, such as "triple choc cookie", will throw a `nomatch` event that can be caught by a `<nomatch>` element to provide guidance or perform some other action as appropriate.

```
#JSGF V 1.0;
grammar foodtype;

<gimmie> = [gimmie | I want | I would like] [some];
<pizza> = <gimmie> pizza | pizzas;
<burger> = <gimmie> [ham] (burger | burgers);
<donuts> = <gimmie> donut | donuts;
```

As the speech-processing system receives input, it checks whether that input falls within the set of constraints defined by the grammar. If the utterance by the user is matched to one of these grammar rules, it is returned to the application for any processing. (As we will see later, there are ways of specifying what is returned to the application, which solve the problem of the somewhat cumbersome response "I want some ham burgers" being returned.) Utterances outside of the grammar need special attention that can be provided by the active `<nomatch>` element, as we will see in more detail in Chapter 5. To sum up, constraining input by grammar helps the speech engine to:

- Reliably recognize speech within a short period
- Provide an application with a single identifier for a range of utterances

Grammar Definition Languages

Unfortunately, at present there is no standard notation for defining a Voice grammar, although attempts for standardization are under way, and hopefully the World Wide Web Consortium will soon finalize its recommended grammar specification. Until then, your choice of grammar syntax for an application will depend firstly on the formats supported by your voice platform, then by individual preference. In this chapter, we discuss two of the most popular grammar formats, JSGF (Java Speech Grammar Format) and GSL (Nuance's Grammar Specification Language). As a member of the Java family, JSGF conforms to Java syntax, while GSL is a proprietary format devised by Nuance software. However, neither JSGF nor GSL are standards specified by any industry consortium.

In general, JSGF will be the easiest to follow for web developers at least, because of its Java syntax, but due to Nuance's highly respected position in the field of speech processing, GSL is often the preferred choice.

Grammars in VoiceXML

These two formats for defining grammars are pre-existing notations that have been borrowed by the VoiceXML specification. Whichever syntax you decide to use, the grammar is included as a child of VoiceXML elements to which it applies, and is contained by the <grammar> element. There is also the special case of the <menu> element, when the grammar for each option is contained within each <choice> element, but we shall be looking at this later. <grammar> elements have several scoping options that can be specified – namely field level, form level or document level, which define the input elements for which the grammar is valid by default. This is covered in detail in the upcoming section *Grammar Scope in VoiceXML Documents.*

There are two main ways of defining a grammar: **inline** or **external**. Inline grammars are specified inside the elements to which they apply, and to avoid spoiling the well-formedness of our VoiceXML document, often need to be enclosed within a CDATA section. An inline grammar can be a complete grammar or just a fragment of a grammar, as in the example below:

```
<field name="connectMuppet">
  <prompt>Which Muppet would you like to speak to?</prompt>
  <grammar type="application/x-jsgf">
    kermit | ([miss] piggy)
  </grammar>
  <nomatch>
    I'm afraid only Kermit and Miss Piggy are available today
  </nomatch>
  <filled>
    <if cond="connectMuppet=='kermit'">
      <goto next="speakToKermit" />
    <else/>
      <goto next="speakToMissPiggy" />
    </if>
  </filled>
</field>
```

When using an inline grammar, the `type` attribute of <grammar> gives the MIME type of the grammar. For example, if the grammar is written in JSGF, as here, then the MIME type will be `application/x-jsgf`. GSL grammars use the `application/x-gsl` MIME type.

The alternative to fully specifying a grammar inside the elements where it is active is to use an external grammar defined in a separate document. They are referenced from a VoiceXML application by the `src` attribute of the <grammar> element. If the above grammar were to be placed in the file `muppets.gram`, then the following line would reference that grammar:

```
<grammar src="grammars/muppets.gram" type="application/x-jsgf" />
```

The main attributes of the <grammar> element include:

- `type`: indicates the MIME type used in the grammar. If omitted, the interpreter engine of the voice platform will sometimes attempt to determine the type dynamically
- `src`: this attribute specifies the URL for external grammar documents
- `scope`: defines the scope for the grammar within the current application, as explained more fully in the next section

There are also the attributes caching, fetchhint, and fetchtimeout. The purpose of these is as follows:

- caching – This attribute indicates what caching to use, and can take one of two values: safe means content is always refreshed; fast means a cached copy may be used if it has not expired.
- fetchhint – This attribute controls the interpreter's cache behavior. It can take one of three values: prefetch means it can fetch the resource in advance when the page first loads; safe means the resource should only be fetched when needed; stream is used for very large files or streaming media, to tell the interpreter that processing may commence before the file has completed downloading. Defaults to the grammarfetchhint property.
- fetchtimeout – The value of this attribute specifies the period to wait before throwing an error.badfetch event.

Grammar elements can be included at a form (dialog) level or within any VoiceXML element that receives user input. Examples of grammar within <field>, <menu>, and <link> elements are given below. (These elements will be covered in more detail in Chapters 4 and 5, but their meaning should be apparent here.)

```
//This snippet shows a grammar in a field
<field name = "color">
  <prompt>
    Please tell me the color you would like for your Woolen Nose Insulator
  </prompt>
  <grammar>Red | Blue| Green | Yellow</grammar>
</field>
```

The simple dialog above specifies an interaction that requests that the user say which one of the available colors they would like for the product ordered.

The <link> element of VoiceXML is a means of specifying a transition available over a varying scope, and is another place where grammars are required. When an utterance matches one of these grammars, the transition of the corresponding link will be followed:

```
//This snippet shows a grammar in a link element
<link next="http://localhost/buyflowers.vxml">
  <grammar type = "Application/x-jsgf" >
    [ buy ] (roses | violets | carnations | flowers)
  </grammar>
</link>
```

Now, whenever the user says "Buy roses", "Flowers" or any other utterance matching this grammar while this link is in scope, it will be triggered taking the user to the external VoiceXML document provided by the next attribute, buyflowers.vxml. Don't worry too much about the syntax for the grammar used here, as it is covered in detail under the headings *Java Speech Grammar Format* and *Nuance- Grammar Specification Language* later on.

Grammars can also be defined within <form> elements using the <grammar> element with a form-level scope. This is required to write mixed-initiative forms, which we will explain in Chapter 5.

In menus, a grammar is implicitly specified by the <choice> element, unlike other elements, where the <grammar> element is required to specify a grammar. A menu's active grammar comprises the set of terms contained by the menu's constituent <choice> elements. Look at this example:

```
<menu>
  <prompt>
    Welcome to Tekey Tips. Please tell me your preferred language.
  </prompt>
  <choice next= "http://techtips.programming.com/java.vxml">Java</choice>
  <choice next ="http://techtips.programming.com/delphi.vxml">Delphi</choice>
  <choice next = "http://techtips.programming.com/cpp.vxml">CPlusPlus</choice>
  <noinput>
    Please tell me the name of your favorite computer language.
  </noinput>
  <nomatch>
    The following languages are available:
    <enumerate/>
  </nomatch>
  <help>
    You may say one of the following:
    <enumerate/>
  </help>
</menu>
```

In the above example, the menu has an implied grammar of `Java | Delphi | Cplusplus`. Note that the `<enumerate>` element in the `<nomatch>` and `<help>` elements causes the voice interpreter to say these allowed utterances out loud using TTS. A typical user interaction with this form could proceed like this:

System:	"Welcome to Techie Tips. Please tell me your preferred language."
User:	"Occam"
System:	"The following languages are available, Java, Delphi, C++"
User:	"Delphi"
System:	*Proceeds to http://techtips.programming.com/delphi.vxml*

DTMF Grammars

In addition to speech input, VoiceXML allows tone input produced by pressing the keys on the telephone handset: the system known as DTMF (Dual Tone Multi-Frequency).

Many applications allow the user to enter inputs using the keypad on their telephone as an alternative to speaking, either in the event that speech recognition is unreliable or undesirable, or simply because many users feel a little uneasy about speaking to a machine. Not only that, but certain hotkeys can enhance an application's usability – for example, assigning the star key as a shortcut to the main menu from anywhere in an application. The following short dialog shows how an application could offer DTMF:

System:	"Welcome. Please press 1 or say 'Check Mail' to check your e-mail. Please press 2 or say 'New mail' to compose a new mail."
User:	*Presses key 1*

The application designer would then define a DTMF grammar in addition to the standard voice grammar, specifying the action to perform when the user presses either 1 or 2. In a way, a DTMF grammar acts like an input validator.

A DTMF grammar can be specified for any of the VoiceXML input elements using the <dtmf> element. For the <menu> element, a DTMF grammar can be defined using the dtmf attribute on <choice> elements within the menu.

Like the <grammar> element, the <dtmf> element also has attributes type, src, and scope that perform the same functions. As with the voice <grammar> element, no standard is specified for writing a DTMF grammar in the VoiceXML specification. The example below, an adaptation of the previous example, is written using JSGF:

```
<field name="color">
  <prompt>
    Please tell me the color you would like for your Woolen Nose Insulator
  </prompt>
  <help>
    Your insulator is handcrafted by machine from the finest draylon, in one
    of the following colors: Red, Green, Blue, Yellow.
  </help>
  <grammar type="application/x-jsgf">
    Red {red} | Blue {blue} | Green {green} | Yellow {yellow}
  </grammar>
  <dtmf type="application/x-jsgf">
    1 {red} | 2 {blue} | 3 {green} | 4 {yellow}
  </dtmf>
</field>
```

Now the user may make their choice either by saying their preferred color, or by pressing keys 1, 2, 3, or 4, which are specified by the DTMF grammar as corresponding to the voice utterances red, blue, green, and yellow by defining JSGF tags (the curly braces, {}, and their contents – for more on these, see the *JSGF Tags* section).

In the following example of a <menu> dialog, we see how the dtmf attribute is used to provide a numeric input to trigger each <choice> element. An (easy) exercise for the reader here would be to modify this to include appropriate text content for the <choice> elements so that the user could either press a number, or ask for a language by name should they prefer:

```
<menu>
  <prompt>
    For English press 1, For French press 2, For German press 3.
  </prompt>
  <choice dtmf="1" next="http://www.mydomain/vxml/english.vxml"/>
  <choice dtmf="2" next="http://www.mydomain/vxml/french.vxml"/>
  <choice dtmf="3" next="http://www.mydomain/vxml/German.vxml"/>
</menu>
```

Grammar Scope in VoiceXML Documents

In general, the scope of the grammar can be thought of as indicating the 'area' for which that grammar is active in the current application. Whilst in that 'area', the VoiceXML engine listens for utterances in the active grammars. By default, a grammar's scope is limited to the elements in which it is defined and any descendant elements without an explicit grammar given. So, if the <grammar> element is contained inside a <field> element, it is valid throughout that field; similarly, a grammar defined in a <form> element is valid throughout that form. An exception to this is a grammar defined within a <link> element: these are valid throughout the parent element that contains the <link> element. For example, if a link is contained in a form, the grammar for triggering it is active throughout the entire parent form.

Grammars defined within forms or menus can be given document scope by using the scope attribute with the value document:

```
<form name="myform" scope="document">
  <grammar src="http://localhost/colors.gram" type="application/x-jsgf" />
</form>
```

Here, as the form scope is set as document, a grammar defined within that form would also scope to document level by default. To specify a dialog-level (that is, form-level) grammar within such a form requires the scope attribute of the <grammar> element to be explicitly assigned the value dialog.

```
<form name="myform" scope="document">
  <grammar src="http://localhost/colors.gram" type="application/x-jsgf" />
  <grammar src="http://localhost/flowers.gram" scope="dialog"
           type="application/x-jsgf" />
</form>
```

This method can be used to avoid overlapping of grammars.

Be aware that grammars given in <choice> elements cannot specify a scope!

Grammars defined in a central root document that is referenced by all other documents in an application (see Chapter 4 for examples of this) will scope to the entire application. In general, the best practice is to minimize grammars of global scope to only those that are truly required for an application. Excessive use of global grammars not only increases the likelihood of overlapping grammars, but may also hit application performance.

Java Speech Grammar Format

We shall now take an in-depth look at usage of the Java Speech Grammar Format, JSGF. As you know, it follows the general conventions of the Java programming language. For instance, semicolons are required at the end of all statements, // can be used to comment out a line of code, and multiple-line comments are enclosed between /* and */. Popular speech processing engines, like IBM ViaVoice, and voice gateways, like HeyAnita, support this format. Here we will explain the basic syntax of JSGF, covering some different constructs and a few other pertinent issues.

Basic Structure of JSGF

A JSGF grammar document consists of a grammar header and a set of grammar rules, called the grammar body. Each rule is by default identified by the tokens representing the actual input expected for that rule.

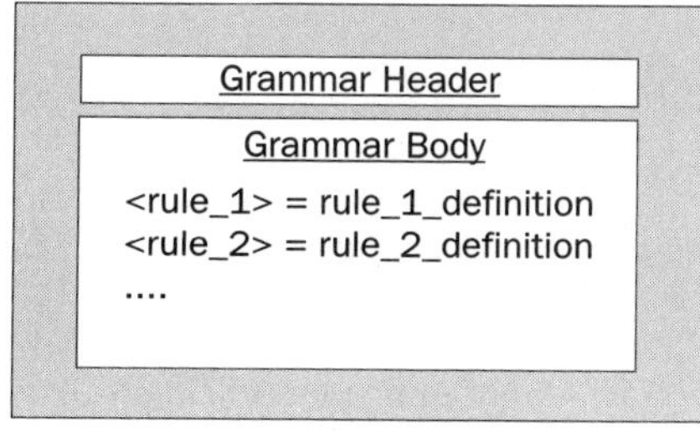

Each JSGF document grammar header starts with a self-identifying header of the following form:

```
# JSGF V 1.0 ISO8859;
```

This indicates the version number (`V 1.0`) and the character encoding used (`ISO8859`). If the encoding is not specified, a reasonable default will be assumed, depending on the platform. After the header comes the keyword `grammar`, followed by the qualified name for the grammar defined in this document.

```
grammar MySite.MyGrammar;
```

JSGF groups together different grammar documents and rules in **packages**, as is the case with other members of the Java family. So, the above line refers to the item `MyGrammar` in the package `MySite`. Similarly, we can refer to individual rules within a particular grammar in this way, as in `MySite.MyGrammar.Rule1`.

After the declaration of the grammar name, `import` statements may be given to make use of rules or grammars from other documents. The `import` statement's syntax is:

```
import <package_name.grammarname.rulename>;
```

So, in order to apply `Rule1` taken from `MyGrammar` contained in the `MyDomain` package, the required usage would be:

```
import <MyDomain.MyGrammar.Rule1>;
```

We can group different rules together using operators, such as the asterisk, so that:

```
import <MyDomain.MyGrammar.*>;
```

will import all rules within `MyGrammar`. An alternative notation to achieve this same effect is to simply use `<MyDomain.Mygrammar>`.

So a JSGF grammar header will look something like this:

```
# JSGF V 1.0 ISO8859;

grammar MySite.MyGrammar;

import <MyDomain.MyGrammar2.Rule2>;
```

Now we've got our header down as required, we can start defining the actual rules for this grammar. A JSGF rule definition obeys the following syntax:

```
public <ruleName> = ruleExpansion ;
```

The definition contains the following parts:

- An optional `public` declaration – this declares the rule as being public
- `<ruleName>` – the name of the rule being defined
- The `ruleExpansion` – this is what must be said to follow the rule

Public rules are useful, because they can be referenced within the rule definitions of another grammar rule in another document, so long as the rule is imported into that document as we showed earlier.

Be aware that, as Unicode string matching is used, rule names are case sensitive. Rule names should begin with an alphabetic character, followed by further characters including Unicode alphanumeric characters, and symbols and punctuation marks from the following list:

```
+ - : ; , = | / \ ( ) [ ] @ # % ! ^ & ~
```

Tokens are the part of a grammar rule that define what the user may say to satisfy that rule, and are most commonly just regular words. JSGF permits tokens to be enclosed in quotation marks, but it is not required. Different tokens can be combined with operators, to make up the `ruleExpansion` in the definition above. The token itself can be delimited by whitespace, a semi-colon, or any of the operators for combining tokens (discussed later). Technical details of a token are given in the final section of this chapter, *Grammar Processing.*

That pretty much covers the basic requirements for writing a JSGF file. To illustrate the key points, I shall introduce a simple quiz program that uses the grammar file below. The grammar is saved as a separate file, `favoriteauthor.gram`, and, to start with, contains just one rule.

```
#JSGF V 1.0 ;
grammar favoriteauthor;

<author> = Marquez; // This is a comment
```

In a VoiceXML document, we could now use the grammar like this:

```
<?xml version ="1.0"?>
<vxml version="1.0">
<form>
  <field name="author">
    <grammar src="favoriteauthor.gram" type="application/x-jsgf" />
    <help>
      Born in Columbia, he was awarded the Nobel prize for literature in 1982.
    </help>
    <nomatch>
      Wrong! Try again!
    </nomatch>
    <nomatch count="4">
      Philistine! It was Gabriel Garcia Marquez!
      <goto next = "http://messages.mydomain//bye.vxml" />
    </nomatch>
    <prompt>"Who is the author of the book Of Love and Other Demons"</prompt>
  </field>
  <block>
    Well done, you got it, you swot.
    <goto next="http://messages.mydomain//winner.vxml" />
  </block>
</form>
</vxml>
```

Here, to follow the rule, the user must say "Marquez" (the expansion), in which case our external JSGF grammar `favouriteauthor.gram` will assign the value `author` to the field with name `author`. Any other input will produce a nomatch error that we can catch to keep tally of bad guesses. You've probably noticed that should the user say "Gabriel Garcia Marquez" rather than "Marquez", such a response will not be recognized as correct: we need to improve our grammar to allow a variety of user responses. We can do this by using operators to enhance our grammar rules, as we will show in the following section.

Smooth Operators

In this section, we will see how we can create more sophisticated rules by using operators to combine tokens. The last example was not very satisfactory, as the grammar rule for the correct author was matched by the author's surname alone. It's possible to change the rule like this:

```
<author> = Gabriel Garcia Marquez;
```

But now, in order to match the rule, the user must say the full name "Gabriel Garcia Marquez", in that exact order. We need to use the | operator to specify a list of alternatives for a particular rule:

```
<author> = Gabriel | Garcia | Marquez;
```

To match the rule now, the user can say "Gabriel", "Garcia", or "Marquez". Note that the | operator is exclusive, so the above rule will not match Gabriel Marquez, say. This isn't quite what we want, but by using parentheses to group different tokens together the rule gets a little better:

```
<author> = ( Gabriel | Garcia ) Marquez;
```

Now, the user can say either "Gabriel Marquez" or "Garcia Marquez" to match this rule, and return a value for any field using this grammar of `author`. But the user cannot say "Gabriel Garcia Marquez", or just "Marquez" with the rule as it currently stands. We need a way of indicating when a token in a rule is an optional utterance. The way to do this in JSGF requires use of the square bracket notation. Any tokens in a rule that are enclosed inside square brackets are optional utterances that may or may not be spoken by the user:

```
<author> = [ Gabriel | Garcia | Gabriel Garcia ] Marquez;
```

This is pretty much what we want, as it allows the user to respond with just "Marquez", "Gabriel Marquez", "Garcia Marquez", or "Gabriel Garcia Marquez". The surname is always required, but the first names, by dint of the square brackets, are optional. However, should the user say "Garcia Gabriel Marquez", they will be rightly scolded for their ignorance.

We can make our grammars more readable and reusable by combining rules using their rule names:

```
<firstNames> = [ Gabriel | Garcia | Gabriel Garcia ];
<author> = <firstNames> Marquez;
```

Note that in JSGF, it is not legal to leave square brackets or parentheses empty.

Unary Operators in JSGF

JSGF also allows the Kleene star, *, and the + character as unary operators. The * operator indicates that the immediately preceding token may be spoken any number of times or omitted entirely.

```
<mumble> = err | umm | ahh
<answer> = <mumble>* <author>
```

So, to match the answer grammar, the user can now say, "umm, ahh, Marquez" or "err, err, umm, Gabriel Garcia Marquez", or just be decisive and say "Marquez".

The unary operator + is similar, except that it indicates the previous token must be spoken at least once. So, going back to the very first example in this chapter, we can come up with this:

```
<order> = ( burgers | pizza | ice cream ) please+
```

Now the user can place an order by saying "burgers please", "pizza please please please", and so on. Rude customers who don't say please will now be caught by the <nomatch> element, where they can perhaps be insulted a little, and cut off!

In JSGF, unary operators must always *come after* the token(s) to which they apply.

JSGF Tags

Tags in JSGF are used to provide clearer identifiers for rule definitions. Your application can then test for these tags rather than the actual user utterance, which will be used by default if no tag is given. JSGF tags are enclosed in curly braces, {}, and like the other unary operators in JSGF, must follow the token or tokens that they apply to.

```
<speakto> = ( George | Bush | George Bush ) {president}
          | ( Dick | Cheney | Dick Cheney ) {vicepres}
```

Here, when the user asks to speak to "George", "Bush", or "George Bush", the grammar will return the value president to the application. Should the user ask for "Dick", "Cheney" or "Dick Cheney", the grammar will return the value vicepres. Unlike other unary operators, there can be more than one tag for a single token, in which case all matching tags are concatenated to produce the returned result.

Operator Precedence

JSGF obeys the following rules of precedence for operators:

- Quoted or Unquoted Tokens
- Grouping Operators () and []
- Unary operators
- Rule Expansions
- | Operator

<void> and <null>

The two special rules <void> and <null> should be mentioned here. The <null> rule is used as a grammar rule to indicate that the user *need not* say anything, while <void> is used as a grammar rule where the user *cannot* say anything. So:

```
<sample> = <rule> | <void>
```

is equivalent to:

```
<sample> = [<rule>]
```

The <void> element can be used to prevent the user answering a prompt:

```
<condition> = <void>
```

Here, the user can't say anything to satisfy the grammar condition because it has been assigned as <void>. However, if the condition were <null>, the rule could be satisfied. These elements can be useful when dynamically creating grammars.

Recursion

Recursion is an effective tool that can represent complex grammars that more closely correspond to natural language. For example, consider the following rule:

```
<myaction> = <action> | (<myaction> and <action> )
<action> = Select | Copy | Delete
```

The recursive myaction grammar allows the user to say "Select and Delete", or even "Select and Copy and Delete". Nested recursion is also allowed in VoiceXML, such as calling different rules from each other. It should be noted that the recursive reference in VoiceXML must appear at the end of the rule. To illustrate, writing the <myaction> rule as below would be illegal because the recursive reference to the rule itself appears on the left-hand side of the expression:

```
<myaction> = (<myaction> and <action>) | <action>
```

Assigning Weights to Tokens

If a developer would like the recognition engine to favor certain utterances over others in a particular situation, it's possible to weight the individual grammar tokens accordingly. This weighting is usually proportional to the expected frequency with which the utterance is spoken.

The weight of a token is given between forward slashes before that token:

```
<action> = /0.5/ Select | /0.3/ Copy | /0.2/ Paste
```

It may be simpler when developing to use numbers such that the sum of the weights for a particular rule is equal to 1, as in this case, but this is not necessary. Here a weighting of 0.5 is assigned to "Select", indicating this option will be uttered around 50% of the time, "Copy" is given a weight of 0.3 so it is generally uttered around 30% of the time, "Paste" has a weight of 0.2, meaning it is the least likely option, uttered around 20% of the time. Note that if we assign probability to one token, then all tokens for that rule must also be assigned probabilities.

By adjusting the weights for available options, we can cause the recognition engine to give preference to certain combinations of words at the expense of other 'competing' combinations. Weighting responses like this requires a lot of insight to get right, and usually involves a fair amount of trial and error to tune optimally. If you get it right, recognition speed and accuracy will increase, but also be aware that weighting responses can reduce the speed of speech processing, depending on the platform used.

Nuance Grammar Specification Language

The Nuance Grammar Specification Language, GSL, is another popular notation for grammar definition. It was originally created by Nuance, and closely resembles JSGF in syntax and internal hierarchy.

GSL grammar rules are defined in the format:

```
.GrammarName GrammarDefinition
```

where `GrammarName` is the name for the grammar, and `GrammarDefinition` defines the tokens for that particular grammar rule. So, the following rule, named `Check_ac`, would match the user utterance 'my checking account':

```
.Check_ac my checking account
```

The initial letter of a grammar name must always be an uppercase letter, but can be followed by uppercase and lowercase characters, digits, and any of the following characters:

```
@ ' _ . - ( )
```

Like JSGF, GSL grammar definitions contain a mix of tokens, operators, and other rule names, separated by tabs, spaces or new line characters. External grammars can be included in a GSL file by the use of an `#include` statement at the beginning.

```
#include grammarfilename.gram

.Grammar_Rule_1 Grammar_Definition_1

.Grammar_Rule_2 Grammar_Definition_2

....
```

As with JSGF, each grammar rule in a document has a fully qualified name of the form `DocumentName.GrammarRule`, where `DocumentName` is the name of the containing grammar file or package.

Grammar Scope in GSL

GSL classifies grammars as sub-grammars and top-level grammars. Basically, a sub-grammar is used to build top-level grammars, while only top-level grammars are accessible by the VoiceXML application document. All top-level grammar rules must begin with a period '.' character.

```
.Colors Primary Secondary
Primary [ Red Green Blue ]
Secondary [ Yellow Cyan Magenta ]
```

Here, we have a top-level grammar named `Colors`, as indicated by the initial period character. It is made up of the two sub-grammars `Primary` and `Secondary`, which as sub-grammars may not be accessed from outside the package where they are defined.

Operators in GSL

Operators are used to combine sub-grammar rules and tokens to allow more sophisticated user responses as with JSGF. Firstly, parentheses are used to concatenate different grammar rules or tokens. All tokens inside the parentheses are required in order to meet that particular rule.

```
.Blacky (Black Cat)
```

Here the user must say "Black Cat" to match the grammar rule.

Also different in usage from JSGF are square brackets, which in GSL indicate that any one of the contained tokens will match that rule when spoken by the user. So, the following rule:

```
.Fruit [ apple banana grapes strawberry pear ]
```

would be matched when the user says "apple", "banana", "grapes", "strawberry", or "pear". One and only one occurrence of the listed tokens inside square brackets is allowed for a rule to be matched.

These operators already enhance the functionality of our GSL grammars quite a bit:

```
.MyCat (Nice [Black White Brown] Cat )
```

This grammar will be matched by any one of the following phrases:

```
"Nice Black Cat"
"Nice White Cat"
"Nice Brown Cat"
```

Unary operators in GSL

There are three unary operators in GSL: the optional operator `?`, the positive closure `+`, and the Kleene closure `*`. Unary operators have highest priority.

> **Unlike in JSGF, GSL unary operators must *precede* the token or grammar rule to which they apply.**

The `?` operator denotes that the following token or grammar rule is optional:

```
.MyCat (?Nice [Black White Brown] cat)
```

The addition of the ? operator to the above rule means that the user can now say things like "Nice White Cat", "Black Cat", and so on. When the + operator precedes a token or grammar rule, that utterance must occur at least once, so for the following example:

```
.MyCat (+Nice [Black White Brown] Cat )
```

"Nice Black Cat", and "Nice Nice Black cat" would be acceptable utterances, but not just "Black Cat". The Kleene star operator is used to precede tokens or grammar rules that may appear any number of times in the user utterance, or may be omitted altogether:

```
.Mycat (*Nice [Black White Brown] Cat)
```

So, the above rule matches "White Cat", "Nice Brown Cat", "Nice Nice Black Cat", and so on.

> **As in JSGF, recursive rules in GSL must place the self-referential token at the end of the rule in order to be valid.**

Nuance GSL Slot Names and Values

As with JSGF, there is a way of specifying the result of the recognition that gets returned to the application with Nuance GSL. In GSL this is done by using a **slot name** and **slot value**, but is analogous to using a tag in JSGF. Take a look at the following example:

```
.Speakto [
          [ George Bush (George Bush) ] {<option president>}
          [ Dick Cheney (Dick Cheney) ] {<option vicepres>}
          ]
```

Here, if the user says "George", "Bush", or "George Bush", the value `president` gets returned to the application. Similarly, if the user says "Dick", "Cheney", or "Dick Cheney", the value `vicepres` gets returned.

The slot names in this example are both `option`, while the slot values are `president` and `vicepres` respectively. Note that on the Tellme gateway, the slot name of `option` is always used, as given above. However, on BeVocal, it is suggested that the name of the `<field>` that the grammar's recognition value should be returned to is used instead. This is necessary for mixed-initiative forms (described in Chapter 5) where the grammar indicates which fields should be filled, but for grammars contained within a single field, it does not matter: in this situation, always using the slot name `option` still works fine.

Grammar Probabilities in GSL

As with JGSF, if we want to favor one particular phrase over another, we can assign a weighting for that phrase, usually based on the probability of it being used by a user. Although if it is done well it can help the speed and accuracy of the processing, providing probabilities is not always appropriate as it can increase the load on the speech processing engine and may thereby adversely affect response time. Probabilities are generally used with the `[ ]` operator for which they are most meaningful, and are associated with a token using the ~ operator, as in this example:

```
.MyCat (*Nice [White~0.1 Black~0.7 Brown~0.2] Cat)
```

Here, a probability of 0.1 (equal to a 10% chance) is assigned to White, 0.7 (a 70% chance) to Black, and 0.2 (20%) to Brown.

We can also use probabilities with + and * operators:

```
+Nice~0.65
```

means the probability of additional occurrence of nice after the first occurrence is 65%, while:

```
*Nice~0.65
```

means Nice is likely to occur one or more times with a probability of 70%.

Use of DTMF in GSL

DTMF can be used in GSL grammars contained with <grammar> element, as well as the <dtmf> element. To demonstrate this, let's look at an example. In this example grammar, we have specified four options for the user to choose from: car, boat, bicycle, and plane. We have also given the user the option of pressing the keys *1* to *4*, respectively, to choose between the four options:

```
<grammar>
[
[car dtmf-1]
[boat dtmf-2]
[bicycle dtmf-3]
[plane dtmf-4]
]
</grammar>
```

Of course, we would need to put this grammar alongside a question prompt such as "What is your favorite method of transport?", and list the options available (within a VoiceXML document!) for it to be of any use to us, but you get the idea. Note that `dtmf-star` and `dtmf-pound` can be used for the * and # keys respectively.

Grammars Defined in Other Files

As mentioned earlier, any top-level grammars in a package can be referenced from other documents by use of the `#include` keyword.

```
#include <grammarfile.grammar>
#include "grammarfile.grammar"
```

The use of the angle brackets here is similar to that for the C++ `#include` directive. In the first case above, the angled brackets indicate that the grammar compiler must first search the default directory for the rule, and then look in other directories. In the second case, however, the compiler only searches the specified directories. Note that including a file more than once will lead to errors, as it is in effect a duplicate declaration.

Built-In Grammars in VoiceXML

Built-in grammars are provided as a part of the VoiceXML language itself, and include both DTMF and voice grammars. They can be used instead of the inline and external grammars we have seen so far, when a grammar of a fairly simple type is needed. They come in various types:

- boolean, for true or false utterances. (In DTMF, 1 is true, and 2 is false.)
- date, for year, month and day inputs. (In DTMF, 14 February 1996 would be 19960214.)
- digits, for strings of individual digits. For example, "three four seven".
- currency, for numbers with a currency indication. (In DTMF * is used for the decimal point.)
- number, for numbers. For example, three hundred and forty seven. (In DTMF, * is used for the decimal point.)
- phone, for a telephone number. (In DTMF, * is used for x, meaning "extension".)
- time, for a time value.

There are two ways in which these grammar types can be used.

Built-in grammars can be included in a VoiceXML document by preceding the src attribute value of a <grammar> element with the builtin: keyword. Below, the means for invoking the built-in Boolean grammar is shown for both the voice grammar, and the DTMF grammar:

```
<grammar src="builtin:grammar/boolean/>
<grammar src="builtin:dtmf/boolean/>
```

Some of the built-in grammars can be parameterized like this:

```
<grammar src="builtin:grammar/digits?maxlength =10" />
```

In this case, we can specify the maximum number of digits that the built-in grammar should permit.

The alternative way of using grammar types is when using the <field> element, which is used to collect user input. The grammar type can be specified using the type attribute of this element, as shown in more detail in Chapter 4.

```
<field name="age" type="number">
  <prompt>
    How old are you?
  </prompt>
  <filled>
    <prompt>
      That old!
    </prompt>
  </filled>
</field>
```

Grammar Processing

We have seen that writing a grammar involves defining a set of tokens to create a general rule. But it is useful to see how the speech-processing engine actually goes about recognizing these tokens when spoken by a variety of previously un-encountered users. In particular, what means does it employ to predict the likely pronunciation of an arbitrary string of characters? This is where the concept of a dictionary comes in.

The speech recognizer software has an **Acoustic Model** that it uses in tandem with its **dictionary** to compile grammar files. An acoustic model is a pattern-matching model used by the speech engine to determine how tokens in a grammar are likely to be said by a user. For maximum efficacy, all the tokens we use in our grammars should be regular words that have their own entry in the dictionary. If a particular token is not found in the dictionary, the speech engine will have to guess how that word may sound, although many engines provide an option for the application developer to create custom dictionaries that define their own particular tokens.

In the standard VoiceXML architecture, grammars in a particular document are loaded by the voice interpreter (the VoiceXML gateway) and then compiled before they can be used for speech processing.

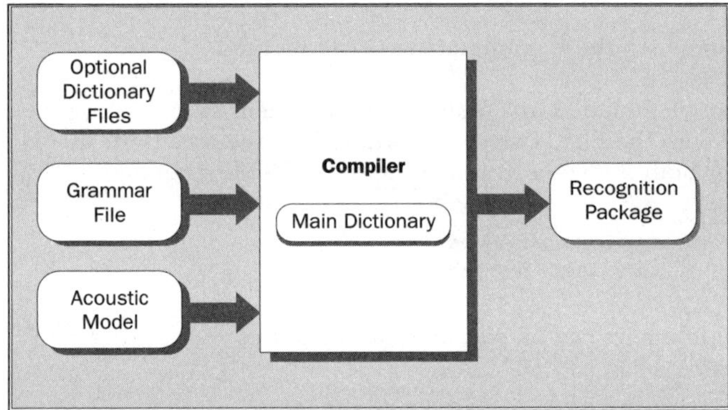

Using Grammar Effectively

The use of an effective grammar is critical for speech-based applications. The most challenging aspect of speech application design is trying to cover as many possible responses as may be encountered. For example, for the question, "Which country are you from?" the user could not only give one of any number of countries, but their phrasing could vary wildly too. They may reply, "India", "I'm from India", "India is my home country" and so on. It's the responsibility of the application developer to predict such cases and to develop suitable grammars to constrain user input without making the interface too clumsy.

The most important thing in a grammar is to be able to identify the key information from a user request. To take the example of a reservation availability system, the inputs that our application requires from the user are the name of the destination city along with the name of the city the user is traveling from. A whole host of extraneous words and phrases could come along with these, such as, "I want to go to...", "Can I fly to..." and so on. It is essential to determine the exact input we require from the user, and also other items that they may say, if we are to design a grammar effectively and efficiently.

However, never try to take into consideration each and every possibility the user may say. That is not practicable and such a grammar will noticeably hinder speech processing, and hence make your application inefficient and a nuisance to use. By devising a well-designed prompt, we can limit the variety of user responses so our grammar can be simpler from the outset.

Mixed-initiative forms are particularly tricky, as you will see in Chapter 5: you need to take extra care to ensure that your form-level grammars don't overlap with field-level ones, which can have unpredictable results. Always try to keep the scope of the grammar in mind, and coordinate it with the overall application design.

Check the capabilities of the speech-processing engine of your platform while designing an application. Always consider factors like dynamic recompilation of grammar and other capabilities of the engine. Even if changes are made to a grammar file, some platforms will not recompile the revised grammar during the lifetime of the document that contains it.

Summary

We've seen what a grammar is and investigated the important role that grammars play in VoiceXML. We have looked at the notation for creating grammars in the two most popular formats, JSGF and GSL, and looked at the different features offered. In VoiceXML, DTMF grammars are used to specify the key presses allowable as input from a user. To be effective, designing and developing a grammar in VoiceXML requires thorough analysis of the speech interface that is to be offered to users, and the sorts of information that we can expect our users to say to the application. This issue is covered in depth in Chapter 6.

Currently, the W3C is working on a specification for a standard grammar format based on JSGF. Nevertheless, GSL is also very popular in voice application development, and it offers a lot of extra features. It is likely that the final grammar standard will incorporate the best aspects of each format, with a few extras thrown in. To finish with, here is a quick reference table comparing operators from JSGF and GSL grammar formats.

Operator	JSGF	GSL
Disjunction: a or b	`a	b`	`[a b]`
Optional: a or no a	`[a]`	`?a`
One or more: a or aa or ...	`a+`	`+a`
Zero or more: no a or a or ...	`a*`	`*a`
Weighting: a with a probability of n	`/n/ a`	`a~n`

```
<?xml version="1.0"?>
<vxml version="1.0">
<form id="foo">
<block>
<prompt>
Hi. My name is Bob
</prompt>
</block>
</form>
</vxml>
```

Basic VoiceXML

This chapter examines the basic elements of VoiceXML markup, illustrated through the development of simple VoiceXML documents and dialogs.

The topics discussed in this chapter include:

- A very brief reminder of XML language and syntax, and how it relates to VoiceXML
- Pointers to online documentation and resources
- The structure of a VoiceXML application, including root documents, documents, and dialogs, and the transitions between these documents and dialogs
- Basic structure of a VoiceXML document – the `<vxml>` and `<meta>` elements
- Delivering content and prompting the user with the `<prompt>`, and `<audio>` elements, and the JSML elements for TTS markup
- Collecting content and user responses with the `<form>` and `<menu>` elements
- Forms containing `<field>`, `<block>`, `<record>`, and other elements
- Menus with the `<enumerate>` and `<choice>` elements
- Using `<option>` elements in a `<field>`
- Form and field variables, the Form Interpretation Algorithm (FIA), and the `<filled>` element and event
- Recognizing input using grammars (speech and DTMF). Grammars are covered by example within the treatment of the `<field>` and `<menu>` elements

Where necessary, the different topics are demonstrated by separate code examples, the techniques from which are then brought together in the last example to produce a complete working application. All examples are available in the code download for this book.

XML Syntax and VoiceXML

VoiceXML is a programming-oriented language for the definition of voice interfaces and dialogs. It builds upon the momentum and acceptance gained by XML at large, and opens up to voice application developers the large toolbox of technologies and utilities that supports XML. "But wait," you might ask, "wasn't XML originally intended as a markup language for data formatting and exchange? Doesn't using an XML vocabulary as a programming language violate the spirit of this?" Well, yes. However, formulating VoiceXML as an XML vocabulary has several advantages, including a wealth of tools, such as validating XML editors, off-the-shelf parser libraries, easy use of valuable XML-related technologies such as XSLT, and the momentum of an open standard and the overall hype surrounding XML.

Because of this fact, using VoiceXML in a context that makes it, essentially, a procedural programming or scripting language can feel a little unnatural. For example, following the rules of well-formed XML in an "if-else" block seems a little off when the "else" is written `<else/>`. Another example is the absence of a "switch" construct in the spirit of the C language. Perhaps the authors of the language DTD just got tired? Client-side computation within the document is limited to ECMAScript. However, the ECMAScript interpreter will be tightly integrated with the VoiceXML interpreter, with many VoiceXML constructs (such as fields) automatically being defined as variables in the ECMAScript context.

Since XML is a markup language built on the rules of the Standard Generalized Markup Language (SGML), and since parsers and interpreters for XML vocabularies are far less forgiving than their equivalents in the HTML world, it is important to remember the rules of XML syntax and well-formed XML. We can summarize the rules of good XML syntax into these basic "commandments":

- Every document must begin with the declaration `<?xml version="1.0"?>`
- A `<stuff>` tag will always be matched and closed by a `</stuff>` tag
- An empty element always must contain the self-closing character "`/`", such as the `<else />` construct
- Attribute values are always quoted, such as `<goto next="#foo" />`. Common, but sloppy, HTML practices such as an `<INPUT TYPE=text>` tag will cause a parse error
- Tag names are case-sensitive

Documentation and Resources

The comprehensive and authoritative specification for the VoiceXML language is the World Wide Web Consortium "Note", available on the Web at http://www.w3.org/TR/voicexml/. This is an excellent resource, and illustrates the use of all the tags in the VoiceXML language. It also includes the official DTD, a detailed description of the Form Interpretation Algorithm, and a reference on JSGF grammar syntax. The document has "Note" status, and is not a Recommendation, because of intellectual property issues with the members of the VoiceXML consortium, and the need to integrate VoiceXML with the work done by the W3C's own Voice Browser Working Group.

Another useful resource is the Java Speech Markup Language (JSML) specification, found at http://java.sun.com/products/java-media/speech/forDevelopers/JSML/. VoiceXML borrows several elements from JSML, as we will see later. Almost as important to the individual developer will be the documentation for the platform they are developing on, especially documentation that explains any places where the platform diverges from the standard!

Remember that some platforms may not comply completely with the 1.0 specification, or may implement their own proprietary elements and attributes.

All of the example code in this chapter was tested using the Motorola Mobile Application Development Kit (MADK) version 2.0, as detailed in Chapter 2. However, all VoiceXML code in this chapter conforms to the 1.0 specification, and should run without modification on any compliant platform.

Structure of a VoiceXML Application

VoiceXML documents can be grouped together into applications: these consist of a root document, together with other documents connected to it through the use of the `application` attribute, as we will see later. Applications contain documents, and documents contain dialogs that are implemented with the various tags. This is illustrated in the diagram below, which also reflects the possible scopes of variables and grammars:

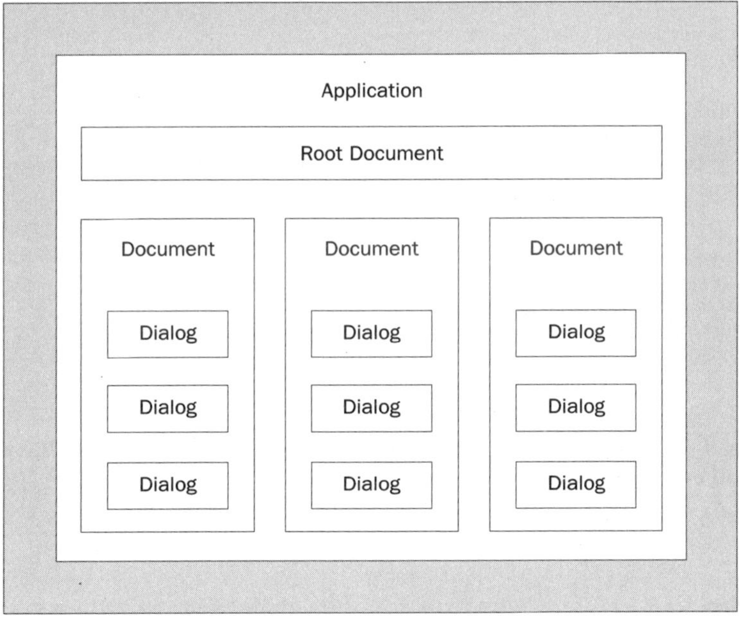

When the application is first executed, the interpreter will load the root document, if any. For example, if processing during the application invokes code in the root document like an event handler (for example, a global error handler) the application will change context to the root document to do processing, then return control back to the document where the event originated.

Root Documents

It is always good practice in programming to bundle common behaviors, variables, and scripts together for access, maintenance, and reusability. In VoiceXML development, the **root document** is the logical place for including this global functionality. This functionality is available in all documents that reference this root document: such documents are called **leaf documents**.

The code below shows a simple root document, called `ExampleRoot.vxml` in the example source code collection. It is also referenced in the document declaration shown below in the next section, *Starting a VoiceXML Document*. This document defines an application-level variable, a common handler for the "telephone disconnect" or hang-up event, and a global grammar equivalent to the built-in "help". Don't worry about the specifics of these items right now. They will be covered in greater detail in Chapter 5.

```
<?xml version="1.0"?>
<vxml version="1.0">
  <var name="FOO" expr="'bar'"/>
  <catch event="telephone.disconnect">
    <submit next="hangup.vxml"/>
  </catch>
  <link event="help">
    <grammar type="application/x-jsgf">
      help
    </grammar>
  </link>
</vxml>
```

Documents

Documents are individual files identified by a URI. They must follow the rules of well-formed XML, and are identified as VoiceXML by the `<vxml>` element. The required structure of valid VoiceXML documents will be covered in more detail shortly, beginning with a look at `<vxml>` and its attributes. The example below is the obligatory "Hello, world".

```
<?xml version="1.0"?>
<vxml version="1.0">
  <form id="foo">
    <block>
      <prompt>Hello, world</prompt>
    </block>
  </form>
</vxml>
```

This is the minimal document that will execute correctly and produce any audible result. All of the elements used will be explained in greater detail later.

Dialogs

Dialogs collect data from or offer choices to a user through the `<form>` and `<menu>` elements, respectively. Actually, this distinction is rather arbitrary, since menu functionality could easily be implemented with a form.

The flow of control through these dialogs can be controlled explicitly with the `<goto>` construct, or implicitly by understanding the Form Interpretation Algorithm (FIA – see *The Form Interpretation Algorithm* section later in the chapter for more details on this). The `<form>` in the example above is an example of implicit control: the interpreter will always execute the first valid dialog in the document, and in this case, it also happens to be the only one.

Moving Between Documents

Using a root document and an application structure implies multiple documents. If nothing else, most applications will probably want to send some information to a server-side application when the user explicitly exits or hangs up, as illustrated by the `<catch>` condition in the sample root document seen previously.

The two elements commonly used to move between dialogs in different documents are the <goto> and <submit> elements. Both allow the use of ECMAScript expressions to compute a destination URL dynamically. The main difference between the two is that the <goto> element will not pass along any of the variable values in the current document, while the <submit> element allows the programmer to specify a namelistof variables to pass. Both will be explained in greater detail in Chapter 5.

Starting a VoiceXML Document

All VoiceXML documents share a basic common structure. Like all XML documents, VoiceXML has a top-level root element.

<vxml>

The root or parent element for the VoiceXML language is the <vxml> element. It has four attributes, the mandatory version and the optional base, lang, and application.

```
<?xml version="1.0"?>
<vxml base="." lang="en-us" application="ExamplesRoot.vxml" version="1.0">
```

The version attribute tells the VoiceXML interpreter what DTD the document should conform to, and by extension, what services the interpreter is expected to provide.

The base attribute defines the base URI to use for relative URLs in document paths. Just as in HTML, this will default to the base URI of the current document.

Languages are specified in the lang attribute using ISO-639 language codes and ISO-3166 country codes. The handling of languages is implementation-specific, and obviously depends on the installation of Automated Speech Recognition (ASR) and Text-To-Speech (TTS) systems in the desired language on the target platform.

Finally, the application attribute is used to refer to a root document and place the document within the context of its application, making this a leaf document as explained previously.

<meta>

The VoiceXML analog of the HTML <meta> element is called, appropriately enough, <meta>. Like its HTML cousin, the VoiceXML <meta> tag lets the programmer include data about the document. Some platforms interpret these in a manner similar to a UNIX environment variable. For example, the "maintainer" line below, when executed on the Motorola Mya platform, will cause information about dialog problems of a certain severity (usually a complete crash), when they occur, to be sent via e-mail to the indicated address.

```
<meta name="maintainer" value="foo.user@fictionalcompany.com"/>
<meta name="author" content="John Doe"/>
```

This particular interpretation of metadata is obviously platform-dependent. Perhaps in the future, voice documents will be indexed for searching based on <meta> keywords, as HTML documents are today.

Delivering Content

Content can be delivered to the user with both Text-To-Speech (TTS) and pre-recorded audio in a number of formats. The availability and type of TTS, and the supported audio formats, vary from platform to platform, but most, if not all, platforms will have TTS services available. The quality of TTS rendered audio varies greatly from vendor to vendor. For pre-recorded audio, the VoiceXML 1.0 standard, suggests several types of 8 kHz 8-bit monaural audio file formats. These data-rate and bit-depth values correspond to telephony standards for a standard voice channel.

Content is delivered to the user via a combination of `<prompt>` and `<audio>` elements, and TTS blocks. Note that there is no inherent distinction made between "prompting" the user in the sense of expecting a response, and the simple delivery of information. Anything that is audible is a prompt.

Text in any dialog-level element will be treated as a TTS prompt. However, it is better form to nest the TTS data inside a `<prompt>` element, especially if TTS is to be mixed with pre-recorded audio. Placing the prompts inside the `<prompt>` element also gives control over certain attributes of prompt behavior, which will be explained later. In the following example, both dialogs will produce the same audible output and are equivalent:

```
<?xml version="1.0"?>
<vxml version="1.0">

  <form id="foo1">
    <block>
      Hi!
    </block>
  </form>

  <form id="foo2">
    <block>
      <prompt>
        Hi!
      </prompt>
    </block>
  </form>

</vxml>
```

<prompt>

As shown previously in the "Hello, world" example, a `<prompt>` element must be contained within a dialog. The `<block>`, `<field>`, and `<menu>` elements are the dialogs most commonly used to serve as parents for prompts. These will be covered in more detail later.

The `<prompt>` element has several attributes. The `bargein` attribute controls barge-in, the ability for the user to interrupt the prompt before it is complete. The user cannot interrupt the prompt when it is set to `false`. The `cond` attribute specifies an ECMAScript condition as to whether to play the prompt, and defaults to `"true"` when not explicity present. The `count` attribute allows the specification of different prompts if the dialog is going to be executed repeatedly. Finally, the `timeout` attribute defines a "grace period" for the user to respond after the prompt has been played. This is in units of seconds or milliseconds, and the minimum timeout effectively allowed would be platform dependent, however most interpreters should ignore values that are outside the allowed range. For example, if a document sets `timeout="1ms"` and the minimum allowed is 100ms, no errors should be thrown.

The example below illustrates a simple TTS-only prompt, using a condition where the bargein is set to false. In this case, explicitly defining a timeout would be somewhat redundant because the user can't say anything. The count attribute is unnecessary, and so defaults to "1".

```
<form id="start">
  <block>
    <prompt cond="(new Date()).getDay() == 0" bargein="false">
      Sorry.  We are closed on Sunday.
    </prompt>

    <prompt cond="(new Date()).getDay() != 0" bargein="false">
      Hello!  Thanks for calling.
    </prompt>
  </block>
</form>
```

So, this example will apologize for being closed if today happens to be Sunday, otherwise it will play a welcome message.

<audio>

Pre-recorded audio is played inside a prompt with the <audio> element. The audio element can have four attributes. The src attribute is required, and is a full or partial URI to the audio file to be played.

The other three attributes, caching, fetchtimeout, and fetchhint, relate to caching and fetching behaviors for optimization. (We saw these attributes previously as attributes of <grammar> in Chapter 3.) These are all optional because the platform the document is executing on will already have a global document cache policy, and any use of the attributes will only apply in a local scope for the given audio file. The values and standard behavior of these properties are discussed in great detail in Section 12.1 of the VoiceXML 1.0 specification. However, actual implementation of caching policies varies widely.

The example below shows the second prompt of the previous example, rewritten to make use of a pre-recorded audio message. It also illustrates the use of mixed TTS and pre-recorded audio. It will play a TTS message, followed by a pre-recorded audio file.

```
<prompt cond="(new Date()).getDay() != 0" bargein="false">
  Hello!  Thanks for calling.
  <audio src="welcome.wav" caching="fast" fetchhint="prefetch"/>
</prompt>
```

The fast caching policy means that the voice browser should use a cached copy if one is available that has not yet expired. Note that this is probably the default policy in any case. A prefetch value for the fetchhint attribute means the VoiceXML interpreter should fetch the audio file as soon as possible; generally before the dialog that references that particular file is executed. This is a good idea if the file is always to be played (such as a welcome message), and is large enough for its load time to cause a perceptible delay.

The <audio> element in the previous example was empty. However, it is also possible to include an alternative TTS message between the opening and closing tags, to be played in case the retrieval of the audio file fails, or the file itself is corrupted. Although the actual availability of this feature can vary by platform, this is good programming practice because the name of the audio file may not be very descriptive. The example overleaf illustrates this. Like the previous example, it will play a TTS message followed by a pre-recorded audio message. However, if the file 123.wav is not available, it will play the alternative message nested inside the <audio> element as a TTS prompt.

```
<prompt cond="(new Date()).getDay() != 0" bargein="false">
  Hello!  Thanks for calling.
  <audio  src="123.wav" caching="fast" fetchhint="prefetch">
    Welcome to our voice service menu.
  </audio>
</prompt>
```

Improving TTS with Speech Markup

After implementing a prompt using the basic constructs described above, a developer might wish to fine-tune the user experience, particularly the quality and tone of the TTS messages. VoiceXML provides five elements that allow the markup of TTS prompts. These are based on the Java Speech Markup Language (JSML) specification. The JSML-based VoiceXML tags are `<break>`, `<emp>`, `<sayas>`, `<div>`, and `<pros>`.

The tags are not actually implemented on every platform, but any VoiceXML 1.0-compliant interpreter should at least allow the tags to be used, even if they are ignored. Text within the ignored tags should still work, and the interpreter should try to make the best possible use of the available TTS to implement at least some of the JSML features.

<break>

The `<break>` element causes a specific pause during TTS playback. In particular, it could be used to replace commas and periods with specific pauses. The `<break>` element has two possible attributes, either `msecs`, an explicit number of milliseconds, or `size`, a subjective and platform-dependent pause with possible values `none`, `small`, `medium`, and `large`. The `<break>` element is always empty.

The example below will play a message followed by a "small" break, another message followed by a break of 5500 milliseconds, and then a final message. Note that, in this example, most TTS platforms will at least attempt to inflect the punctuation properly. So, the period at the end of each sentence will be interpreted to cause some kind of pause, dependent upon the TTS engine. However, it might be wise to strip the punctuation altogether and use explicit `<break>` elements to control the flow of speech.

```
<prompt bargein="true">
  You can say help at any time.
  <break size="small"/>
  You can say operator to be transferred to a
  representative between 8 AM and 5 PM PDT.
  <break msecs="5500"/>
  Say status to check your account.
</prompt>
```

<emp>

The `<emp>` element lets you place special emphasis on, or de-emphasize, parts of a TTS prompt. It has one optional attribute, `level`, which has four possible values: `strong`, `moderate`, `none`, and `reduced`. If the `level` attribute is omitted, the value defaults to `moderate`. The example below builds upon the previous one. The actual user experience in using the `<emp>` element will differ significantly by TTS implementation. In the future, the TTS may be smart enough to identify what are, in the example below, the object nouns of the sentences, and emphasize them accordingly, because that is how normal human speech is inflected.

```
<prompt bargein="true">
  You can say <emp level="strong">help</emp>
  at any time.
  <break size="small"/>
  You can say <emp level="strong">operator</emp>
  to be transferred to a representative between
  8 AM and 5 PM PDT.
  <break msecs="5500"/>
  Say <emp>status</emp> to check your account.
</prompt>
```

<sayas>

The <sayas> element suggests a correct pronunciation to the TTS program, by identifying the marked up text as a general category of phrase, using the class attribute. Valid classes are phone, date, digits, literal, currency, number, and time. The literal class causes the prompt to be read literally, for example the number "15" would be read as "one five".

A complete replacement phrase can be given using the sub attribute. Also, a phonetic spelling in the Unicode International Phonetic Alphabet (IPA) can be provided with the phon attribute.

The example below again extends the previous prompt, using the <sayas> to improve typically weak TTS rendering of time of day, and giving a complete replacement phrase for the time zone. Even with the class identification, it might be better to either use the sub attribute to give a complete and verbose proper pronunciation, or rewrite the prompt to use more explicit wording; for example, saying "eight o'clock" instead of "8:00". That will be the only way to guarantee consistent interpretation of the sentence if different TTS systems will be used.

```
<prompt bargein="true">
  You can say <emp level="strong">help</emp>
  at any time.
  <break size="small"/>
  You can say <emp level="strong">operator</emp>
  to be transferred to a representative between
  <sayas class="time">8:00 AM</sayas> and
  <sayas class="time">5:00 PM</sayas>
  <sayas sub="Pacific Daylight Time">PDT</sayas>
  <break msecs="5500"/>
  Say <emp>status</emp> to check your account.
</prompt>
```

<div>

The <div> element identifies speech as either "sentence" or "paragraph" using its required type attribute. The TTS engine can use this information to change the rhythm of speech to a more natural sounding cadence. The example below identifies the whole prompt as a paragraph.

```
<prompt bargein="true">
<div type="paragraph">
  You can say <emp level="strong">help</emp>
  at any time.
  <break size="small"/>
  You can say <emp level="strong">operator</emp>
  to be transferred to a representative between
  <sayas class="time">8:00 AM</sayas> and
  <sayas class="time">5:00 PM</sayas>
```

```
    <sayas sub="Pacific Daylight Time">PDT</sayas>
    <break msecs="5500"/>
    Say <emp>status</emp> to check your account.
  </div>
  </prompt>
```

<pros>

The prosody of the rendered speech can be altered with the `<pros>` element. This allows fine-tuning of speech rate, volume, and intonation. The attributes that control these features are `rate`, `vol`, `pitch`, and `range`, which respectively control the speaking rate (in words per minute), volume (normalized, with a range from 0 to 1), pitch, and pitch range for the TTS voice. These attributes, and their legal values are explained in complete detail in the JSML specification.

There are currently no platforms that support all of these features. If this level of playback control is needed for prompting, moving to pre-recorded audio or libraries of pre-recorded concatenated speech would probably give a better, more reliable user experience, especially if the application has to run on multiple platforms. The example below shows these four attributes in use:

```
  <prompt bargein="true">
    <pros rate="160" vol="0.5" pitch="+10%" range="-10%">
    This is a fast, loud prompt that has a higher pitch
    than the default voice and a smaller range.
    </pros>
  </prompt>
```

Collecting User Input

Dialogs are interactions that collect input from the user. They are implemented with the `<form>` and `<menu>` elements. Generally, the `<form>` is used to collect data with a series of questions, while the `<menu>` is a kind of short-cut `<form>` to ask the user one question and offer several alternative destinations with the `<choice>` element.

The examples in this section use a variety of built-in, inline, and external grammars to illustrate the information gathering capabilities of the form. The code developed here demonstrates a prototype for a system to let a user request a taxi dispatch by voice. This is what is called a directed form, meaning the form elements are executed sequentially.

Form Basics by Example

The form is by far the mainstay component of the VoiceXML document. Each form can implement a self-contained, multiple-step dialog using several nested `<field>` elements. In this chapter, we will look at its uses to process data, define local event handlers, collect data using built-in and user-defined grammars, and record user audio input.

The form can also implement mixed-initiative dialogs and, named sub-dialogs, transfer calls, and invoke platform-specific binary code such as Nuance SpeechObjects. These advanced `<form>` concepts will be covered in Chapter 5.

The <block>

The `<block>` prompts the user or processes data, but does not collect input. Blocks can be named with the `name` attribute, initialized to a value using the `expr` attribute, or "guarded" in the conditional sense with the `cond` attribute. If the block has a value assigned via `expr`, it will not be executed unless the variable identified by `name` is explicitly cleared in some other processing routine within the same `<form>` by the use of a `<clear>` element. Blocks are most commonly used as unconditional sections of code with none of these attributes.

Let's examine the example below, which can be found in the sample code in the file `AcmeTaxi.vxml`. The form must have an `id` and this must be unique within the document. The `scope` attribute defines the scope of the grammars referenced within the form. In this case, they are scoped to "`dialog`" and will not be valid outside the particular form.

The `<block>` performs some initial calculation. In this case, the conditional guard `cond` attribute of the block is used to check if the current time is outside normal business hours. If it is, the system will inform the user and hang up with the `<exit/>` tag. Notice that the greater-than and less-than comparison operators (and the logical-and (`&&`) operator in later examples) have to be escaped in the VoiceXML document, because >, <, and `&` are reserved characters in XML. Of course, we would hope that a real cab company is open after 6 PM!

```
<?xml version="1.0"?>
<vxml lang="en-us" version="1.0">
  <form id="get_me_a_taxi" scope="dialog">
    <block cond="( ((new Date()).getHours() &lt; 6) ||
                   ((new Date()).getHours() &gt; 18) )">
      <prompt>
      Sorry, we are closed right now. Please call later.
      </prompt>
      <exit/>
    </block>
```

The <field>

The next part of the example prompts the user for their phone number using a `<field>`. The `<field>` element has an optional `type` attribute. The `type` attribute lets the user access one of the VoiceXML built-in grammars; see the *Built-In Grammars in VoiceXML* section of Chapter 3 for more details on these.

Let us examine the example below in detail. The `name` of the field, "`ph`" becomes a locally scoped ECMAScript variable of the same name, which will contain the value returned by the speech recognizer when a 'good' value is returned. In this case, the "`phone`" type is a grammar that will accept several common forms of spoken telephone numbers.

The grammar will need to vary by language because of the different formats of telephone numbers in different countries. Specifying a supported language with the VoiceXML `lang` attribute of the `<vxml>` element will assign appropriate native language grammars to the built-in types.

The incremental prompting will be used if there is a misrecognition event or the user does not respond. When the user responds with a phone number that is valid according to the built-in grammar, the system will play the number back and move on to the next unfilled field in the dialog.

The `<filled>` element defines a behavior for the case where the speech recognizer matches the grammar and returns a value to the field. This implicit navigation is an example of the FIA in action. The FIA and the behavior of the `<filled>` element and event will be covered in more detail later in this chapter.

```
<field name="ph" type="phone">
  <prompt count="1">
    Thank you for calling the Acme Taxi Company.
    What is your phone number?
  </prompt>
  <prompt count="2">
    Please say your phone number.
  </prompt>
  <prompt count="3">
    Please tell me your phone number. I need it to
    begin your taxi request.
  </prompt>
  <filled>
    <prompt>You said <value expr="ph"/>.</prompt>
  </filled>
</field>
```

The next question also uses a built-in type. Again, the system plays back the user input in order to confirm the response. Repeating the user's utterance is a good way to reduce both user frustration and the possibility of incorrect data being collected.

```
<field name="pickup_time" type="time">
  <prompt>What time do you need to be picked up?</prompt>
  <filled>
    <prompt>You requested pick up at
      <value expr="pickup_time"/>.
    </prompt>
  </filled>
  </field>
```

The next step uses the built-in `boolean` type, which is probably the quickest way to get a simple yes or no answer. It also illustrates several important features of the `<field>`. The conditional guard `cond` must evaluate to `true` in order for this field to be executed. This means the system will only prompt customers about sharing rides during the busy hours of the day. When the `modal` attribute is `true`, it means that any global grammars in this application will not be valid during the execution of this `<field>`.

```
<field name="share"
   type="boolean"
   modal="true"
   cond="( ((new Date()).getHours() &gt; 10) &amp;&amp;
       ((new Date()).getHours() &lt; 13) )">
  <prompt>
    Do you mind sharing a ride?  Say yes or no.
  </prompt>
  <filled>
    <prompt>You said <value expr="share"/>.</prompt>
  </filled>
</field>
```

Inline and External Grammars: Custom Field "Types"

Obviously the number and scope of the built-in types is limited to a very small set of functionality. The true power of speech recognition comes with the capability for custom application-specific grammars. The next step of the dialog demonstrates an inline JSGF grammar. A `<field>` that does not specify a `type` must contain a `<grammar>` element. The `type` of a grammar is a MIME type that tells the interpreter the format language of the grammar. We will recall from Chapter 3 that common grammar types are `application/x-jsgf` and `application/x-gsl` for JSGF and Nuance GSL respectively.

This sample grammar uses a CDATA (character data) section, even though the grammar in this example does not contain any reserved characters. It is a good idea to use a CDATA delimiter with an inline grammar, especially if the document and the contents of the grammar are being generated dynamically. For more on the specifics of grammars, see Chapter 3. Note that this particular example is a grammar fragment. It does not refer to any XML reserved characters, non-terminals, or rules outside its own definition.

```
<form>
  <field name="pickup_where">
    <nomatch>
      <goto next="#record_street"/>
    </nomatch>
    <grammar type="application/x-jsgf">
      <![CDATA[<
      lake and wabash { law } |
      wabash and lake { law } |
      main and first { maf } |
      first and main { fam } |
      airport { air } |
      ([the] mall) { mall }
      ]]>
    </grammar>
    <prompt count="1" timeout="1s">
      Where do you need to be picked up?
    </prompt>
    <prompt count="2" timeout="1s">
      You can say lake and wabash, main and first, airport,
      and mall.
    </prompt>
    <filled>
      <prompt>
        You said <value expr="pickup_where"/>.
      </prompt>
    </filled>
  </field>
</form>
```

The street grammar shown is rather small. Any real city street grammar is going to be quite large. It is probably wise to store the grammar externally, since it will most likely be generated dynamically from a database of some sort. The `<grammar>` source above can be replaced with a URI reference to the source.

```
<grammar src="/relative/path/to/grammar/pickup_location.jsgf"
         type="application/x-jsgf"/>
```

DTMF-Only Grammars with <dtmf>

Now let's recap on DTMF grammars. Sometimes the voice interface design may call for limiting user input to DTMF digits only. In these cases it is possible to specify DTMF-only grammars using the `<dtmf>` element. In this example, let's suppose that the dialog designer wants to use a DTMF sequence "1 2 3" to indicate that the user wishes to confirm the taxi request. The DTMF sequence will be far less prone to misrecognition problems than any spoken confirmation.

```
<field name="confirm_request">
  <dtmf type="application/x-jsgf">
    1 2 3
  </dtmf>
  <prompt>
    Press one two three on your phone to
```

```
      confirm your request.
    </prompt>
    <filled>
      <prompt>
        We appreciate your business!
      </prompt>
    </filled>
  </field>
```

The <dtmf> element has the same attributes and behavior as the <grammar> element. The DTMF grammar can also be loaded from an external URI using the src attribute. The only difference between them is the restriction of input to DTMF tones.

Recording User Responses with <record>

You may have noticed the use of the <nomatch> element in the pickup_where field above. This lets the developer assign a custom handler for the case where the voice recognizer detects a user response but cannot find a satisfactory match in the current active grammar. This element is covered in greater detail in Chapter 5, but is used here to illustrate another feature: the ability to sample a recording from the user. For this example, we can imagine that even the largest and most carefully prepared city street grammar may still have gaps. Why not record the user's request and send it to a human in these cases? There will probably still be a human taxi dispatcher in the loop at some point.

```
<?xml version-"1.0"?>
<vxml>
<form id="record_street">
  <record name="pickup_location" maxtime="10s" beep="true"
      finalsilence="4000ms" dtmfterm="true" >
    <prompt>
      At the tone, please say the name of the place
      where you would like to be picked up.
    </prompt>
  </record>
  <block>
    <prompt bargein="false">
      You requested pick up at
      <value expr="pickup_location"/>
    </prompt>
  </block>
</form>
</vxml>
```

The <record> element will sample the user's voice into a local variable called pickup_location, its name attribute. It will beep to prompt the user to begin recording, record for a maximum time of ten seconds, and stop recording either on a DTMF key press or a user silence of four seconds. The block following the recording will play the user's voice back to them (no doubt prompting the user to think, "Do I really sound like that?").

This example is obviously functionally incomplete. The VoiceXML interpreter needs to submit this data to a program or servlet somewhere that will process the sound file into an e-mail attachment to send to the taxi dispatcher, or some other method of delivery to a human agent.

In this example we looked at the use of the <form>, <block>, <field>, <record>, <grammar>, and <filled> elements. Now let's move on to the other major type of dialog, the menu.

Menus with <menu>, <choice>, and <enumerate>

The elements shown up to this point could be combined to create a menu where a user is offered a list of choices, and the application branches to a different dialog (perhaps a different <form>) to execute that choice. However, VoiceXML provides the <menu> and its associated elements as convenient shorthand for this task, including several shortcuts to make the job easier.

<menu>

Like the <form> element, the <menu> element has optional attributes id and scope. The id attribute lets the menu be a link target from elsewhere in the document, or from another document. Just as in a form, the scope attribute controls the scope of grammars. The menu also has a third optional attribute, dtmf, which can be set to true or false, false being the default. See below, in the <choice> section, for more explanation of dtmf.

<choice>

A <menu> element contains one or more <choice> elements. Each <choice> contains a simple inline grammar fragment that doubles as the description of the choice. A <choice> element requires a next, expr, or event attribute, and can have optional dtmf, caching, fetchhint, fetchtimeout, and fetchaudio attributes. The next or event or expr attribute defines the branch destination if the user picks this particular choice. The next attribute is a literal destination URI, while the expr attribute is a computed URI based on the value of the expression when evaluated. The event attribute lets the user response throw an event rather than cause a transition to a specific dialog. The concept of events will be treated in greater detail in Chapter 5.

The dtmf attribute, with numeric values 1 to 9, specifies a DTMF keypad alternative to the speech grammar contained in the <choice>. If the dtmf attribute of <menu> is set to true, the first nine choices will automatically be assigned DTMF alternatives 1 through 9 sequentially. If the dtmf attribute of <menu> is set to false or omitted, the dtmf attribute (if given) of the individual <choice> elements will be used instead.

The caching, fetchhint, and fetchtimeout attributes are related to the cache performance policies for retrieving the document at the URL specified in the next or expr attributes. Just as in our prior discussion of the <audio> element, the caching and fetch policies can be set in different scopes (including platform-wide) and support for the different options may vary from platform to platform. The fetchaudio attribute points to an audio file to be played to the user while the system is fetching the next document.

Automatic Prompting with <enumerate>

The <enumerate> element, which has no attributes, creates a prompt based on the choices that are contained in the menu. The content of the <enumerate> element is a template that is used to generate the prompt given the value of the choice. If <enumerate/> is used as an empty element, then a default template specific to the platform is used. This simple default template would take the character data from each <choice> and concatenate them into one prompt. The example overleaf shows an <enumerate> with a nested template that is similar to the kind of default behavior that can be expected.

This menu demonstrates the use of all three of the major menu elements. This is found in the file AcmeMenu.vxml. When executed, the VoiceXML interpreter will automatically generate the complete prompt: "Welcome to Acme Corporation. Here are your choices. Say taxi or press one. Say rocket backpacks or press two. Say free bird seed or press three."

```
<menu id="main_menu" scope="dialog" dtmf="false">

    <prompt>
      Welcome to Acme Corporation. Here are your choices.
      <enumerate>
        Say <value expr="_prompt"/> or press
      <value expr="_dtmf"/>.
      </enumerate>
    </prompt>

    <choice dtmf="1" next="AcmeTaxi.vxml">
      Taxi
    </choice>

    <choice dtmf="2" next="AcmeAerospace.vxml">
      Rocket back packs
    </choice>

    <choice dtmf="3" next="AcmePetFood.vxml">
      <prompt>
        <audio src="/path/to/prompts/petfood.wav">
          Free bird seed
        </audio>
      </prompt>
    </choice>

    <choice dtmf="4" next="#more_info">
        More information about Acme.
    </choice>
</menu>
```

Grammars

Note that grammar for the menu prompt is generated automatically from the content of the <choice> elements, as phrases where all the component words are optional. So, in addition to saying "free bird seed", the user could also say "free bird", "free seed", "bird seed", "free", "bird", or "seed". This means that it is important that the sets of all the words in each of the choice phrases do not have any ambiguities or overlaps. In the case of choice three, the system will play the audio file if it is available, but use the TTS alternative text nested in the <audio> element to generate the actual grammar.

Using <option> Elements in a <field>

The <field> equivalent of the <choice> element nested in a <menu> is the <option> element. This is used to offer the user a limited set, or option list, of possible values, and fill the field variable with the result. Like the <choice> element, the <option> element has a dtmf attribute that can be used to set an alternative DTMF grammar. It also has a value attribute, which is assigned to the field variable if that option is selected.

The example below collects a user response and sends the value from the option list to a server to request a new document, presumably a dynamically created document with relevant information based on the user request. The prompt is generated with the <enumerate> element, exactly as in the case of the <menu>. The grammar for this field is created from the option values in exactly the same way that the menu grammar was created from the choice elements in the previous example.

```
<form id="more_info">
  <field name="information_request">
    <prompt>
```

```
        You can request more information
        in a number of areas.
        <enumerate/>
      </prompt>

      <option dtmf="1" value="investor">
        investor prospectus
      </option>

      <option dtmf="2" value="tree_hugger">
        environmental impact statement
      </option>

      <option dtmf="3" value="job_seeker">
        employment with acme
      </option>

      <filled>
        <submit next="/imaginary/process_request"
                method="post"
                namelist="information_request"/>
      </filled>
    </field>
  </form>
```

This example uses the <submit> element. This is used to request a new document from a server, specifying a method (HTTP GET or POST), and a namelist of local variables to send with the URI request. The <submit> element will be covered in greater detail in Chapter 5.

Form Interpretation

Each <form> in the document can implement a dialog of one or more steps, as the examples so far have shown. When a form contains multiple **form items**, such as <block>, <field>, and <initial> items, the VoiceXML interpreter must implement an algorithm to select among the items and determine their order of execution. This is called the **Form Interpretation Algorithm**, or FIA. The FIA is explained in exhaustive detail in Appendix C of the VoiceXML 1.0 Specification.

This section will discuss the basics of the FIA, and how it relates to the flow of control in a dialog. Although it might seem rather complex, especially if you read the full description (several pages of C-style pseudo-code) in the appendix mentioned, the fundamentals of the FIA follow the rules of common sense. We have already seen several aspects of the FIA in action in our previous examples. For example, the taxi request example code depends on the implicit execution order of the <field> dialogs in its main <form>. One of those items, the "share" field, relied on the conditional guard of its cond attribute to skip over that question in certain circumstances.

Form and Field Items

Each <form> contains one or more **form items**. Form items are the elements in the form that can be considered for execution by the FIA. All form items have three common, but optional, attributes, which have been seen previously. They can be named with the name attribute, can be initialized with an expression in an expr attribute, and can have a guard condition specified with an expression in the cond attribute.

Form items are further classified as **control items**, which include the <block> and <initial> elements, and **field items**, which include <field>, <record>, <transfer>, <object>, and <subdialog> elements. These relationships are shown in the diagram below:

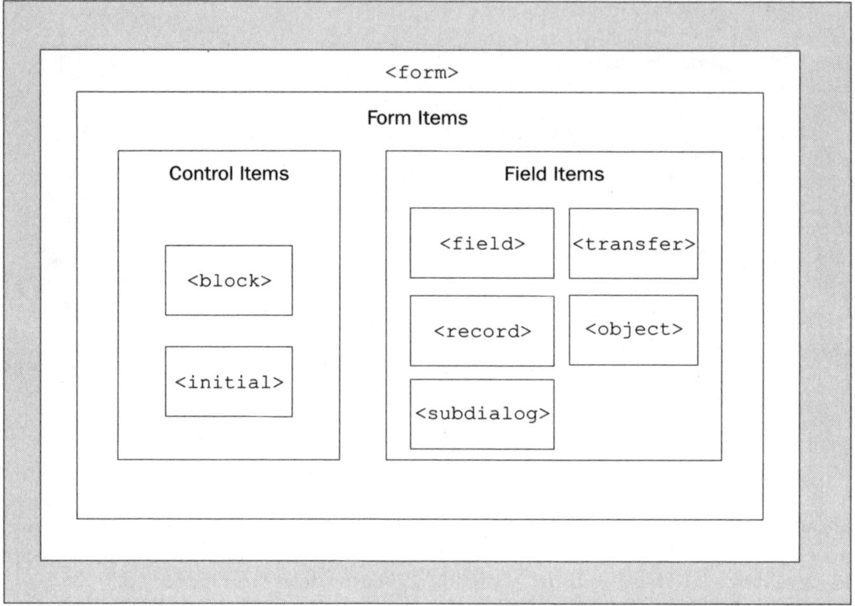

Control Items

Control items can be used to process data and initialize variables. The <block> element carries out a procedure of some kind, but does not gather user input, as has already been demonstrated in previous examples. The <initial> element sets up the <field> items for mixed-initiative dialogs by prompting the user for some input that matches form-scoped grammars. Mixed-initiative dialogs are explained in greater depth in Chapter 5.

Field Items

Field items, including the most common, <field>, are used to prompt the user to collect data from a grammar, and have event handlers to deal with cases such as misrecognition. The event handlers are often implicit, such as the automatic re-prompting in the case of a <nomatch>, or are inherited from a root document, such as the hang-up event handler shown in the sample root document at the beginning of this chapter. All of these elements assign the result of the user utterance to a local variable whose name matches the name attribute of the field item. The kind of data assigned to the variable depends on the type of field item. We have already seen two: the <field> itself, which gets the value returned by the ASR system, and the <record> tag, which actually holds the sound samples recorded.

Shadow Variables of <field>

The <field> element offers an additional interesting capability. The variable named by the name attribute of the field has three "shadow" variables: confidence, utterance, and inputmode. confidence is a floating-point number from 0.0 to 1.0, which represents the "certainty" of the ASR system that the match is correct. utterance is a raw text string that transcribes what the ASR system heard. The transcription given could vary by platform for the same utterance – this might be helpful when a grammar has many alternative phrases defined for the same command. Finally, inputmode is the mode of the response, either voice or dtmf.

In the taxi example, we used a DTMF mode confirmation step to reduce the chance that misrecognition would result in false taxi requests being processed. The same effect could be achieved with a voice grammar, if the confidence of the resulting utterance is compared against a high threshold. The sample below illustrates this. This is a voice replacement for the DTMF confirmation step of the taxi example. Although the `if-else` and `throw` constructs won't be covered in detail until Chapter 5, the behavior should be pretty obvious. If the confidence is less than 60% (actually a fairly high value), the VoiceXML dialog will treat the response as a `nomatch`. The confidence threshold itself will probably be adjustable at a platform level, possibly even on a document basis, but the shadow variables allow for fine-tuning of the behavior at the lowest level.

```
<field name="voice_confirm_request" type="boolean">
   <prompt>
     Would you like to confirm this request?
   </prompt>

  <filled>
    <if cond="voice_confirm_request$.confidence &gt; 0.6">
      <goto next="/some/script"/>
    <else/>
      <throw event="nomatch"/>
    </if>
  </filled>
</field>
```

The <filled> Element

When the recognizer returns a response, the FIA looks for application-defined code to execute. This code is contained in the `<filled>` element. It has two optional attributes, `namelist`, and `mode`. The `namelist` attribute contains a space-delimited list of the form items to which this `<filled>` element applies. The mode is either `all`, or `any`. If it is `all`, the handler will execute only when all the items in the `namelist` are filled, and one of them has been filled by the last user utterance (the default behavior). If it is `any`, the handler will execute if the last user utterance matched any of the items in the `namelist`.

The `<filled>` element can be contained at the field-item level, as shown above, or at the form level itself with a `namelist`. When it is at the field-item level, it cannot specify a mode.

The example below shows a `<filled>` handler with a `namelist` of one item. Once the user answers, the system will respond, rather untruthfully, "I didn't quite understand you". This is part of a larger dialog we'll look at later in our discussion of the FIA.

```
<filled namelist="one">
  <prompt>I didn't quite understand you. </prompt>
</filled>

<field name="one" type="boolean">
  <prompt>Say yes or no.</prompt>
</field>
```

The example below shows an inline equivalent to the handler above.

```
<field name="one" type="boolean">
  <prompt>Say yes or no.</prompt>
  <filled>
    <prompt>I didn't quite understand you. </prompt>
  </filled>
</field>
```

The <clear> Element

The `<clear>` element clears both the value and prompt counter for one or more form items. It has one optional attribute, `namelist`, which is a list of form items to clear. The example below illustrates its use. In this case, if the field were the first or only item in a form, it would execute repeatedly since its value will never stay assigned.

```
<field name="infinite_loop" type="boolean">
  <prompt>Say yes or no.</prompt>
  <filled>
    <prompt>I didn't quite understand you. </prompt>
    <clear namelist="infinite_loop"/>
  </filled>
</field>
```

The Form Interpretation Algorithm

This discussion of the Form Interpretation Algorithm (FIA) follows very closely the order of the presentation of material in Appendix C of the VoiceXML 1.0 specification. This is recommended reading for a complete understanding of all the nuances of form-item processing.

As mentioned previously, the interpreter uses this algorithm to determine the order of execution of the forms and form items in the document. The FIA can be roughly broken into the initialization phase, which occurs once when the form context is entered by the interpreter, and the selection, collection, and processing phases, which compose a "main loop" that repeats continuously as long as the current form remains active. These phases are illustrated in the diagram that follows.

The FIA also:

- Activates and deactivates grammars by scope, including issues such as the modal attribute
- Selects the prompt to play, based on prompt counters
- Handles the case where the user enters a form based on an utterance in another form that matches the current form's grammar. See the *Initialization Phase* section overleaf
- Leaves a form based on a match to a grammar other than the most local ones
- Fills multiple fields from one utterance
- Processes the catching of any thrown events

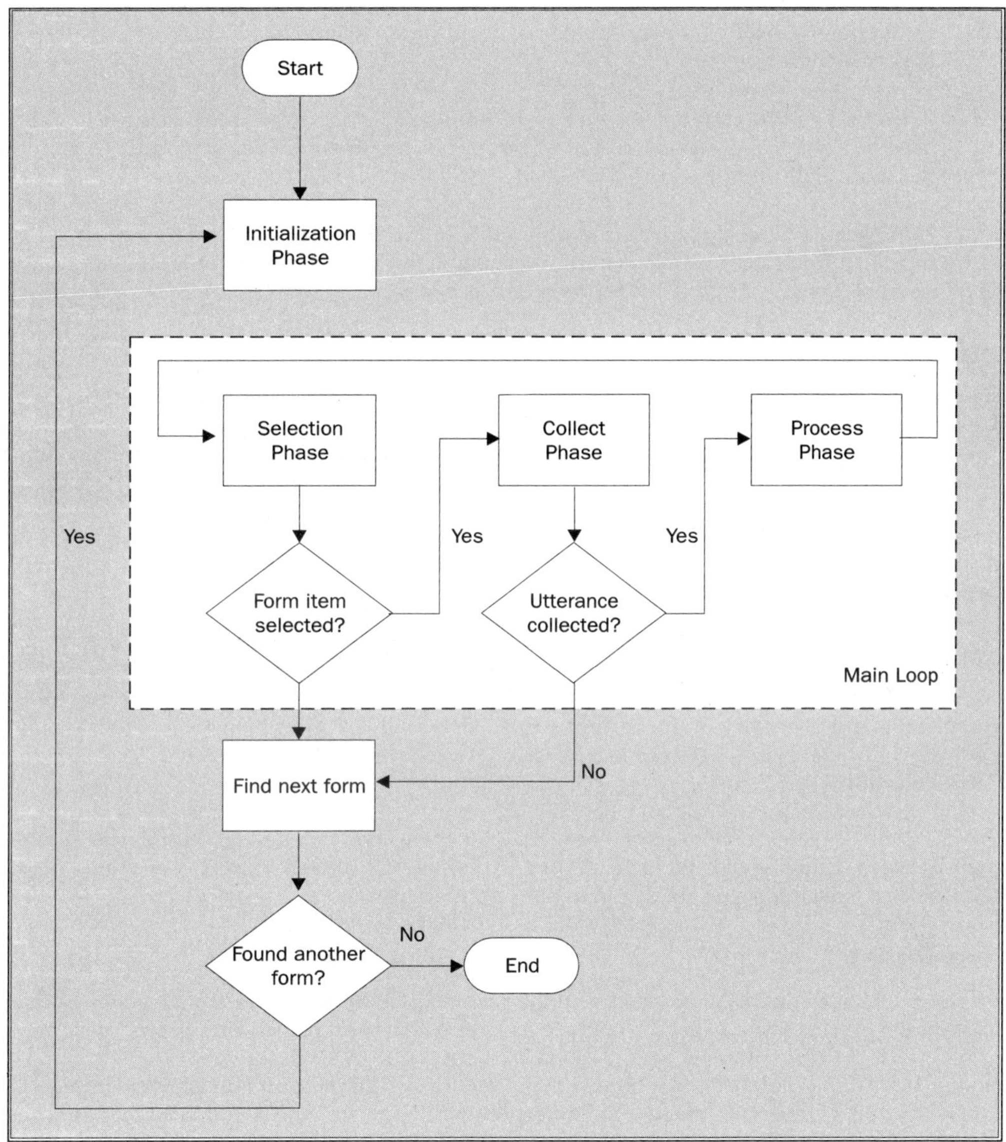

Initialization Phase

When the interpreter enters a form, it is initialized (which means that the state of the form from any previous visits while the user has been interacting with the current document is lost). Initialization consists of the following steps:

1. In document order, set each `<var>` or form item variable to `undefined` or the value of its `expr` attribute.

2. Create a prompt counter for each field item and `<initial>` item, and set it to 1. This is used to track the `count` attribute of the `<prompt>` element for sequential prompting in the same field item.

3. If the grammar of this form is visible outside the form, and the user entered the form by a match to this grammar elsewhere, then enter the main loop at the processing phase, because there is already an utterance to process.

Selection Phase

The selection phase chooses the next form item to execute in the current form. This is a fairly simple process. If the last iteration of the loop ended with a `<goto nextitem>`, which gives an explicit form item target, then that item is executed. Otherwise, the interpreter looks for the next form item with an unsatisfied guard condition.

If no suitable form item is found (presumably because they've all been visited already) the interpreter exits the form with an implicit `<exit/>`. Once an item has been selected, the algorithm enters the collection phase.

Collection Phase

The collection phase starts by choosing the prompts to play to the user. Then it activates all of the grammars that are necessary in the current scope, such as global grammars from a root document, all the way down to the most local grammar. Finally, it executes the form item. This final step depends on the particular form item.

For a `<field>`, it collects an utterance or throws an event. For a `<record>`, it records the utterance or throws an event. If the item to be executed is a `<block>`, the block's implicit variable is set so that the block won't be executed again on this pass through the form.

Process Phase

After a user utterance has been collected, or if the user entered this form item from a grammar in another form item, the process phase begins. The process phase is shown graphically in the block diagram opposite.

First, the algorithm will handle any events that were thrown in the previous phase. These could include `<noinput>` and `<nomatch>` events. The interpreter will execute any handler defined for the events. These handlers could involve leaving the context of the FIA, or returning to an earlier phase such as the selection phase, for example, in the case of a re-prompt.

Next, the interpreter identifies the context of the grammar that was matched. If the match came from a grammar other than the local form-item grammar, the FIA will exit and execution will continue in a new form item. Otherwise, the execution will proceed in the current form item.

Finally, the interpreter will look for `<filled>` handlers to execute. It will identify which items have just been filled in the most recent loop and user utterance, in order to satisfy the `namelist` constraint on the `<filled>` handler as explained above. These items include `<filled>` elements where the current form item is part of the `namelist`, and `<filled>` elements that are children of the current form element.

Then it will filter out <filled> elements that don't meet the test of the mode attribute. Finally, the <filled> handlers will be executed in document order.

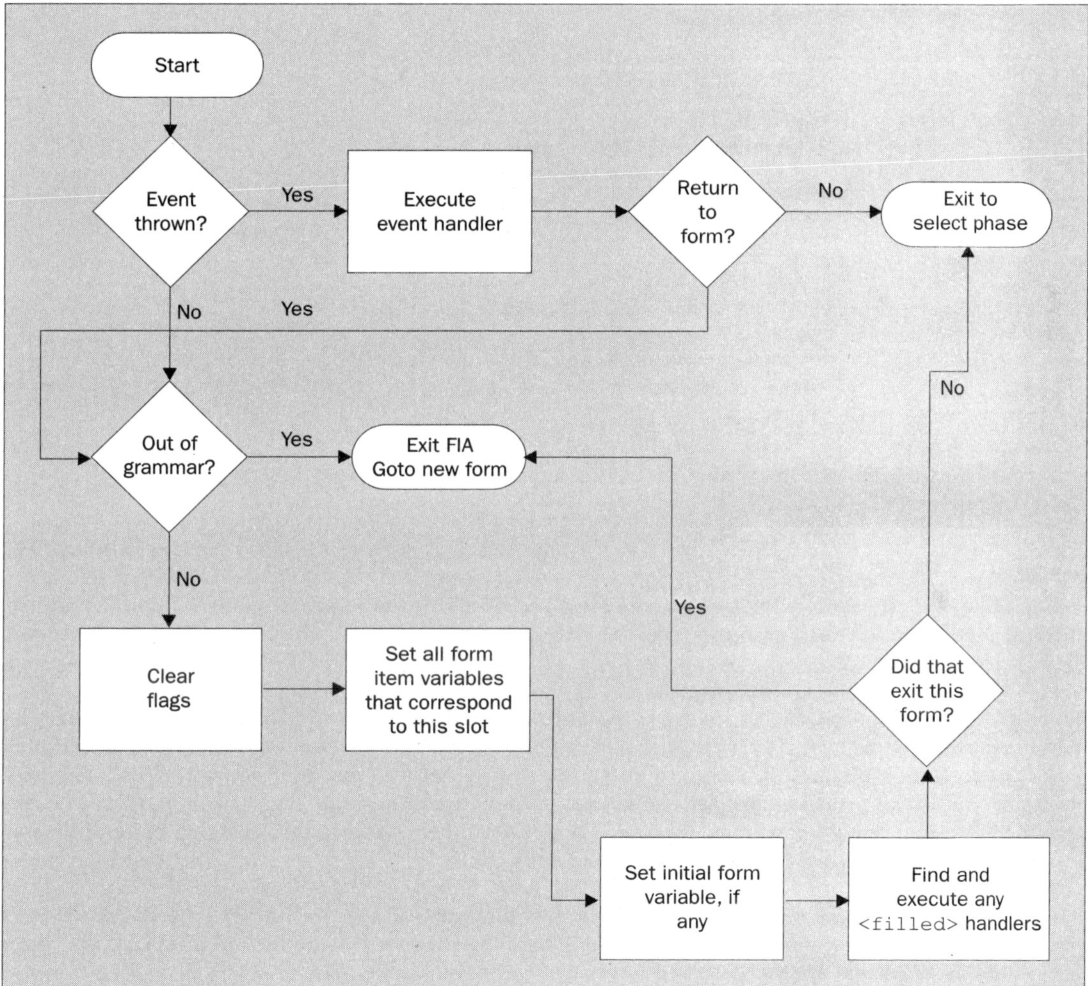

A FIA Example

Let's examine a simple VoiceXML document that depends entirely on the FIA for the control of transitions between dialogs:

```
<?xml version="1.0"?>
<vxml lang="en-us" version="1.0">

  <form id="start">
    <block name="welcome">
      <prompt>
        Hi!
      </prompt>
    </block>
```

```
      <filled namelist="one">
        <prompt>I didn't quite understand you. </prompt>
      </filled>

      <field name="one" type="boolean">
        <prompt>Say yes or no.</prompt>
      </field>

      <field name="two" type="boolean">
        <prompt>Did you just say yes or no?</prompt>
        <filled>
          <prompt>Ah.  I thought so.</prompt>
        </filled>
      </field>

      <block name="liar" cond="two != one">
        You are a liar!
        <clear namelist="one two liar truthful"/>
      </block>

      <block name="truthful" cond="two == one">
        Thanks for telling the truth.
        <clear namelist="one two liar truthful"/>
      </block>
    </form>
  </vxml>
```

When the interpreter enters the form, all of the variables are completely cleared. So, the FIA will select the first form item to execute, in this case the `block` called `welcome`. The user will hear the greeting "Hi!" once and only once.

Since there was no grammar, and no response, the FIA will skip over the collection and process phase, and move directly to the `field` called `one`. The computer will say, "Say yes or no." The interpreter will enter the collection phase and wait for a yes/no response. Assume that the user says "Yes". The FIA will then proceed to the processing phase. In this case, the FIA will find one `<filled>` handler to execute, the one defined directly before `field one`. The user will hear the prompt, "I didn't quite understand you", something of a white lie on the part of the computer.

The FIA will move to the selection phase again, this time identifying the `field two` as the next to execute, by virtue of its order in the document. The FIA will enter the collection phase. Again, there are no grammars active except the yes/no grammar of the `field two`. The user will hear the prompt, "Did you just say yes or no?" Assume that the user says "Yes", again. The FIA will proceed to the processing phase. In this case, the FIA will find one `<filled>` handler to execute, the one that is a child element of the `field two`. The user will hear the prompt, "Ah, I thought so."

The FIA will cycle back to the selection phase. This time, there are only two choices. The guard condition on the `block liar` will evaluate to `false`, while the condition on the `block truthful` will evaluate to `true`. The FIA will select `block truthful` to execute. The user will hear the prompt, "Thanks for telling the truth." There is no grammar active, so the FIA will skip to the process phase, where it will execute the `<clear>` element that is part of the block.

By clearing all of the form items except the `block welcome`, the user will never hear the welcome message after the first time, and will loop through the dialogs continuously, being called truthful or a liar, until they escape by hanging up or using a global command like "goodbye".

Summary

In this chapter, we looked at the fundamental building blocks of VoiceXML documents and applications. We learned how to prompt the user with audio or Text-To-Speech, and improve Text-To-Speech performance with the JSML elements. We implemented dialogs with the <form> and <menu> elements, and used option list, built-in, inline, and external grammars to collect user input through the <field>, <record>, and <block> elements. Finally, we took a look at the Form Interpretation Algorithm, and its method of dialog control.

These are the basics of VoiceXML. With just a few missing pieces (dynamic generation of documents, server-side programs to handle the user responses, and of course the actual platform) we now have enough understanding to build working applications.

```
<?xml version="1.0"?>
<vxml version="1.0">
<form id="foo">
<block>
<prompt>
Hi. My name is Bob
</prompt>
</block>
</form>
</vxml>
```

5

Advanced VoiceXML Markup

VoiceXML is designed for telephone-based and voice-enabled dialogs that feature both client- and server-side scripting for manipulating data. It provides useful functionality like: event handling for helping the user and handling errors; navigation within the same document and to another document; phone transfer and disconnection; manipulation of properties to affect platform behavior; and allowing both the computer and the user to direct the conversation.

This chapter covers several groups of elements that are used to build dialogs with these features and this functionality, in different sections:

- *Programming Elements* introduces the programming elements used to manipulate client-side data and guide selective execution
- *Event Handling* discusses how the event handling elements can be used to provide assistance to the user and handle errors
- *Navigation* describes the elements that lead to conversation transitions
- In *Objects*, we discuss using platform-specific server-side objects to fulfill data access and processing tasks on a server
- *Properties* explains how the properties can be set up to affect the platform behavior by means of the `<property>` element
- *Mixed-Initiative Forms* discusses mixed-initiative forms that allow both the computer and user to direct the conversation

Programming Elements

VoiceXML allows the use of the ECMAScript (European Computer Manufacturers Association script) language for manipulating data and execution on the client-side. Bear in mind that ECMAScript can be thought of as the standardization of what is called JavaScript by Netscape, and JScript by Microsoft. Of course, by "client" we are actually referring to the voice browser (for example, on the voice gateway), not on the phone itself! The programming constructs that ECMAScript provides, such as variables and branching statements (for example, `if...else`), are important building blocks of an application. This section discusses how the variables and branching statements can be used to build an application.

Variables and Expressions

The variables and expressions used in VoiceXML are exactly equivalent to the ECMAScript variables and expressions specified in the *ECMAScript Language Specification* (which can be found at http://www.ecma.ch/ecma1/stand/ecma-262.htm).

Variables

A variable needs to be declared before it can be used. A declared variable has a scope, and a scoped variable can only be accessed within its scope. Variable declaration, scope, and access are covered in the following discussions.

Variable Declaration

There are two ways to declare variables. Firstly, we can declare a variable by using `<var>`:

```
<var name="user"/>
```

where `user` is the variable name. We can also initialize a variable when we declare it:

```
<var name="user" expr="'Mike Fraser'"/>
```

Here, the variable `user` is declared and initialized to the string "`Mike Fraser`". Note the two sets of quotes, single, and double – this is because we are declaring our variable value as an ECMAScript string, which itself needs quotes round it to be recognized as such when being used by our ECMAScript functions. If a variable is not initialized explicitly when declared, it is initialized to the ECMAScript `undefined` value.

Secondly, as we have already seen in Chapter 4, we can declare a field item variable when declaring a field in a form:

```
<field name="user">
...
</field>
```

Variables declared by these two methods are interchangeable – they can both be used in calculations or assigned values in the same way.

After a variable is declared, it can be assigned a new value by using the `<assign>` element:

```
<assign name="user" expr="'Susan Fraser'"/>
```

The variable user is set to the string "Susan Fraser". Using the <assign> element overwrites the old value of the variable if it has one.

Variable Scope

Variable scoping defines the availability of a variable in a particular part of a VoiceXML document. A variable can be declared in five different scopes: **anonymous, dialog, document, application,** and **session.**

A variable has an **anonymous scope** when it is declared inside a <block>, <filled>, or event handler element. The variable can only be used inside that particular element. For example:

```
<?xml version="1.0"?>
<vxml version="1.0">
<form>
  <block>
         <!-- Declare the variable user. -->
    <var name="user" expr="'Mike Fraser'"/>
    <prompt>
      Hi, <value expr="user"/>
    </prompt>
  </block>
</form>
</vxml>
```

The variable user is declared in the <block> element and can *only* be used in that <block> element. The following use of the variable user is *incorrect*:

```
<?xml version="1.0"?>
<vxml version="1.0">
<form>
  <block>
    <var name="user" expr="'Mike Fraser'"/>
  </block>
  <block>
    <prompt>
      <!-- user can not be accessed here. -->
      Hi, <value expr="user"/>
    </prompt>
  </block>
</form>
</vxml>
```

A variable has **dialog scope** if the variable is declared inside a <form> or <menu> element using the name attribute or a child <var> element. A dialog-scoped variable can be used anywhere inside the dialog in which it was declared, but cannot be accessed outside that dialog:

```
<?xml version="1.0"?>
<vxml version="1.0">
<form>
  <!-- declare the variable user in a dialog -->
  <var name="user" expr="'Mike Fraser'"/>
    <field name="answer" type="boolean">
      <prompt>
    <!-- user has dialog scope.  It can be accessed here. -->
        <value expr="user"/>, is that true?
      </prompt>
  </field>
  <block>
    <prompt>
      <!-- answer has dialog scope. It can be accessed here. -->
```

```
      You told me <value expr="answer"/>
    </prompt>
  </block>
</form>
</vxml>
```

In the above example, the variable user is declared explicitly by the child element <var> of the form, and the variable answer is declared by the <field> element. Both of them have a dialog scope and thus are accessible from anywhere in the form.

A variable has a **document scope** when it is declared by a <var> element that is a child of the <vxml> root element. A variable with document scope can only be accessed from within the same document:

```
<?xml version="1.0"?>
<vxml version="1.0">
<var name="user" expr="'Mike Fraser'"/>
<form>
  <block>
    <prompt>
      Hi, <value expr="user"/>
    </prompt>
  </block>
</form>
</vxml>
```

In the above example, the variable user is declared as having document scope, and thus can be used anywhere in this document but not in any other.

A variable that is declared by a <var> that is a child of the <vxml> element *in the root document* has **application scope**. It is available to any documents of the application. For example, the variable user is declared in the root document (root.vxml):

```
<?xml version="1.0"?>
<vxml version="1.0">
  <!-- user has an application scope. -->
  <var name="user" expr="'Mike Fraser'"/>
</vxml>
```

It can then be accessed in any leaf document of the application:

```
<?xml version="1.0"?>
<vxml version="1.0" application="root.vxml">
<form>
  <block>
    <prompt>
      <!-- user is accessed here. -->
      Hi, <value expr="user"/>
    </prompt>
  </block>
</form>
</vxml>
```

When the user dials into the system, the VoiceXML interpreter creates a group of read-only variables that will exist until the session is over; they're not defined in the document. These variables are called **session variables**, and these variables have **session scope**. There are four such session variables:

- `session.telephone.ani` stores the caller's phone number
- `session.telephone.dnis` stores the phone number the caller dialed
- `session.telephone.iidigits` contains caller line identification information
- `session.telephone.uui` provides user-to-user information

Note that whether a session variable has a valid value depends on whether the corresponding telephone service is supported. The following example plays back the caller's phone number:

```
<?xml version="1.0" ?>
<vxml version="1.0">
<form>
  <block>
    <prompt>
      Your phone number is
      <sayas class="phon"><value expr="session.telephone.ani"/></sayas>
    </prompt>
  </block>
</form>
</vxml>
```

If two variables in different scopes are declared to have the same name, the VoiceXML interpreter will use the one that has the narrower scope.

```
<?xml version="1.0"?>
<vxml version="1.0">
<form>
  <!-- user has a dialog scope. -->
  <var name="user" expr="'Mike Fraser'"/>
  <block>
    <!-- user has an anonymous Scope. -->
    <var name="user" expr="'Susan Fraser'"/>
    <prompt>
       <!-- use the user that has an anonymous scope. -->
      The user is <value expr="user"/>.
    </prompt>
  </block>
</form>
</vxml>
```

The document plays "The user is Susan Fraser", *not* "The user is Mike Fraser".

However, sometimes we want to access a variable from a different scope. To do so, we need to attach a prefix to the variable, as shown in the example below (the first document is the root document `root2.vxml`):

```
<?xml version="1.0"?>
<vxml version="1.0">
  <!-- this variable has application scope. -->
  <var name="user" expr="'Anybody'"/>
</vxml>
```

```
<?xml version="1.0"?>
<vxml version="1.0" application="root2.vxml">
  <!-- this variable has document scope. -->
  <var name="user" expr="'Fraser Family'"/>
```

```
<form>
  <!-- this variable has dialog scope. -->
  <var name="user" expr="'Mike Fraser'"/>
  <block>
    <!-- this variable has anonymous scope. -->
    <var name="user" expr="'Susan Fraser'"/>
    <prompt>
      The anonymous user is <value expr="user"/>.
      The dialog user is <value expr="dialog.user"/>.
      The document user is <value expr="document.user"/>.
      The application user is <value expr="application.user"/>.
    </prompt>
  </block>
</form>
```

The document plays like this:

System:	"The anonymous user is Susan Fraser."
	"The dialog user is Mike Fraser."
	"The document user is the Fraser family."
	"The application user is anybody."

Variable Access

A variable can be accessed in a `cond` or `expr` attribute's expression. In the previous examples, you saw how a variable could be accessed in an `expr` attribute. The following example shows how the variable `number` can be accessed in both `cond` and `expr` attributes (the `<if>` and `<else>` elements will be discussed later in the *Branching Elements* section):

```
<?xml version="1.0"?>
<vxml version="1.0">
<form>
  <!-- Assign a random number to the variable -->
  <var name="number" expr="Math.random()"/>
  <block>
    <!-- Access number in cond attribute -->
    <if cond="number == 0">
       <prompt>
         The value of the variable is zero.
      </prompt>
     <else/>
      <prompt>
         <!-- Access number in expr attribute -->
        The value of the non-zero variable is <value expr="number"/>.
      </prompt>
    </if>
  </block>
</form>
</vxml>
```

Expressions

An expression is a representation that evaluates to a value. Expressions can be used in `expr`, `cond`, `destexpr`, and `expritem` attributes, and also contained in the `<script>` element.

The `expr` attribute works with many VoiceXML elements including `<assign>` and `<value>`. The value of the `expr` attribute can be any valid ECMAScript expression. The following is a list of examples of valid expressions:

```
"3.14"
"'Mike Fraser'"
"true"
"var * 2 * 45"
"var != 0"
"var + '  ' + 'Susan Fraser'"
```

The `cond` attribute is used to specify the conditions for executing a particular part of the document. The value of the `cond` attribute can be any Boolean expression that evaluates to either `true` or `false`. For example, `"var1 > 0 && var2 < 0"` is a valid Boolean expression. Remember that ">", "<" and "&&" need to be escaped to `">"`, `"<"`, and `"&&"` in a VoiceXML document, because it has to abide by the rules of XML.

The `destexpr` attribute works with the `<transfer>` element, which is used to transfer a phone call to another phone number. The value of the `destexpr` attribute is an expression that evaluates to the URL of the destination. The following example shows how the `destexpr` works with the `<transfer>` element to transfer the current phone call to another phone number (`18001234567`):

```
<?xml version="1.0"?>
<vxml version="1.0">
<form>
  <var name="URLprefix" expr="'phone://'"/>
  <block>
    <prompt>
      This is call transfer test.
    </prompt>
  </block>

  <!-- destexpr expression evaluates to phone://18001234567 -->
  <transfer name="services" connecttimeout="300"
      destexpr="URLprefix + 18001234567" />
</form>
</vxml>
```

The `expritem` attribute works with the `<goto>` element to transition to another form item in the same form. The value of the `expritem` attribute evaluates to the name of the form item to transition to.

```
<?xml version="1.0"?>
<vxml version="1.0">
<form>
  <field name="order" type="boolean">
    <prompt>
      Do you want to go block 1 first?
    </prompt>
    <filled>
      <!-- expritem's value evaluates to a block name -->
      <goto expritem="(order)? 'block1' : 'block2'"/>
    </filled>
  </field>

  <block name="block1">
    <prompt>
      You are in block 1.
    </prompt>
```

```
  </block>

  <block name="block2">
    <prompt>
      You are in block 2.
    </prompt>
  </block>
</form>
</vxml>
```

The example shows how to use the `expritem` attribute to transition from one form item to another. One scenario could be:

System:	"Do you want to go block 1 first?"
User:	"No."
System:	"You are in block 2."

Client-side scripting can also be achieved in a VoiceXML document by using the `<script>` element. Expressions are important building blocks in JavaScript.

Branching Elements

The branching element `<if>` allows selective execution of certain parts of a VoiceXML document; its `cond` attribute determines which part of a document should be executed based on one or more conditions. The value of the attribute `cond` evaluates to a Boolean value `true` or `false`. The `<elseif>` and `<else>` elements are the optional children of the `<if>` element. Take a look at the following example that demonstrates these branching elements:

```
<?xml version="1.0" ?>
<vxml version="1.0">
<var name="number" expr="Math.random()"/>
<form>
  <block>
    <!-- IF structure -->
    <if cond="number &gt; 0.9">
      <prompt>
        The number <value expr="number"/> is greater than 0.9
      </prompt>
     </if>

    <!-- IF-ELSE structure -->
    <if cond="number &gt; 0.1">
      <prompt>
        The number <value expr="number"/> is greater than 0.1
      </prompt>
    <else/>
      <prompt>
        The number <value expr="number"/> is between 0 and 0.1
      </prompt>
    </if>

         <!-- IF-ELSEIF-ELSE structure -->
    <if cond="number &lt; 0.5">
      <prompt>
        The number <value expr="number"/> is less than 0.5
```

```
      </prompt>
      <elseif cond="number == 0.5"/>
      <prompt>
        The number <value expr="number"/> is 0.5
      </prompt>
      <else/>
      <prompt>
        The number <value expr="number"/> is greater than 0.5
      </prompt>
    </if>
  </block>
</form>
</vxml>
```

Event Handling

The VoiceXML processor expects constrained input utterances, so the user needs to know what to say at any point during a conversation. However, the user may not know exactly what to say, so the system needs to provide help instructions when the user asks for assistance. When an error such as nomatch or noinput occurs, an event will be thrown and should be caught by its corresponding event handler. The following discussion introduces how to provide the user with assistance by using the <help> element and how to throw, catch, and process an error or event.

Helping the User

The user is allowed to ask for assistance whenever they get lost and don't know what to do next during a conversation. Whenever the user asks for assistance, for example, says "Help", a help event is thrown and then caught by the <help> element. The grammar for assistance is platform-specific, and may include "Help", "Shoot", etc.

```
<?xml version="1.0"?>
<vxml version="1.0">
<form>
  <field name="action">
    <prompt>
      Welcome to the email service. How may I help you today?
    </prompt>
    <grammar>
      [compose check]
    </grammar>
        <!-- Provide instructions on how to proceed -->
    <help>
      Say compose or check.
    </help>
    <filled>
    <prompt>
      You said <value expr="action"/>.
    </prompt>
    </filled>
  </field>
</form>
</vxml>
```

In the example, the <help> element gives the user the instructions on what to say next. A scenario could be:

System:	"Welcome to the e-mail service. How may I help you today?"
User:	"Help."
System:	"Say compose or check."
User:	"Check."
System:	"You said check."

Handling Errors and Events

When an error or event occurs, its corresponding event handler catches and handles the error or event. An error or event can be thrown by the platform, the VoiceXML interpreter, or the `<throw>` element and caught by a built-in event handler, or the `<catch>` element.

<nomatch> and <noinput> Elements

When the system fails to match the user input with the corresponding grammar or has not received an input from the user for a particular period of time, a `nomatch` event or a `noinput` event will be thrown and then caught by the `<nomatch>` or `<noinput>` element respectively. How long the system will wait for the next input before it throws a `noinput` event can be set by using the `timeout` attribute in the `<prompt>` element or by using the `<property>` element (see the *Properties* section). The default `timeout` is platform-specific.

```
<?xml version="1.0"?>
<vxml version="1.0">
<form>
  <field name="action">
    <prompt timeout="3s">
      Welcome to the email service. How may I help you today?
    </prompt>
    <grammar>
      [compose check]
    </grammar>
        <!-- Provide instructions on how to proceed -->
    <help>
      Say compose or check.
    </help>
    <nomatch>
      Sorry, I didn't get that. Please say compose or check.
    </nomatch>
    <noinput>
      Sorry, I didn't hear anything. Please say compose or check.
    </noinput>
    <filled>
      <prompt>
        You said <value expr="action"/>.
      </prompt>
    </filled>
  </field>
</form>
</vxml>
```

This example demonstrates how the system catches `nomatch` and `noinput` errors and handles them as well. A possible conversation could be:

System:	"Welcome to the e-mail service. How may I help you today?"
User:	"Send e-mail."
System:	"Sorry, I didn't get that. Please say compose or check."
User:	*does not respond*
System:	"Sorry, I didn't hear anything. Please say compose or check."
User:	"Compose."
System:	"You said compose."

<error> Element

When the VoiceXML interpreter encounters an error, it throws an `error` event. To catch an `error` event, we use the `<error>` element. There are several pre-defined errors, including:

- `error.badfetch` – It failed to fetch a document
- `error.semantic` – A run-time error occurred, for example a zero denominator, string bounds error, or reference to an undefined variable
- `error.noauthorization` – The user is not authorized to perform the requested operation
- `error.unsupported.format` – The requested resource has a unsupported format
- `error.unsupported.element` – The platform does not support the element

The `<error>` element catches all these errors. The following example shows how the `<error>` element catches an error when an attempt is made to use a variable before it is declared:

```
<?xml version="1.0" ?>
<vxml version="1.0">
<form>
  <error>
    <prompt>Error occurred</prompt>
  </error>
  <block>
    The variable <value expr="myvar"/> is not declared.
  </block>
</form>
</vxml>
```

The `error.semantic` error is thrown and caught by the `<error>` element. "Error occurred" is uttered by the system.

<throw> and <catch> Elements

The events that have been discussed so far are thrown either by the platform (`help`, `nomatch`, and `noinput`) or by the VoiceXML interpreter when it determines an error has occurred. All these events are pre-defined. However, we can also define our own events and use the `<throw>` and `<catch>` elements to throw and catch them. Consider the following sample:

```
<?xml version="1.0"?>
<vxml version="1.0">
<form>
  <field name="number" type="number">
    <prompt>
      Tell me a non-zero number.
    </prompt>
        <!-- The invalid _number event is caught here -->
    <catch event="invalid_number">
      <prompt>
        Zero is not allowed.
      </prompt>
    </catch>
    <filled>
      <if cond="number == 0">
          <!-- invalid_number is thrown here -->
        <throw event="invalid_number"/>
      </if>
      <prompt>
        You said <value expr="number"/>
      </prompt>
    </filled>
  </field>
</form>
</vxml>
```

In this example, an `invalid_number` event is thrown when the user inputs "zero":

System:	"Tell me a non-zero number."
User:	"Zero."
System:	"Zero is not allowed."

The `<throw>` and `<catch>` elements can also be used to throw and catch pre-defined events, including `exit`, `help`, `nomatch`, `noinput`, and `error`. The following example shows how to catch a pre-defined event `nomatch`:

```
<?xml version="1.0" ?>
<vxml version="1.0">
<form>
  <catch event="nomatch">
    I'm afraid you must say yes or no.
  </catch>
  <field name="action" type="boolean">
    <prompt>
      Should we continue?
    </prompt>
  </field>
</form>
</vxml>
```

A possible conversation could be:

System:	"Should we continue?"
User:	"Go ahead."
System:	"I'm afraid you must say yes or no."
User:	"Yes."

The <catch> element can also be used to catch more than one type of event:

```
<?xml version="1.0" ?>
<vxml version="1.0">
<form>
  <catch event="nomatch noinput">
    Please say yes or no.
  </catch>
  <field name="action" type="boolean">
    <prompt>
      Should we continue?
    </prompt>
  </field>
</form>
</vxml>
```

A possible conversation could be:

System:	"Should we continue?"
User:	does not respond
System:	"Please say yes or no."
User:	"Yes."

Actually, the <help>, <nomatch>, <noinput>, and <error> elements are just the shorthand notations of the event handlers <catch event="help">, <catch event="nomatch">, <catch event="noinput">, and <catch event="error">.

Each <catch> element, including <catch>, <help>, <nomatch>, <noinput>, and <error>, has a count attribute, which allows our code to handle the event thrown in a different way each time the event is thrown. For example, the system could use different prompts for successive noinput events. The following example shows how the count attribute works:

```
<?xml version="1.0"?>
<vxml version="1.0">
<form>
  <field name="shares" type="number">
    <prompt>
      The number of shares to buy?
    </prompt>
    <nomatch count="1">
      Please tell me the number of shares you want to buy.  For example, one
      hundred.
```

```
      </nomatch>
      <nomatch count="2">
        Please repeat the number of shares you want to buy
      </nomatch>
    </field>
  </form>
  </vxml>
```

A possible conversation could progress like this:

System:	"The number of shares to buy?"
User:	"I don't want to buy any chairs."
System:	"Please tell me the number of shares you want to buy. For example, one hundred."
User:	"One zero zero."
System:	"Please repeat the number of shares."
User:	"One hundred."

An event handler doesn't have to be in the same element within which the event is thrown, because an element inherits event handlers specified in its ancestor elements. For example, if an event is thrown in a form item and the form item doesn't have a <catch> element to catch that event, but the form itself does, the event will be caught by the form-level <catch> element. Therefore, an event thrown in a form item may be caught in the same form item, in the form, in the document, or in the application.

Navigation

A conversation doesn't have to be limited to a single dialog; indeed, it could be quite boring if it did! It can transition to another dialog (subdialog) and return to the original place, to another URL destination, to another dialog or form item, or to another URL destination when matching a particular grammar. This section introduces the elements that allow the conversation to shift from one place to another in this way.

The <subdialog> Element

In addition to dialogs, VoiceXML provides the function-like <subdialog> element, used as a subdialog of the current dialog. The <subdialog> element can be considered as a function call in a programming language; it invokes a new interaction and returns to the original point in the original document when it is finished. All local variables, grammars, and information are saved before the execution goes to the subdialog and restored when it comes back. The <subdialog> element is very useful when an application needs to return to the calling document after performing a particular task. It can also be used to create a library of reusable dialogs to be shared among the documents in the same application and among different applications. The <return> element is used in a subdialog to return values to the calling document.

The <param> element included within a <subdialog> element is used to pass a parameter from the caller to the subdialog. Each parameter passed by the calling document needs to be declared in the subdialog using the <var> element. The return values are stored in the name attribute of the <subdialog> element as a list of properties, and the src attribute of the <subdialog> element specifies the URL of the subdialog.

```
<?xml version="1.0"?>
<vxml version="1.0">
<form id="main">
  <block>
    <prompt>
      Before calling the sub dialog.
    </prompt>
  </block>

  <!-- Calling subdialog info with parameter name -->
  <subdialog name="result" src="#info">
    <param name="name" value="Susan Fraser"/>
   </subdialog>

  <block>
    <prompt>
      You are back to the main dialog.
      The social security number is <value expr="result.ssn"/>
      and phone number is <value expr="result.phone"/>
    </prompt>
  </block>
</form>

<!-- Subdialog defined here -->
<form id="info">
  <var name="name"/>    <!-- Parameter passed to this subdialog -->
  <var name="ssn" expr="''"/>
  <var name="phone" expr="''"/>
  <block>
    <prompt>
     You are in sub dialog.
    </prompt>
    <if cond="name=='Susan Fraser'">
      <assign name="ssn" expr="'123-45-6789'"/>
      <assign name="phone" expr="'1-800-1234567'"/>
      <elseif cond="name=='Mike Fraser'"/>
      <assign name="ssn" expr="'987-65-4321'"/>
      <assign name="phone" expr="'1-800-7654321'"/>
    </if>
        <!-- Return variables ssn and phone to caller -->
    <return namelist="ssn phone"/>
  </block>
</form>
</vxml>
```

This document plays the following sequence of prompts:

System:	"Before calling the subdialog."
	"You are in subdialog."
	"You are back to the main dialog."
	"The social security number is 123-45-6789 and phone number is 1-800-1234567."

Note that the subdialog doesn't have to be in the same document as the calling `<subdialog>` element. If a subdialog is in another document, say `info_dialog.vxml`, the `src` attribute of the `<subdialog>` element in this example would be set to `info_dialog.vxml#info`.

The <submit> Element

When we need to submit values to the document server we can use the <submit> element. The next attribute of the <submit> element specifies the URL to which the values are submitted and the namelist attribute specifies the values to submit. If the namelist is not supplied, all the named field item variables are submitted. Once executed, the <submit> element doesn't necessarily return control to the calling document. If the next attribute specifies an ASP script that generates a well-formed VoiceXML document, for example, execution will continue with the generated VoiceXML document.

```
<?xml version="1.0" ?>
<vxml version="1.0">
<form>
  <var name="user" expr="'Mike Fraser'"/>
  <field name="pin" type="digits">
    <prompt>
      What is your pin?
    </prompt>
    <filled>
      <!-- Submit user and pin to server side script -->
      <submit next="http://www.yoursite.com/yourscript.asp"
              namelist="user pin"/>
      </filled>
    </field>
</form>
</vxml>
```

The example shows that when the pin is collected from the user, the user's name and PIN are both submitted to the server-side script yourscript.asp. If the namelist attribute wasn't specified, pin would be the only variable submitted.

Note that the default method of submitting the values is using GET. However, the POST method can be specified using the method attribute of <submit>.

The <goto> Element

The <goto> element is another way to direct the execution to another dialog. Using <goto nextitem> or <goto expritem> passes execution to another form item (for example, <field> or <block>) in the same form, while using <goto next> or <goto expr> passes execution to another dialog in the same document or a different document.

```
<?xml version="1.0"?>
<vxml version="1.0">
  <form id="form1">
    <block name="block0">
      <prompt>
        You are in block 0.
      </prompt>
            <!-- Transition to another form item -->
      <goto nextitem="block2"/>
    </block>

    <block name="block1">
      <prompt>
        You are in block 1.
      </prompt>
            <!-- Transition to another form -->
```

```
      <goto next="#form1"/>
    </block>

    <block name="block2">
      <prompt>
        You are in block 2.
      </prompt>
    </block>
  </form>

  <form id="form2">
    <block>
      <prompt>
        You are in form 2.
      </prompt>
    </block>
  </form>
</vxml>
```

This example replays the prompts in the following order:

System:	"You are in block 0."
	"You are in block 2."
	"You are in block 1."
	"You are in form 2."

The <link> Element

In addition to the <subdialog>, <submit>, and <goto> elements, VoiceXML provides another element, the <link> element, for execution transition. The <link> element specifies one or more grammars scoped to the element that contains the <link> element. When the user input matches one of the grammars, the execution transitions to the URI specified by the next attribute, or an event specified by the event attribute is thrown.

The <link> element can be specified at the application level (in the root document), document level (as a child of the <vxml> element), form level (as a child of a <form> element), or included as a child of a form item. The following example, which includes a root document root3.vxml and a leaf document foo.xml, shows how the <link> element works:

```
<!-- root3.vxml -->
<?xml version="1.0"?>
<vxml version="1.0">
<!-- Transition to a form item in foo.vxml when the grammar is matched -->
  <link next="foo.vxml#quit">
    <grammar> (i want to quit) </grammar>
  </link>
</vxml>
```

```
<!-- foo.vxml -->
<?xml version="1.0" ?>
<vxml version="1.0" application="root3.vxml">
  <!-- Transition to form help when the grammar is matched -->
  <link next="#help">
```

```
    <grammar>(i need help)</grammar>
  </link>

  <form>
    <field name="test">
      <!-- Throw help event when the grammar is matched -->
      <link event="help">
        <grammar> (i don't know what to say) </grammar>
      </link>
      <help>
        <reprompt/>
      </help>
      <prompt>
        To get help, say I need help.
        To quit the system, say I want to quit.
      </prompt>
    </field>
  </form>

  <form id="help">
    <block>
      <prompt>
        You are in the help form.
      </prompt>
    </block>
  </form>

  <form id="quit">
    <block>
      <prompt>
        Thanks for using the service. Goodbye.
      </prompt>
      <exit/>
    </block>
  </form>
</vxml>
```

Let's take a look at some of the conversations that could develop using the above document:

System:	"To get help, say I need help. To quit the system, say I want to quit."
User:	"I need help."
System:	"You are in the help form."

System:	"To get help, say I need help. To quit the system, say I want to quit."
User:	"I want to quit."
System:	"Thanks for using the service. Goodbye."

System:	"To get help, say I need help. To quit the system, say I want to quit."
User:	"I don't know what to say."
System:	"To get help, say I need help. To quit the system, say I want to quit."

Call Transfer and Disconnection

During a conversation, we may need to transfer the user to another phone number or disconnect from the user. To accomplish these tasks, we can use the <transfer> and <disconnect> elements.

The dest attribute of the <transfer> element specifies the destination phone number and the name attribute stores the outcome of the transfer. The name attribute can have the following values:

- busy – The endpoint refused the call
- noanswer – There was no answer within the specified time
- network_busy – The intermediate network refused the call
- near_end_disconnect – The call went through but was terminated by the caller
- far_end_disconnect – The call went through but was terminated by the person called
- network_disconnect – The call went through but was terminated by the network

The following example shows that the current call will be transferred to the operator at 18001234567 if the user inputs "yes".

```
<?xml version="1.0" ?>
<vxml version="1.0">
<form>
  <field name="talk" type="boolean">
    <prompt>
      Do you want to talk to the operator?
    </prompt>
    <filled>
      <if cond="talk">
        <prompt>
          One moment please.
        </prompt>
        <!-- Transfer to phone number 18001234567 -->
        <transfer name="services" dest="phone://18001234567">
          <filled>
            <!-- Prompt the user if it is busy -->
            <if cond="services == 'busy'">
              <prompt>
                Sorry, the phone line is busy. Please call back later.
              </prompt>
            </if>
          </filled>
        </transfer>
      <else/>
        <prompt>
          Goodbye.
        </prompt>
        <!-- Disconnect from the user -->
        <disconnect/>
        <prompt>
          You should not hear this.
        </prompt>
      </if>
    </filled>
  </field>
</form>
</vxml>
```

Objects

Data access and processing are necessary in many applications. For example, you may need to find a list of flights in a travel application, or verify a credit card number in an e-commerce (or v-commerce) application. One way to do this is using the <object> element. The <object> element invokes a platform-specific object with or without parameters and brings back an ECMAScript object with one or more properties to the VoiceXML document.

The following is a platform-dependent example taken from the BeVocal site (http://www.bevocal.com) that runs on the BeVocal platform:

```
<?xml version="1.0"?>
<!DOCTYPE vxml PUBLIC "-//BeVocal Inc//VoiceXML 1.0//EN"
"http://cafe.bevocal.com/libraries/dtd/vxml1-0-bevocal.dtd">
<vxml version="1.0">
<form id="form1">
  <object classid="speechobject://bevocal.cafe.SOCityState" name="cityState"/>

  <field name="yesno1">
    <prompt><value expr="cityState"/>
        <audio src="is_that_correct.wav"> is that correct?
        </audio>
    </prompt>
    <grammar>[yes no]</grammar>
    <filled>
      <if cond="yesno1=='no'">
        <clear namelist="cityState"/>
      </if>
    </filled>
  </field>

  <block>
    <assign name="city" expr="cityState.city"/>
    <assign name="state" expr="cityState.state"/>
  </block>

  <object classid="speechobject://bevocal.cafe.SOStreet" name="streetName">
    <param name="cityName" expr="cityState.city" />
    <param name="stateName" expr="cityState.state" />
  </object>

  <field name="yesorno2">
    <prompt><value expr="streetName"/>
      <audio src="is_that_correct.wav"> is that correct?
      </audio>
    </prompt>
    <grammar>[yes no]</grammar>
    <filled>
      <if cond="yesorno2=='no'">
        <clear namelist="streetName"/>
      </if>
    </filled>
  </field>

  <object classid="speechobject://bevocal.cafe.SOStreetNumber"
          name="streetNumber">
    <param name="cityName" expr="cityState.city" />
    <param name="stateName" expr="cityState.state" />
    <param name="streetName" expr="streetName.street"/>
```

```
    </object>

    <field name="yesorno3">
      <prompt>You said <value expr="streetNumber"/>
        <audio src="is_that_correct.wav"> is that correct?
        </audio>
      </prompt>
      <grammar>[yes no]</grammar>
      <filled>
        <if cond="yesorno3=='no'">
          <clear namelist="streetNumber"/>
        </if>
      </filled>
    </field>
  </form>
  </vxml>
```

The `classid` attribute specifies the location of the object's implementation and the `name` attribute stores the result. The `<param>` elements are used to pass the parameters from the VoiceXML document to the object. One of the conversations of this example could be:

System:	"Name a city and state."
User:	"Sunnyvale, California."
System:	"Sunnyvale California. Is that correct?"
User:	"Yes."
System:	"Say a street name in Sunnyvale."
User:	"Mathilda."
System:	"Mathilda. Is that correct?"
User:	"Yes."
System:	"Say a street number or say I don't know."
User:	"157."
System:	"You said 157. Is that correct?"

The first object `SOCityState` asks for the name of a city and state. When the user inputs "Sunnyvale California", the city and state names are returned to the document and included in the prompt for confirmation in the document: "Sunnyvale California. Is that correct?" Then the object `SOStreet` is invoked with the city and state names as parameters and asks for a street name in Sunnyvale. This indicates that the object `SOStreet` has received the city and state names. The errors that occur in an object are handled within the object.

A more detailed discussion of SpeechObjects can be found in Chapter 10.

Properties

The <property> element is used to control the platform's behavior, including recognition process, barge-in, timeout, caching policy, and document fetches, etc. It can be defined at application level (in the root document), document level (as a child of the <vxml> element), dialog level (as a child of the <form> or <menu> element), or at form-item level (as a child of a form item). A <property> defined at lower level overrides a <property> defined at higher level.

The <property> element can be used to specify the speech recognizer properties. For example, it can be used to set the confidencelevel property, which has a value between 0.0 and 1.0. Results are rejected when the recognition engine's confidence level falls below this confidencelevel setting. The default value is set to 0.5.

The bargein and timeout properties for a prompt can be set by using the <property> element. When bargein is set to false, interruption of system prompts by the user is not allowed. The default value is true. The timeout property is set to specify how long the platform has to wait for an input before throwing a noinput event.

Both voice and DTMF inputs are allowed by default. With the <property> element, we can choose to use only one of them (for example, we could turn off speech recognition when the application is used in a noisy environment). To turn off speech recognition, set the inputmodes property to "dtmf". To turn off DTMF, set it to "voice". You may set it to "dtmf voice" to allow both voice and DTMF, which is the default.

The <property> element can be used to specify the caching policy, which could be either fast or safe. The fast policy fetches a document when the document is expired and the safe policy fetches a document when it is expired or modified. The default caching policy is fast. To set the caching policy to safe, use <property name="caching" value="safe"/>.

When it takes a while to fetch a document, the <property> element can be used to set the fetchaudio property to the URI of an audio file to play while the system is fetching the document. No audio will be played by default.

The <property> element can also be used to specify whether an audio, document, grammar, object, or script should be pre-fetched and specify the timeout period for the fetches.

The following document shows the use of the <property> element:

```
<?xml version="1.0" ?>
<vxml version="1.0">
  <!-- set recognition confidence level to 0.7 -->
  <property name="confidencelevel" value="0.7"/>
  <!-- barge-in is not allowed -->
  <property name="bargein" value="false"/>
  <!-- set caching policy to safe -->
  <property name="caching" value="safe"/>
  <form id="number_form">
    <field name="mynumber" type="number">
    <!-- set timeout to 5 second -->
      <property name="timeout" value="5s"/>
      <prompt>
        Tell me a number. For example, one hundred.
      </prompt>
      <filled>
        <prompt>
```

```
            You said <value expr="mynumber"/>
          </prompt>
          <goto next="#dtmf_menu"/>
        </filled>
      </field>
    </form>
    <menu id="dtmf_menu">
      <!-- only DTMF is allowed -->
      <property name="inputmodes" value="dtmf"/>
      <prompt>
        For math press 1, for science press 2, for music press 3.
      </prompt>
        <choice dtmf="1" next="#math"> math </choice>
        <choice dtmf="2" next="#science"> science </choice>
        <choice dtmf="3" next="#music"> music </choice>
    </menu>

    <form id="math">
      <block>
        <prompt>
          You've chosen Math.
        </prompt>
      </block>
    </form>

    <form id="science">
      <block>
        <prompt>
          You've chosen Science.
        </prompt>
      </block>
    </form>

    <form id="music">
      <block>
        <prompt>
          You've chosen Music.
        </prompt>
      </block>
    </form>
  </vxml>
```

In this example, the `inputmodes` property is set to "`dtmf`" in the `<property>` element in the menu, so the application will only accept input from the keypad of the phone; speech input is ignored by the VoiceXML application.

Mixed-Initiative Forms

A conversation between a computer and a user doesn't always have to be computer-directed, with the computer asking questions and the user answering. Using the `<initial>` element and form-level grammars allows both the computer and the user to direct a conversation. A form that allows the user to direct the conversation by including one or more `<initial>` elements and form-level grammars is a **mixed-initiative** form.

When the input utterance matches the form-level grammar and one of the form-item variables is filled in the `<initial>` element, the execution moves on to the next form item that has not been filled. The fields in a mixed-initiative form can be filled in any order, and more than one field can be filled by a single utterance.

Here's a grammar document, `foo.grammar` (written in Nuance GSL):

```
Object [
   (Color Item)
   Color
   Item
]

Color [
   red  {<color red>}
   blue {<color blue>}
]

Item [
   ball {<item ball>}
   box  {<item box>}
]
```

Here's a VoiceXML document containing a mixed-initiative form:

```
<?xml version="1.0" ?>
<vxml version="1.0">
<form>
  <!-- Form level grammar -->
  <grammar src="foo.grammar#Object"/>

  <initial>
    What object do you want?
  </initial>

  <!-- Ask for color -->
  <field name="color">
    <grammar src="foo.grammar#Color"/>
    <prompt>
      What is the color of the object, red or blue?
    </prompt>
  </field>

  <!-- Ask for item -->
  <field name="item">
    <grammar src="foo.grammar#Item"/>
    <prompt>
      What is the name of the object, ball or box?
    </prompt>
     </field>

  <block>
    <prompt>
      You said <value expr="color"/> <value expr="item"/>.
    </prompt>
  </block>
</form>
</vxml>
```

The grammar rule `foo.grammar#Object` is the form-level grammar, which matches the following utterances and cause the corresponding field variable(s) to be set when a match occurs:

red ball – (color is set to red and item is set to ball).
red box – (color is set to red and item is set to box).
blue ball – (color is set to blue and item is set to ball).
blue box – (color is set to blue and item is set to box).
red – (color is set to red).
blue – (color is set to blue).
ball – (item is set to ball).
box – (item is set to box).

The fields can be filled in any order:

System:	"What object do you want?"
User:	"Box."
System:	"What is the color of the object, red or blue?"
User:	"Blue."
System:	"You said blue box."

or:

System:	"What object do you want?"
User:	"Red."
System:	"What is the name of the object, ball or box?"
User:	"Ball."
System:	"You said red ball."

A single utterance can fill in more than one field:

System:	"What object do you want?"
User:	"Blue ball."
System:	"You said blue ball."

A form-level grammar in a mixed-initiative form is active when the user is in another dialog. Once the input utterance matches the form-level grammar, the execution will be directed to the mixed initiative form.

```
<?xml version="1.0" ?>
<vxml version="1.0">
<form id="mixed_init_form">
  <!-- For level grammar -->
  <grammar src="foo.grammar#Object"/>

  <initial>
    What object do you want?
  </initial>
```

```
    <!-- Ask for color -->
    <field name="color">
      <grammar src="foo.grammar#Color"/>
      <prompt>
        What is the color of the object, red or blue?
      </prompt>
     </field>

       <!-- Ask for item -->
    <field name="item">
      <grammar src="foo.grammar#Item"/>
      <prompt>
        What is the name of the object, ball or box?
      </prompt>
    </field>

    <block>
      <prompt>
        You said <value expr="color"/> <value expr="item"/>.
      </prompt>
      <goto next="#confirm"/>
    </block>
  </form>

  <form id="confirm">
    <field name="todo" type="boolean">
      <prompt>
        Do you want to continue?
      </prompt>
      <filled/>
    </field>
  </form>
  </vxml>
```

When the user is in the form `confirm` and inputs "ball" in responce to the question, the execution will be directed to the form `mixed_init_form`.

Summary

The elements and their related attributes covered in this chapter are the most useful ones in VoiceXML in building telephone-based and voice-enabled dialogs. The following groups of elements have been discussed:

- Programming elements used to manipulate client-side data and selective execution
- Event-handling elements used to help the user and handle errors
- Elements leading to dialog transitions
- Object elements used to access and process data
- Property elements used to manipulate platform behavior
- Mixed-initiative forms used to allow both computer- and user-directed conversations

```
<?xml version="1.0"?>
<vxml version="1.0">
<form id="foo">
<block>
<prompt>
Hi. My name is Bob
</prompt>
</block>
</form>
</vxml>
```

6

Good Application Design

An application design defines the interaction interface that determines how the entire system is presented to the user. Voice-enabled interfaces will combine elements of directed and mixed-initiative dialog, and allow for both voice and non-voice input. By incorporating speech into a system, we hope to take advantage of the communication methods found in natural language that people are already used to. Thus, voice application design should be based on good understanding of the communication protocols obeyed by people in their daily lives.

A good interface has to help people get their job done in an effective and efficient way with satisfaction. Effectiveness means that the user gets the results desired and efficiency ensures that they get them quickly and without effort. Determining the best way of interacting with the user so that they get their work done effectively and efficiently is the primary goal of speech interface design.

The objective of this chapter is to provide you with the basic principles of creating a user interface for a voice-enabled application. Seven separate issues are covered, each under its own heading.

A General Process outlines the general procedure of speech user interface design.

Prompting provides advice for constructing prompts. A good interface is capable of handling various aspects of user interaction, including:

- quickly obtaining particular items of information from expert and novice users alike
- providing assistance for the user when required
- leading the user to provide an answer that matches the grammar
- seeking confirmation from the user before any significant transaction is executed
- guiding the user so that tasks can be achieved speedily
- avoiding causing offense to the user
- the appropriate use of DTMF and barge-in
- good application of the consistency rules

Error Handling discusses how errors can be handled. A speech user interface is different from a graphic user interface in that audio information is temporal, and therefore must rely on the user's memory. This is something that the designer really needs to be aware of. Besides, a speech user interface relies on speech recognition technology, which is not error free. There's always a relatively high chance of mistakes from either the user or the system that must be dealt with. A well-designed user interface will always handle error prevention and error recovery well, and it is something that should never be underestimated when devising a speech user interface.

Grammar presents some basic techniques in grammar design. As one of the major components of a speech interface, grammars can greatly affect usability, by offering flexibility, avoiding confusing input, and allowing the user to drive a dialog according to their personal preferences.

Application Personality describes what to consider when creating an application personality. Users often tend to ascribe a particular personality to a voice-enabled application – even if personality was not an issue during the interface design. However, this is something to take advantage of, as by giving the system the right personality you can make the user feel comfortable and at ease.

Learning examines learning techniques. To design a system that sounds inviting, it's possible to incorporate learning functionality into the interface. A system that remembers preferences and details of the user during the course of one or more interactions, applying that knowledge to later interactions, could be said to have intelligence. That is, an intelligent interface learns how to serve a particular user in the way they prefer, increasing the level of user satisfaction.

Usability Testing rounds things up by looking at the procedure of usability testing. When you have determined how to implement the user interface, or perhaps have implemented a prototype or even the full system, you should conduct an evaluation test to get feedback from users. This step is very important as it can reveal hidden usability flaws.

A General Process

A user interface defines how users see a system and, if it is any good, it enables users to accomplish a task effectively and efficiently. However, a good interface doesn't just happen, it requires the designer to follow a process for success, and this section suggests just such a process for applying to speech user interface design.

We can divide the process into four basic phases: analysis, design, implementation, and evaluation. When necessary, the entire design process iteratively cycles through these phases.

Analysis

During the analysis phase, you need to define the scope of the application, identify who will be using the system, evaluate users' requirements and expectations, and formulate the usability plan.

Define the Scope of the Application

First of all, you need to know what the application is setting out to do. Is it a business application, a healthcare application, or an education application? Does it provide e-mail service, travel service, or driving directions? What tasks should the application be capable of? What hardware and software are used currently, and what will be used in the system? So, to define the scope of the application, we must answer the following questions:

- What is the goal of the application?
- What tasks can the application help users to accomplish?
- What technology is most appropriate?

Identify the Users

Who the system is targeting affects the interface design decision. People from different backgrounds have different expectations and habits when interacting with the system, and will act differently when the unexpected occurs. You need to answer at least the following questions about potential users:

- Will they already have experience of a speech interface?
- What are their expectations for the system?
- Will they use the system frequently, or only on occasion?
- Do they have prior knowledge of this sort of application?
- What is their likely age range?
- What are their professional backgrounds likely to be?
- In what environment will they be using the system?
- What might possibly be their speaking styles?
- Whether the accents they have can be handled by the speech recognition package you have?

These questions determine the nature of prompting, dialog flow, application personality, terminology, and grammar for the application, and indicate where DTMF and barge-in should be used.

Write up a Usability Plan

Interface usability has three aspects: effectiveness, efficiency, and user satisfaction. As I like to put it, a good interface design is able to guide the user to get the job done efficiently with satisfaction. This requires the designer to identify the usability objectives and determine how best to set about achieving these. The following is a list of issues you should consider when writing up your usability plan:

- Will it be able to help users to get their job done? If this isn't clear, users will have less motivation to try out and persevere with the system.
- Will users be able to accomplish their tasks quickly using the system?
- Is the system easy to use? In other words, it is user-friendly?
- Is the system easy for a new user to learn?
- Does the system have a suitable personality?
- What other things can increase user satisfaction for this particular application?

All these issues influence whether a user is willing to come back to the system.

Design

During the design phase, we need to develop ways of achieving our usability objectives in the light of the understanding of the application that the initial analysis has provided.

Users, especially those who already have experience of similar applications, will have established a mental model of the interface and tend to bring expectations to the new system. For example, users who are familiar with e-mail services with either text or graphic interfaces will be looking for the same basic functionality in your voice-enabled e-mail system. So, we need to develop a conceptual model of the system consistent with the user's mental model, or that allows the user to easily develop a mental model to aid their understanding of the application.

To construct a conceptual model, we write down as many scripts and possible task scenarios as we can think of. The scripts and scenarios should include the design of prompting, error handling, grammar, and application personality, discussed later in the chapter.

During this phase of the design, it is also important to look into the cost of the system. Different applications have different system requirements. Although VoiceXML is designed to handle voice and DTMF input, and TTS and audio file output, not all applications need all these features. Some applications might be better designed not to use voice recognition but to rely solely on DTMF. Other applications, such as a wake-up call service, may only require the system to replay audio files. If your budget allows, making full use of the features provided by VoiceXML should be encouraged since they enhance the usability. However, if the system happens to be designed on a tight budget, avoiding using expensive speech recognition and TTS packages increases the possibility of success.

Implementation

With the completion of the documents developed in the design phase, you may start implementing the interface or submit your design to the implementation team. Of course, implementation should be guided by the design, but it is very common for a design to miss details that become apparent during the implementation phase. If that happens, you need to be ready to receive feedback from the implementers and revise your design accordingly.

Evaluation

Evaluation can be conducted at any time during the design. The goal of evaluation is to collect opinions from other usability engineers and feedback from potential users to highlight problems in the design.

Different approaches are developed for interface evaluation. One of them is known as the Wizard of Oz (WOz) technique, which allows us to collect objective data and subjective opinions from real users. The WOz technique is introduced in the final section, in this chapter *Usability Testing*.

Other usability evaluation approaches are around that may be useful here, such as 'Heuristic Evaluations' and 'Walkthroughs'. The Heuristic Evaluation approach requires that expert evaluators trace through the entire design to winkle out usability problems. Walkthroughs are simpler; you 'walk' someone, such as a coworker, 'through' the interface as though they were using the system to accomplish a set task, asking questions about the interface along the way.

Prompting

Prompting is a major issue in speech interface design. Prompting design is concerned with communicating with users effectively and efficiently. Designing prompts appropriately reduces errors, increases user satisfaction, and enhances system productivity. This section discusses how to guide different users, be they experts or novices, to quickly get tasks done, to lead them into providing responses that match the grammars, to seek confirmation from the user when a significant transaction is about to be executed, to provide feedback to the user, to avoid offending the user, and to use DTMF and barge-in appropriately.

Tapered Prompts

Tapering prompts is the shortening of prompts each time they are presented to the user. Essentially, you start with a more detailed prompt and then taper it when subsequently fired. This is for those cases where you need to ask for the same piece of information over and over. For example,

System:	"We are going to send the package to your home. Please tell me your home address, including zip code and state."
User:	*Says their home address, but the system fails to understand.*
System:	"Sorry, please repeat your full home address."

When the system fails to recognize the user's input, it tapers the prompt. This is based on the assumption that the user heard the prompt that explains why his home address is needed. Use of tapered prompts can make dialogs brief, concise, and efficient.

Tapered prompts can be used when the system needs to ask for more than one piece of information. To use tapered prompts, start with a long prompt to ask the user to input all pieces of information, and then give another shorter prompt for the pieces that are still missing. For example,

System:	"Please tell me your name and address."
User:	"My name is Mike Green."
System:	"And your address?"

In this example, when the name of the user has been filled, it uses a shorter prompt to ask for the address. This gives the user a chance to input all pieces of information in a single utterance. Typically, this type of tapered prompt is used in forms in which a mixed-initiative dialog is followed, as described in Chapter 5.

Incremental Prompts

These are the inverse of the tapered prompt. For a particular input, the system may start with a short prompt. If the user doesn't respond or fails to respond correctly, the system replays a prompt that conveys more information about how to respond. If this still doesn't work, further prompts can be fired that supply more detailed instructions on what to do. This approach works well for both experts and novices since experts have the chance to move fast, and novices get necessary information as required. For example:

System:	"How many would you like?"
User:	"What?"
System:	"How many shares do you want to buy? For example, one hundred."
User:	"I guess at least a thousand."
System:	"I'm sorry, I still didn't get that. Please enter the number of shares you would like to buy using your keypad."

Leading Prompts

Usually, to a particular question, there are widely varying answers. For example, in a stock application, answers to "The current price is $45. Would you like to trade?" could include:

- Yes, I would like 1000 shares.
- Of course I want to buy.
- Sell 1000 shares please.
- No, I think I'm going to wait.

A comprehensive grammar is required to handle this variability of input. However, it is always difficult for a designer to write a grammar that covers all possible answers to a particular question. Too many grammar mismatches will quickly discourage the user, so you need to avoid prompts that can have widely varying responses. Use prompts that let the user follow the lead of the question. One way to do this is to put important words, especially words you expect the user to include in the response, at the end to steer the user's response. For example, instead of using "The current price is $45. Would you like to trade?" a preferable prompt would be, "The current price is $45. Do you want to buy, sell, or quit?" The user is then very likely to say one of the words "buy", "sell", or "quit".

Prompts should always be specific, because a general prompt usually leads to imprecise or vague responses. For example, we should avoid prompts like this one:

System:	"Welcome to the X Stock System. How may I help you today?"
User:	"Oh hi! I was just wondering if you could tell me the price of United Beet."

Since the question is too general, the answers can vary wildly, especially when the system talks to novice users. Even if the system talks to expert users, the response to the question can vary from user to user. To improve this, make the question be specific. For example,

System:	"Welcome to the X Stock System. Please give the company name for stock information."
User:	"United Beet."

Since the question only asks for the company's name, the answer is very likely going to be just the name of a company.

Confirmation

Current speech recognition technology cannot guarantee that the system heard exactly what the user said. People are going to feel more comfortable if they know that the system understands what they have said, what it is about to do, and what it is doing. In many cases, it is necessary for the system to be sure that what it will do is what the user really wants, especially when the next action could result in irrecoverable consequences. Confirmation and feedback can ensure that the user has been heard correctly. There are two basic types: explicit confirmation and implicit confirmation.

Explicit confirmation plays back the user's request message to double-check that they have been heard correctly. For example,

System:	"Please state the number of shares you would like to buy."
User:	"100."
System:	"You want to buy 100 shares in Microsoft, is that correct?"

Explicit confirmations are especially useful when the next action could cause effects that cannot be undone as in this example. However, too many unnecessary confirmations could impact on system productivity, make the interface too verbose, and annoy the user. Thus, explicit confirmations should only be used when the next action could cause irrecoverable damage.

In some other circumstances, it is necessary for the system to assure the user it heard what the user has said and is about to perform the task requested by the user. Usually, this type of action won't cause any permanent damage. This is when implicit confirmation is best used. For example:

System:	"What would you like to do next?"
User:	"List all messages sent by Anne Brimacombe."
System:	"One moment please while I get the e-mails sent by Anne Brimacombe for you."

Here, an **implicit confirmation** is used. The user will know the e-mails they is going to hear are from Mike Green and not anyone else. An implicit confirmation can be used when it is necessary to inform the user about the results of a particular task. The use of implicit confirmation helps avoid confusion without the extra time cost of asking the user's confirmation.

Brief Prompts

Psychologists have found that, in general, people can only hold between five and nine chunks of information in their heads at a time. If you don't believe me, use a long complex prompt and expect the user to remember everything they've been told; you will soon find it doesn't work that way! If the message is delivered with synthesized speech, the situation can be even worse. Use brief prompts and only deliver necessary information to the user. When we need to instruct the user on how to say the next command, we should consider moving the instructions to a help prompt, rather than repeating them everywhere, to make prompts shorter and less confusing.

There is another reason to use brief prompts: brief prompts can encourage the users themselves to be brief, making the dialog more efficient and easier to interpret.

Polite Prompts

Speech recognition-based applications are relatively prone to errors. Errors can arise due to grammar mismatch, problems with the user's accent, background noise, no user response, and other limitations of the technology. Whenever an error occurs, *never* blame the user; always let the system take the blame. This automated good-naturedness is, in fact, one of the biggest potential advantages of automated voice systems – if you've ever had to deal with rude or impatient operators at traditional call centers, how has that made you feel about the company concerned? Never make the user feel it is their fault when something goes wrong, even if they must have been acting like a complete blundering fool. When the system fails to recognize what it has heard, or has waited for a response for too long, don't use a prompt like "You haven't provided the right information, please say news, sports, or weather", "Use one of the allowed words news, sports, or weather only" or "You forgot to say please". Instead, go for ones such as, "Oops, my mistake. Could you please repeat what you said using the keywords news, sports, or weather," or "Sorry, I missed that. Please repeat which service you require, news, sports, or weather."

Menus

When you plan to list a group of items in a menu, you need to take the user's limited memory into account. Remember that people can only hold between three and seven chunks of information in memory, and that items presented in the middle of a list are more likely to get forgotten than those listed at the two ends. Ideally, you should never have more than five options in a menu, as it becomes increasingly difficult for a user to remember all the options when their number exceeds this. To list three or four items at most in a menu is preferable.

When asking the user to choose what to do next from a menu, list the available commands after the function description. So for example, avoid using:

System: "Say delete to delete this message; say forward to forward this message to a person"

The commands *delete* and *forward* occur before the function descriptions. Users are likely to forget these keywords once they've heard the function description. The above example would be better as follows:

System: "You may delete this message or forward it. Please say delete or forward."

Always put frequently used items first in a menu, and sometimes it's worth letting the user know when the end has been reached with a prompt or an auditory icon.

On entry to a menu, the system should tell the user where they are. Examples are:

System: "You have reached the main menu, please say one of the following options: ..."

System: "You have 2 new messages. Please say one of the following: read, delete, reply, forward."

In the above examples, an expert user may decide to barge in immediately on discovering which menu is currently active.

Auditory Icons

An auditory icon is a musical fragment that is associated with a particular event and object, and can provide useful feedback to the user. Keeping the user posted in this way can make them feel more comfortable. For example, when the user has asked the system to do a particular task, by hearing the corresponding auditory icon, they know that the system has heard correctly and the desired process is underway.

A few seconds pause could cause the user to become concerned. Pauses can occur when the system didn't hear the input and is still waiting, or when the system did hear, and is busy processing or retrieving data. It's important to distinguish between these two situations. If the system is still waiting for input although the user has assumed that the system heard what they said, a `noinput` event will end up being thrown. On the other hand, if the system is processing the user's input but the pause makes the user believe the system didn't hear and then repeat the request, the user could either miss the next prompt since they are talking, or a recognition error could occur if the system is listening for something else. Auditory icons can be used to distinguish a "processing delay" from "waiting for input". For example:

System:	"Welcome to Kingsbury Pallets. Who would you like to talk to?"
User:	"Jon Towers."
System:	*Plays Greensleeves as the call is put through to Jon Towers.*

When the user hears the in-progress auditory icon, they know the system has the person's name and is now transferring their call to them. The user recognizes that auditory icons indicate a processing delay, so that any pauses without sound indicate the system is awaiting input. An alternative to using an auditory icon is to use a spoken prompt to let the user know when processing is about to take place. For example:

System:	"Welcome to Kingsbury Pallets. Who would you like to talk to?"
User:	"Jon Towers."
System:	"One moment please while you are transferred."

However, auditory icons can put the user at ease and make the dialog livelier.

Another use of auditory icons is to play adverts when the system is busy processing input, helping generate revenue from your application. This can be achieved using the `fetchaudio` attribute of various VoiceXML elements to create effects such as this:

System:	"Welcome to Kingsbury Pallets. Who would you like to talk to?"
User:	"Jon Towers."
System:	"You are being connected. Have you ever tried Snack-o-Bran cereal? It's a wholesome treat that keeps you going all day!"

Different auditory icons may suggest different events. For example, an auditory icon sounding like typing on a computer keyboard could be used when the system has received input and is processing data.

Use of DTMF

Current speech-recognition technology is quite error-prone. When the system has failed to recognize a particular input several times, encourage the user to use the keypad. For example,

System:	"Do you want me to delete this message?"
User:	"Yep, kill it."
System:	"Sorry, I missed what you said. To delete the message, say yes; otherwise, say no."

User:	"Okay."
System:	"Sorry, still no luck. To delete the message, press 1; otherwise, press 2."

When the user needs to input confidential information, such as a password, social security number, or credit card number, you should not ask the user to input using speech. When privacy is a concern, DTMF input is much more suitable.

Since DTMF input has a lower error rate than speech, use DTMF for final confirmation of a significant transaction. For example,

System: "You wish to buy 1000 shares. Press 1 to confirm, or 9 to cancel."

When the application is likely to be used in an environment where DTMF input is not convenient (for example, while the user is driving a car), we should allow both speech and DTMF until the system has failed to recognize the speech several times.

Note that the letters Q and Z do not show on some telephone keypads; they are supposed to occupy the same keys as PRS and WXY. The user should be told where to find them if absolutely necessary, but if possible avoid using them altogether.

A similar issue to bear in mind is that keys 5 and 8 are adjacent to all other numbers on a keypad, and so are most likely to be hit accidentally. Therefore, it's a good idea to avoid their use for actions that could cause irrecoverable consequences.

When asking the user to input multiple keys, use the word "enter", and when asking the user to type one key only, use the word "press". For example:

System: "Please enter your password."

System: "If you would like to delete the message, press 1; otherwise, press 9."

Consider using an application-level DTMF grammar of "1" for "yes" and "9" for "no", with perhaps the "#" key to indicate the termination of input when required, "*" to exit a menu and return to the previous one or to insert a decimal point in numeric input, and "0" to connect to a human operator.

Use of Barge-in

Users feel more in control of an exchange if allowed to interrupt prompts to input information, rather than having to wait for the prompt to complete. This technique, known as barge-in, can also have the effect of making the system more productive. Users, especially experienced users, can get impatient if they must wait for each prompt to finish before being able to talk to the system. Thus, barge-in should always be enabled, unless the user needs to hear the entire prompt for a particular reason.

So, when designing a prompt, don't put important information the user needs to hear after an utterance that sounds like the end of the prompt, since the user could miss the important information by barging in, or attempting to if that prompt does not allow barge in.

When you want to encourage the user, especially an expert, to use barge-in, precede the prompt with a cue that leads the user to respond with an expected utterance. For example,

System:	"You have reached Barney's Voice Services. How may I help you today?"
System:	*Brief pause*
System:	"Please say weather, recipes, caterpillar racing news, or mail Barney"

An experienced user is very likely to barge in when or even before they encounter the pause.

Background noises can be treated mistakenly as user barge-in. If the application is likely to be used in a noisy environment, you may need to avoid using barge-in altogether. For example, people may use a driving direction service when driving a car. The background noises may be mistaken for an input, and so barge-in should probably be switched off.

Consistency

Interface consistency is a fundamental quality of a usable application. Speech interface consistency includes consistent use of terminology, personality, DTMF, etc. People will pick up implicit rules as they interact with the system. Overall consistency makes the learning process smoother, and helps users predict what will happen and what they need to do, which in turn helps build confidence in using the system.

Interfaces should be consistent in:

- Terminology: use the same words rather than synonyms to refer to an object or event. So, use "To delete the message, say delete" rather than "To remove the message, say delete."
- Personality: To convey a particular personality to the user, use the same wording, attitude, and style in all dialogs in an application.
- Use of DTMF: assign the same key to the same word or action. For example, you may assign "1" to "yes" and "9" to "no" across the application:

System: "Would you like to make an appointment? If yes, press 1; otherwise, press 9."

System: "Would you like to go back to the main menu? If yes, press 1; otherwise, press 9."

There are other things that you need to be aware of during prompting design:

- People have trouble remembering long and complex messages delivered in synthesized speech. Use prompts recorded in human speech as much as possible.
- Use terminology in the prompts that all potential users will understand.
- Avoid compound questions since they can be too verbose and confusing for users, like this one:

System: "Would you like to book a ticket, or would you like to check your luggage?"

- Use tones to tell the user it is their turn to input when appropriate, as in:

System: "Please say your message after the tone."

- Use tones to let the user know the system has received input when appropriate, as in:

System:	"Please enter your social security number."
User:	*Types their social security number on the keypad.*
System:	*Plays a tone.*

- Do not overuse tones however, as they can make the system sound unnatural.
- Keep the interface as simple as possible rather than trying to offer all things to all people.

Error Handling

There are always going to be errors made by either the user or the system that a good design must effectively cater for. There are the following basic types of error:

- The user responds using words that don't match the grammar
- Background noise leads to recognition failure
- The system fails to recognize the speech input correctly, perhaps because the user has an accent that the system has difficulty understanding
- The user starts speaking too early
- The user speaks too late or not at all

Errors make users frustrated if they are not handled well, making error handling a very important issue in speech interface design. This section discusses both error prevention and error recovery.

Error Prevention

Some situations are naturally error-prone, and the goal of error prevention is to avoid putting the user in such situations. Therefore we must design the interface with error prevention in mind. There are several things that can be done to reduce the number of errors that occur:

- It's important not to overload the user's memory. The nature of audio information means that it is easy to overload the user's working memory, leading to the user misunderstanding the question, forgetting the information, or getting frustrated by a system that delivers too much of it at a time.
- Allowing DTMF when the system asks for a digit string input, such as the number of shares in a stock trade can reduce the number of errors. This is especially important if the system has already failed to recognize voice input for that particular item.
- Use comprehensive grammars – recognition fails on grammar mismatch. Although it is almost impossible for a designer to write a grammar to handle all possible utterances, create the grammar to work appropriately with a corresponding prompt, which must attempt to constrain input, while including as many possible utterances as you can think of.
- Minimize background noise. Usually, it is not up to the system to decide the physical environment of the user. However, if the nomatch event has occurred a lot more than the noinput event, it probably implies that there is background noise causing recognition failure. If this happens, prompt the user to move away from the noise if possible. This works well when the noise can be avoided and the user doesn't realize that background noise impedes recognition.
- Let the user know they can get help. This instructive information can be included in the initial greeting, as in, "Welcome to the X e-mail service. Say help at any time for assistance."

Error Recovery

VoiceXML has built-in mechanisms for handling nomatch and noinput errors, and for offering assistance whenever the user requests it. A nomatch error occurs when the input fails to match the activated grammar(s). A noinput error occurs when the system is expecting input and fails to detect anything after waiting for a specified period of time. Usually, a nomatch or noinput happens when the user doesn't know what to say to the system.

An error might occur anywhere in a dialog. So for each field, the help event should be caught and both nomatch and noinput errors should be handled. We can specify that nomatches and noinputs may only occur a given number of times, say, three times for nomatches and two times for noinputs. After this, we can have the system transfer the user to a human operator. A good idea to aid the user is to include an example of correct input in the prompt when a help, nomatch or noinput event is thrown. In the last occurrence of nomatch and noinput, mention the option of DTMF input, which is helpful to users with an accent or who are still unsure of what to say after a couple of tries. If this still doesn't work, consider taking the user back to the main menu, to an error-handling dialog, or a human operator.

Grammar

Writing good grammars has a dramatic impact on usability. The discussion here gives some suggestions that can be applied to grammar design.

Use form-level mixed-initiative grammars whenever possible. Users feel more comfortable if they feel they are in control of the system, not the other way around. One method previously discussed is to use barge-in so the user may interrupt the machine. The other method is to use mixed-initiative grammars to allow the user to direct the dialog. The use of mixed-initiative grammars lets a single sentence uttered by the user fill multiple fields in any order, which enhances overall interface flexibility and system efficiency.

Take advantage of grammars that allow global commands. For example, put a link in the root document to let the user go to a particular application or the main menu at any point during conversation:

```
<?xml version="1.0"?>
<vxml version="1.0">
  <link next="http://www.mysite.com/main.vxml">
    <grammar> main menu </grammar>
  </link>
  <link next="http://www.mysite.com/email.vxml">
    <grammar> email </grammar>
  </link>
   <link next="http://www.mysite.com/stock.vxml">
    <grammar> stock </grammar>
  </link>
...
</vxml>
```

In this example, execution will jump to `main.vxml` whenever the user says "Main Menu" or `email.vxml` whenever the user says "E-mail".

Use dynamic grammars, that is, generate or modify grammars on the fly at run time. This is useful when the grammar to use cannot be determined when the VoiceXML document is written and needs to be based on the user's input. Dynamic grammars typically require the system to connect to a server to create the grammar, you may need to use the <object> element or server-side scripts to achieve this. For example, in an e-mail application, different people have different contact lists, and the system needs to create the grammar for input once it has found out to whom it is talking.

```
<?xml version="1.0"?>
<vxml version="1.0">
  ...
  <!--form asks for the user's name and password-->
  <form id="user">

   <!--field asks for the user's name -->
    <field name="username">
      <prompt>
        Your name?
      </prompt>
      ...
    </field>

    <!--field asks for the user's password -->
    <field name="password">
      <prompt>
        And your password?
      </prompt>
      ...
    </field>

  </form>

<!--form sends the email -->
<form id="send">

  <object classid="method://email/generate_nicknames_grammar"
          name="nicknames">
    <param name="user" expr="username"/>
    <param name="psword" expr="password"/>
  </object>

  <!--field asks for the recipient's nickname -->
  <field>
    <prompt>
      To whom is the message to be sent?
    </prompt>
    <grammar src="nicknames.gram" type="application/x-jsgf"/>
  </field>
</form>
  ...
</vxml>
```

This code invokes a hypothetical user-defined server-side method `generate_nicknames_grammar` to generate a grammar and store it in the file `nicknames.gram` according to the current user.

Use the user's terminology in grammars. For instance, if a particular feature is associated with existing terms, using these terms in your grammar will increase the likelihood of matching. For example, in an e-mail application, you should include 'delete', 'reply', 'compose', 'send', and 'forward' in the grammar, and avoid other terms not commonly used in that context.

Allow the user to phrase their input in multiple ways to increase the flexibility of the interface.

It's important to include non-verbal vocalizations in grammars. Use of 'err', 'um', and so on is common in human to human interaction, so we shouldn't expect the user to speak without these, even though they are aware they are talking to a machine: "Uh, I would like to make an appointment with Mr, err, Towers."

Avoid including words that have different meanings but similar pronunciations in the same grammar – try to use only phonetically distinct words. For example, a grammar that matches both "That's correct" and "That's incorrect" risks the system doing the opposite of what the user actually wants.

Application Personality

A successful voice-enabled application usually gives the user a sense of dealing with a real personality, even if the system was not intentionally designed to embody a personality. We should take advantage of this to increase system usability. If the personality of an application is perceived by the user as fitting a suitable image, the user will feel more comfortable, and be willing to come back again.

Prompting and "tone" design can dramatically affect the interface personality. Define the interface personality based on the nature of the application; particular personalities are more appropriate to some applications than to others. So a financial application might sound authoritative and trustworthy, a help center application sound friendly, and an entertainment center application sound pleasant and funny. In business applications, avoid using a cute or over-familiar tone. Focus on what needs to be done and making the interface concise and efficient. An online shopping service needs a personality that is polite, friendly, and helpful, avoiding hurried or high-pressure phrasing. Choose the right voice for the application.

Sometimes it can be effective to give the application a name, such as Mary, Bob, (or even Hal!), although some users are likely to be irked by this. This can suggest to the user that the system plays a normal character that the user could encounter in their daily life. The user can then employ dialog constructs pretty much like the conversation between two real people, giving the user a starting point for interacting with the system. It also helps the system designer predict how the user will interact with the system.

In a similar vein, consider using "I" when the system refers to itself since it can make the user feel more at ease with the system.

However, it's important not to try to fool the user into thinking they are talking to a person. A prompt is typically a pre-recorded speech. A fluently talking system can lead people to believe that the system expects only similar fluent input (which is usually not true) and the user may hesitate to talk to the system or expect the system to understand more than it is capable of. If users believe they are talking to a person, they are likely to provide responses without any constraint at all, and cause recognition failure. To avoid this, an initial greeting can let the user know that they are talking to a machine. For example, start an interaction with "Welcome to the X voice service system." When users know they are speaking to a machine, they will speak more carefully, briefly, and precisely.

Learning

An application can be designed in a way that doesn't differentiate novice and expert users, doesn't take into account individual differences, and doesn't offer flexible responses. That is, it has no intelligence at all. However, if we wish to design an application that stands out from the others, we really need to incorporate some intelligence into the system. In order to sound intelligent, an application should collect knowledge about particular users, learn about them, and use that collected knowledge to serve the user in a better way in future interactions.

In a speech interface, two types of learning can be implemented: on-site learning and profile-based learning. On-site learning occurs during a single interaction; whereas profile-based learning is based on historic information collected when the user registered with the system and from previous interactions with the system. This section introduces how to incorporate these two types of learning in your interface design.

On-site Learning

One of the objectives of on-site learning is to identify whether users are novice or expert, and use that information to select appropriate prompts for a given user. For example, if the user is identified as a novice, the prompt could be "Please tell me when you plan to leave. For example, July 1st." However, if the user is identified as an expert, the prompt could be simply, "Your departure date, please."

To identify whether a user is a novice or an expert, you may make the system track how many times the user has asked for assistance, or how many times the user has failed to respond or failed to respond correctly at any point in the dialog. With this information, the system should be able choose an appropriate prompt to play for that particular user.

The next example demonstrates how to make the system learn about the user and choose appropriate prompts for different users.

```
<?xml version="1.0"?>
<vxml version="1.0" >
  <!-- Initialize Variables -->
  <var name="error_count" expr="0"/>

    <!-- form dialog demonstrates how to perform on-line learning in an email
    application -->
    <form>

     <field name="action">
      <prompt>
        What do you want to do with the message?
      </prompt>

       <grammar>
          read [again]              {read}
          reply [to the sender]       {reply}
          forward                 {forward}
          delete [it]                 {delete}
      </grammar>
      <dtmf type="application/s-jsgf">
          1 {read} | 2 {reply} |3 {forward} | 4 {delete}
      </dtmf>
```

```
<!-- Increase the number of errors by 1 when the user asks for help -->
<help>
  <assign name="error_count" expr="error_count + 1"/>
  What do you want to do with the message? You can choose read, reply,
  forward, or delete.
</help>

<!-- increase the number of errors by 1 when a nomatch event is
 thrown -->
<nomatch count="1">
    <assign name="error_count" expr="error_count + 1"/>
  Say one of the following. Read, reply, forward, or
      delete?
</nomatch>
<nomatch count="2">
  <assign name="error_count" expr="error_count + 1"/>
    Please say what you want to do with the message: select one of the
    following actions: read, reply, forward, or delete.
</nomatch>
<nomatch count="3">
    <assign name="error_count" expr="error_count + 1"/>
    To reread the message, press 1; to reply, press 2; to forward,
    press 3; to delete, press 4.
 </nomatch>

 <!-- increase the number of errors by 1 when a noinput event is
  thrown -->
 <noinput count="1">
   <assign name="error_count" expr="error_count + 1"/>
   What do you want to do with the message? Read, reply, forward,
   or delete?
 </noinput>
 <noinput count="2">
   <assign name="error_count" expr="error_count + 1"/>
   To reread the message, press 1; to reply, press 2; to forward,
   press 3; to delete, press 4.
 </noinput>

  <filled>
    <if cond="action == 'read'">
      <!-- Add code here for processing read again -->
    <elseif cond="action == 'reply'"/>
      <!--Add code here for processing reply -->
    <elseif cond="action == 'forward'"/>
      <goto next="#forward"/>
    <elseif cond="action == 'delete'"/>
      <!--Add code here for processing delete -->
     </if>
  </filled>
 </field>
</form>

<!--form that forwards a message to a list of recipients-->
<form id="forward">
   <var name="address_list" expr="''"/>
```

```
        <field name="address">

          <prompt cond="error_count &lt; 3 &amp;&amp; address_list.length == 0">
            And the recipient is?
          </prompt>

          <prompt cond="error_count &gt;= 3 &amp;&amp; address_list.length == 0">
            Say the recipients one at a time, or say "Done" when you're through.
          </prompt>

          <prompt cond="address_list.length &gt; 0">
            The next recipient?
          </prompt>

          <grammar src="email_address.gram" type="application/x-jsgf"/>
          <!--Add code for error handling and assistance here -->

          <filled>
            <if cond="address != 'done'">
              <assign name="address_list" expr="address_list + ' ' +
              address"/>
              <clear namelist="address"/>
            <else/>
              <!--Add code here for processing the address list to forward -->
            </if>
          </filled>
        </field>
      </form>
    </vxml>
```

In this example, when the user has not responded correctly three times when telling the system what to do with the current e-mail, the system will include more instructive information in the next prompt requesting the address list to forward to.

When navigating the dialog, the user can enter a form more than once. Using tapered prompts when the user re-enters a form increases application flexibility and efficiency. The next example illustrates that the system remembers whether the user has ever entered the form before and plays a tapered prompt for users returning to the form.

```
<?xml version="1.0"?>
<vxml verion="1.0" >
  <var name="form_send_entered" expr="0"/>
  ...
  <form id="send">

    <block>
      <assign name="form_send_entered" expr="form_send_entered + 1"/>
    </block>

    <prompt cond="form_send_entered &gt; 1">
      Recipient?
    </prompt>

    <prompt cond="form_send_entered &lt;= 1">
```

```
        Please tell me the recipient's name or email address.
      </prompt>
    ...
    </form>
    ...
  </vxml>
```

The user is not the only factor that the system can learn about. As we've said, background noise impairs speech recognition, and when barge-in is allowed in a prompt, extraneous noise can be mistaken for a speech input. This means the user will miss what the system is trying to say, and the interpreter will take the detected noise as user input, and a nomatch event will be thrown. If we detect that there is too much noise on the background, we can adapt by turning off barge-in (the `bargein` attribute is `true` by default) to ensure the user hears the prompts.

For example, say the user wants to find directions when driving a car and calls a driving direction service center; traffic and other background noise can cause trouble. The following example shows how the system can disable barge-in when it seems there might be background noise impeding the interaction with the user.

```
  <?xml version="1.0"?>
  <vxml verion="1.0" >
    <!-- Initialize Variables -->
    <var name="nomatch_count" expr="0"/>
    <var name="noinput_count" expr="0"/>
    ...
    <!—form receives start location and destination location →
    <form id="locations">

      <field name="location_from">

        <prompt bargein="false" cond="nomatch_count > 0 &&
         nomatch_count * 100.0 / (nomatch_count + noinput_count) >= 80" >
          What is your starting address, including city and state.
          For example, 1234 Palm Tree, San Jose, California.
        </prompt>

        <prompt cond="nomatch_count == 0 ||
         nomatch_count * 100.0 / (nomatch_count + noinput_count) < 80" >
          Tell me your starting address, city, and state. For example, 1234
          Palm Tree, San Jose, California.
        </prompt>

        <grammar src="location.gram" type="application/x-jsgf"/>

        <help>
          <reprompt/>
        </help>

        <nomatch>
          <assign name="nomatch_count" expr="nomatch_count + 1" />
          <reprompt/>
        </nomatch>

        <noinput>
          <assign name="noinput_count" expr="noinput_count + 1"/>
```

```
            <reprompt/>
         </noinput>

         <filled>
            <!—Add code here for processing →
         </filled>
      </field>
   </form>
   ...
</vxml>
```

The idea is that if the nomatch event has been thrown many times, but only a few noinput events have been thrown, we will assume that there is background noise, and disable barge-in to make sure the prompt is played in full. An alternative way to do this is to make the prompts shorter to reduce the chance of interruption when the background noise is detected. For example, the system might ask for the street, city, and state separately.

Profile-based Learning

It may be an option to add functionality to the application based on each user's profile collected during previous visits. A user who has logged onto the system many times can be considered an expert who requires only shorter prompts.

It is generally not possible for a designer to include all possible input in a grammar. However, it might be possible to collect phrases preferred by a user during interactions and incorporating them in future grammars for that user (for example, by using dynamic grammars created on the fly for the user). If a system understands or even uses a particular user's terminology itself, it could appear more inviting, or even more intelligent, to the user. The system can also perform better since the user's input is more predictable and thus recognition errors can be reduced.

Usability Testing

The final phase of the iterative design process sets out to test the usability of an interface; whether the interface can help the user reach their desired goal efficiently.

One of the approaches available for usability testing is the Wizard of Oz technique. This test is named for the eponymous character from the movie *The Wizard of Oz.* This character, you may recall, hid himself behind a curtain where an array of knobs and dials allowed him to create spectacular effects giving the impression that he was some wondrous being. In speech usability testing, the WOz technique means we can test a design even though the real system doesn't actually exist. Subjects participate in the test, interacting with what they believe to be a computer that may in fact be a hidden human, our wizard. For interfaces already developed, the WOz technique can still be used to evaluate the system to highlight possible weak points. In that case, the subjects interact with the real system under close supervision.

You can conduct a WOz test before any system prototype even exists, or when an existing, mature system requires improvement – or at any point in-between. However, when you are finished developing an application, to ensure its success, you need to conduct some sort of usability testing to iron out any design flaws you've overlooked.

Another way to test the usability of an existing application is to record the conversations that result from its use, allowing analysis to be made of how users react to prompts, and where errors occur. Look out for this functionality on voice gateway products.

Summary

In order to reliably produce a good application design, we have seen the need to follow a systematic process, with the emphasis on usability engineering approaches. The protocols evolved over eons of human-to-human communication should be applied and respected in human-to-machine interactions. Well-designed prompting, error handling, grammars, an appropriate personality, and embedded learning ability can dramatically increase a system's chance of success. The role of evaluation testing, which can effectively uncover usability flaws of a design, should not be underestimated in the process of creating a workable system that will win the support of real-world users.

```
<?xml version="1.0"?>
<vxml version="1.0">
<form id="foo">
<block>
<prompt>
Hi. My name is Bob
</prompt>
</block>
</form>
</vxml>
```

7

VoiceXML with XSLT (HTML and WML)

This chapter examines the use of the Extensible Stylesheet Language for Transformations (XSLT) as a tool for the generation of VoiceXML. I intend to illustrate a complete, end-to-end example of implementing a voice interface for a client-server database via XML and XSL. The case study will demonstrate the power of XSL for simultaneously delivering multiple interfaces to the same data by developing HTML and WML front ends also.

The setting for our case study is MyRubberBands.com. It is a fictitious company, purporting to be the "premier rubber bands web site on the Internet". In their infinite wisdom, senior management has decreed that adding WML and voice functionality to the existing order status web site is do-or-die. MyRubberband's competitors have just rolled out their own WAP/voice access solution, and an all-out effort is necessary to catch up. Follow the programmers as they embark on their project to quickly roll out an equivalent capability.

The chapter is organized as follows:

- *A Very Brief Overview of XSLT*, explaining what it is, what it does, where it works, and where it doesn't.
- *Documentation and Resources.* It's important to produce more in-depth documentation of XML/XSLT, and pointers to software that can be used for the example code.
- *MyRubberbands.com – A Case Study.* Step inside the world of a cash-strapped dot-com! We will define requirements, and explore a few of the issues involved, such as voice interface design and application flow.
- *A Look at the Legacy Database.* A schema is given for a basic customer and order-tracking database. We will examine this in some detail, in particular looking at places where it may be unsuited to a voice interface.

- *Creating a Markup Language.* A markup language will be developed to represent the data. It may seem odd to take a perfectly good, normalized relational database, and put it into XML form, but the benefits of standardizing data interchange are far reaching.
- *VoiceXML by XSLT.* Stylesheets can also be used to generate personalized dynamic grammars in JSGF format.
- *WML with XSLT*, or how to access your information on a pretty tiny display. Figuring out why a user would actually want to do this is left as an exercise for the reader.
- *HTML with XSLT.* Parts of the existing web site can be replaced by the new system and generated by the transformation of XML, going some way towards a unified code base.

So, read on...

A Very Brief Overview of XSLT

This section very briefly discusses XSL, its benefits and its disadvantages. For obvious reasons, we cannot explore XSLT in depth here, but the section on resources and documentation provides some pointers for further reading.

What is It?

XSLT is an XML-based scripting language for transforming structured input written in one XML vocabulary to structured output written in another XML vocabulary, or in some general text form. An example of the latter would be transforming XML to formatted plain text, or another format such as Portable Document Format, but the example in this chapter illustrates the former output method.

XSLT treats the document to be transformed as a set of nodes. An XSLT **stylesheet** defines a set of rules, or **templates**. When a template matches one of the nodes in the source document, the output structure given in the template is created in the transformed document.

XSLT uses the W3C XPath specification as a language to query XML data. XPath is strongly analogous to SQL, and lets us specify complex rules to match nodes in a document.

Advantages

Using XSLT to process XML offers certain advantages, including the following:

- It is a recognized W3C standard. A well-written XSLT stylesheet will run on any XSLT processor to produce identical output.
- It is platform independent. A variety of XSLT processors are available, supporting the development of custom applications in programming languages such as Perl, Java, VB, and C++.
- It itself conforms to XML syntax. All of the utilities used for the development of XML, such as parsers and validation tools, can be used with XSLT.
- It allows a clean separation of data and presentation.
- There is no need to parse XML for most applications. If the purpose of the application is to produce a structured document as output, XSLT is an ideal medium. The complexity of a Document Object Model (DOM)-based parser is completely hidden from the stylesheet developer by the XSLT processor.

- Transformations allow for the creation of documents completely tailored to a target device. If you need to support multiple voice platforms that allow for slightly different features, XSLT can be made adaptable. Likewise, a WML document generated for a WAP-enabled phone with a large display can be created that is different from one for a phone with a small display, by applying a different stylesheet, or the same stylesheet but with new parameters, to the same source data.

Shortcomings

In spite of its many positives, XSLT is not a panacea. It is not the right solution for every situation, and is not even practicable in some cases. The following are its more obvious failings:

- The Document Object Model (DOM) parser at the heart of most XSLT processors places a heavy overhead on both CPU and memory use. Even engines based on the Simple API for XML (SAX) parser technology have relatively large memory and CPU footprints. The result is that dynamic conversion by XSLT may not be practical for some applications with large XML source documents, or for applications that have high throughput. For example, when transforming a 20 MB source document of my own using a Java DOM-based XSLT engine, the JVM gobbled up a full 256 MB of heap memory!
- Algorithms are all – a poorly written stylesheet, relying on excessive recursion for a very large document, can have an execution time orders of magnitude larger than a more efficiently written one. An early transform I wrote for the aforementioned 20 MB source file would have taken many hours to complete, but when rewritten, executed in just a few minutes.
- Like VoiceXML itself, XSLT is really just a programming language based on XML syntax, and as such, leaves a lot to be desired. In particular, it feels deficient in its handling of variables and loops, partly deriving from its declarative, rather than the more common procedural, form.

Nevertheless, for a lot of applications, and for getting off to a quick start when processing XML, it is just the ticket – especially when you consider that XSLT is a relatively new technology so that processors should still have plenty of performance improvements possible. Use of an XSLT processor avoids the startup overhead of using a full parser API from a compiled language, making it more suited to dynamic web applications.

Documentation and Resources

The key document defining XSL is the W3C Recommendation, available at http://www.w3.org/TR/XSL. XSL is split into two parts, XSL-FO, a stylesheet language with very precise notation for accurately laying out documents, and XSLT, a language centered on specifying transformations from one XML format to another. For a detailed and comprehensive treatment of XSL as a document-processing language, I can highly recommend the *XSLT Programmer's Reference* by Michael Kay published by Wrox Press. The stylesheets in this chapter were written for Michael Kay's popular Instant Saxon for Windows, a free and complete implementation of the XSLT standard available from http://users.iclway.co.uk/mhkay/saxon/.

The VoiceXML and WML examples shown here were developed using MADK, the Motorola Mobile Application Development Kit available, without charge, from the MAGNET Network at http://www.motorola.com/developers/wireless. This package allows the simulation of both VoiceXML and WML applications on the desktop. The VoiceXML code shown is completely generic, and should run on any reasonably compliant platform that supports the JavaSpeech Grammar Format, JSGF.

The hypothetical legacy database is implemented with MySQL, an open source client-server relational database management system. SQL code for the schema and a set of sample data is included in the code download for this book.

An XML schema is used to represent an export of the legacy database instead of a Document Type Definition (DTD) because the schema standard is now complete, and increasing numbers of developers will be looking for the extra power schemas offer, especially as new development tools become available. An excellent primer on schemas is available from the W3C at http://www.w3.org/TR/xmlschema-0/.

The validity of the schema for the sample application was checked using the online XML Schema Validation (XSV) tool, available on the Web at http://www.w3.org/2001/03/webdata/xsv/. This preview release tool can validate a document supplied, or referred to by URL, against the current schema namespace.

Scripts to export the database to XML format have been written using the Perl language, and Data Base Interface (DBI) library. The Perl script shown was developed on Windows using Active State Perl, but should run on any platform, Unix or Windows. Many commercial databases, such as SQLServer 2000, are capable of exporting directly to XML, and so this step would not be needed.

MyRubberBands.com – A Case Study

Now let's turn to the implementation of the voice interface for our legacy application. To do this, we will step inside the rarified atmosphere of a fictional cash-strapped dot-com. In the aftermath of the stock market meltdown, where our heroes saw their market valuation drop by over 95%, senior management, led by CEO Dr. Todd, has decided that the company's only future lies in creating new business and new opportunities for revenue, and providing voice access to their services should be a part of that.

Business Requirements

With their competitors rolling out both voice and WAP access to services, MyRubberBands.com has no choice but to follow suit or lose market share in the cutthroat world of elastic band marketing. Due to market pressures, the new system must be up and running as soon as possible, and given this short development cycle, the requirements have been scaled back to providing simply voice and WAP access to a customer's order status data.

However, some thought can still be given to the future. Rather than develop a quick and dirty "throwaway" voice interface, by putting in a little extra work now, the engineers can build a reusable infrastructure. By exporting their database to an XML format, they access the power of XSL to create VoiceXML and WML interfaces, and are able to transparently replace parts of the existing HTML site with dynamically created pages.

System Architecture

The following figure is a block diagram showing the existing components of the system, and the relationships to the new XML/XSLT system required to implement the voice interface.

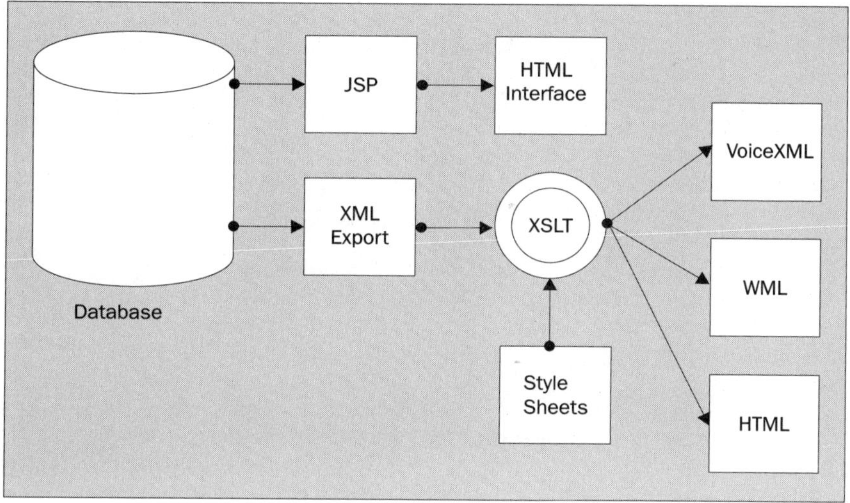

This drawing is not complete in all areas. For example, no method for user login and authentication is given, because such a system would already exist for an e-commerce site, and because although XML/XSLT would be helpful for creating device-specific login code, we are not going to examine on-the-fly transformation (inside a web server, for example) in this particular study.

Designing a Voice Interface

With these rather vague requirements in mind, we can start making some design decisions, and sketch out a rough model for the envisaged user interaction with the voice interface. The goal is to make the user experience simple and intuitive.

- There will be a main menu of options. This is the entry point to the application, and the user can always return to it with a single voice command.
- Online help will always be available. This will use the VoiceXML `<help>` tag to simplify implementation, and also to overload any built-in help that may be offered by the voice platform.
- The number of available options from the main menu should be kept to a minimum. The total number of states should also be minimized. This means that the behavior of the current command should not depend on what the previous command issued was. For example, the word "menu" should always refer to the main menu in every context.
- The top-level commands from the main menu should always be active. If the main menu offers the command "foo", the user should be able to say "foo" at any point in later dialogs with the same result.

The following state diagram illustrates these design goals. The main options are "order status", "product list" (with a link to voice ordering via the existing phone service bureau), and "more information" to access a frequently-asked-questions list. For a more detailed examination of the issues to consider when designing voice applications, refer to Chapter 6. The order status menu leads to a variable number of additional choices, depending on the number of records in the user's order history.

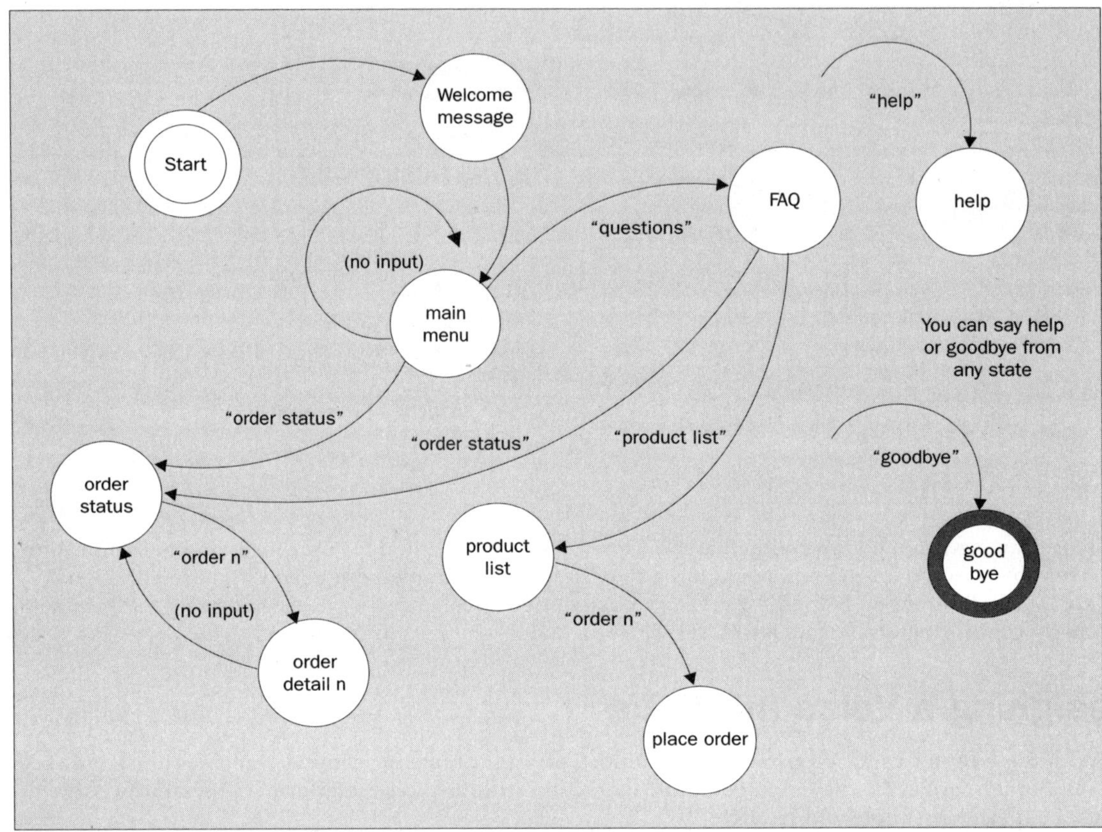

Note that to make the diagram more readable, transitions to the main menu are not shown, since as already stated the main menu can always be reached from any state. Also, the universal transitions to the help and goodbye states are not enumerated to reduce the number of arrows that have to be shown.

The user will enter the system, hear a personalized welcome message, and drop directly into a main menu where they will loop until they end the session by hanging up and or saying goodbye. The interface is intended primarily to deliver information to the user, rather than to collect it. Rather than depend on the implicit VoiceXML form interpretation algorithm, all transitions between forms will be explicitly stated when the document is generated. This issue will be covered in greater detail later.

A Look at the Legacy Database

Naturally, our fictional rubber band sales team already has a database-driven e-commerce web site. Like all legacy databases, it has evolved over time into a hodgepodge of tables, some of which were hastily knocked together to implement poorly-defined requirements. We will assume that the company is operating a traditional Java Server Pages (JSP)-based web site, although we will not look at any specific code examples from that.

A Rubber-Banded Database Schema

The figure below shows part of the layout of the database, including the tables required to export the customer data we want in XML form.

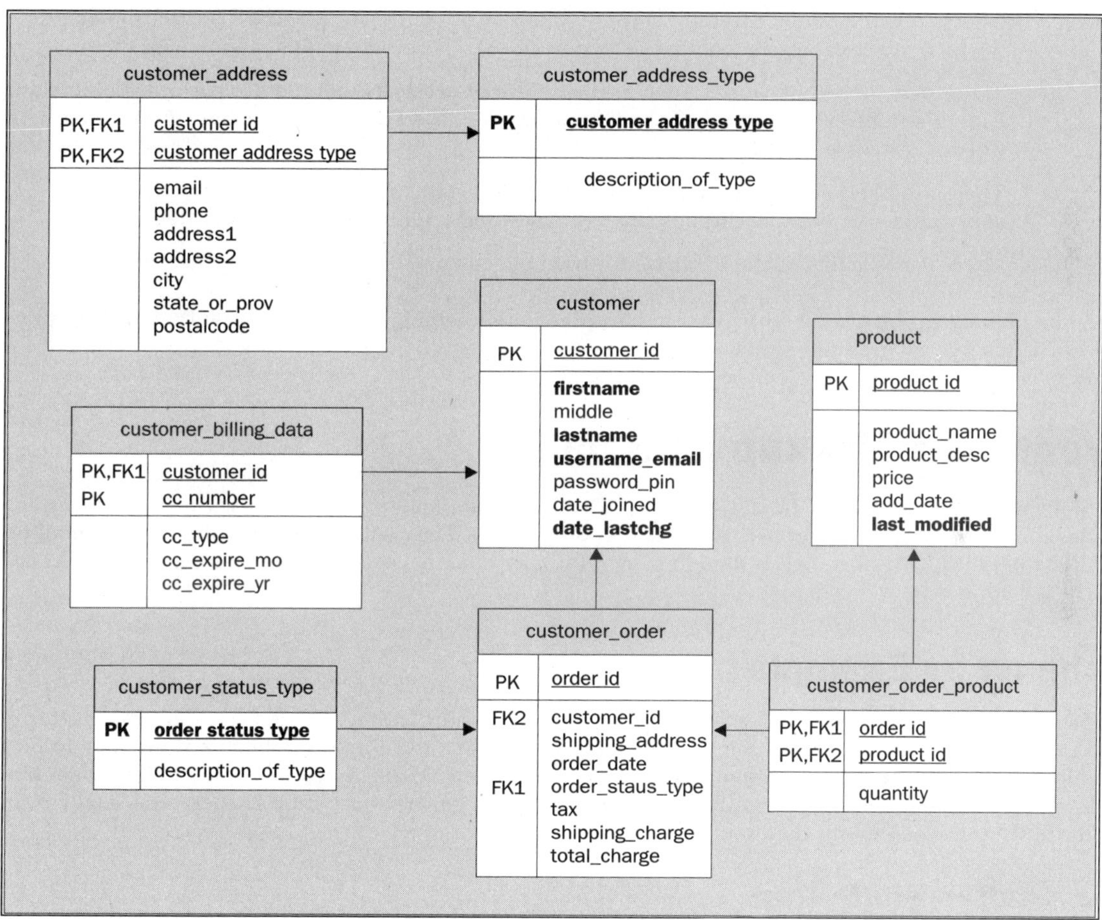

This is a fairly bland schema, and it lacks every single detail necessary for an online business. However, it is complete enough for our purposes, as it contains all the data required for making order status information available by voice. A SQL file to create this schema, and populate it with some sample data, is provided with the code download.

Database Schema Problems

There are a few items that have been left out of this database to simplify the task of implementing a workable voice interface system. The following are the main shortcomings:

- To log the user in by voice, the user password or personal identification number (PIN) has to be constrained to either a strict numeric sequence, or a simple word or phrase in the target customer population's native language. There may be many existing users that have "good" passwords (that is., non-dictionary) that will not be practical for voice authentication. While the user could spell the password letter by letter, voice recognition of single letter utterances is far less reliable than a carefully chosen grammar of words. As discussed further in Chapter 10, the recognizer can easily confuse "e", "g", "c", with other letters that rhyme with them.
- There may be certain words, such as the names of products that require custom pronunciation data to render properly using Text To Speech (TTS). An automated means of replacing such words is discussed in Chapter 8.
- There are likely to be places, such as in the order status table, where the description is appropriate for web site display, but is not worded appropriately for audio delivery.
- There is no facility in the database for tracking customer activity on the voice system.

None of these problems are critical enough to prevent launching the voice service; they will simply restrict the overall usability of the application.

Creating a Markup Language

Since most of the tables in the database are relevant to the requirements of the various interfaces, the developers plump for a "verbose" approach to their XML. They will dump all of the data from all of the tables into XML form, even though some of it may be unnecessary in the VoiceXML, WML, or HTML contexts.

Schema by Example

Sometimes the easiest way to flesh out requirements is to start with a trial and error approach. It is not the optimal approach perhaps, but we must remember that a developer's timetable is unlikely to permit a lengthy requirements definition or documentation process. Most companies today follow some kind of Rapid Application Development (RAD) process, so we're going to just jump in there and start writing the XML to represent our data set.

The <stuff></stuff> Trap

A content publisher I have worked with recently discontinued a flat file data feed in favor of a new XML-based format. Where records in the old format were non-descript comma-separated lists of the form `X, Y, Z`, the new record format actually consisted of XML elements like this: `<stuff>X, Y, Z</stuff>`. The markup contains no meaningful description of the data whatsoever, missing out on the real benefit afforded by XML, and in fact now requires considerably more effort to parse correctly. With this in mind, let's make sure our XML uses descriptive tag names, and doesn't employ any formatting inside each element.

MyRubberbandsML by Trial and Error

The first thing any XML dialect needs is a top-level element. Since we might want to export all the customers in the database, or only one at a time, let's add an attribute on the top level element to describe what kind of data feed this XML document constitutes.

```
<myrubberbands export_type="single">
```

The thing we are most interested is a customer record, because that will be the set of data needed to generate the voice interface for querying order status. Since we might have more than one customer in a file, each individual <customer> and their associated order history will be contained by a <customer_record> element. Note that the time stamps are in XSL's standard format, and won't translate easily for rendering by a TTS engine. The <customer_record> element that starts here is very lengthy, and is not closed until the associated addresses and order history that follows have been given.

```
<customer_record>
  <customer id="1">
    <firstname>John</firstname>
    <middle>Quincy</middle>
    <lastname>Public</lastname>
    <username_or_email>jqp@foo.foo.com</username_or_email>
    <password_or_pin>bar</password_or_pin>
    <date_joined>2001-05-18T16:17:15</date_joined>
    <date_lastchg>2001-05-18T16:17:15</date_lastchg>
  </customer>
```

As shown in the database schema, a customer can have one or more addresses. The XML representation should preserve the foreign key relationship with the customer table, and this relationship should not be dependent on the position of the elements. In this case, for example, both the customer profile and all associated addresses are nested within the <customer_record> tag. This is why all of the <customer_address> elements carry the customer_id attribute inside: it mirrors the relationship between the customer and customer_address tables in the database schema.

In this case, the database schema allows the customer_address table to store real physical addresses like billing and shipping addresses, or e-mail addresses for alternative methods of customer contact. Hence, the <customer_address> element can contain the optional <email> element.

```
<customer_address   address_type="Ship To Address"
        customer_id="1">
  <address1>4321 La Place Ct</address1>
  <address2>Ste 306</address2>
  <city>Carlsbad</city>
  <state_or_prov>CA</state_or_prov>
  <postalcode>92008</postalcode>
  <email></email>
   <phone>7605551212</phone>
</customer_address>
```

Since the main objective of the voice application is to allow the user access to their order history and status information, it makes sense to include the history inside the <customer_record> scope. In this case, because we will need to enunciate the order time, and because we'd rather not use XSL's limited text processing capabilities, we'll add the attribute sayas to the <order_date> element. This provides a pronunciation that can be used with the VoiceXML <sayas> tag for TTS. However, the desired pronunciation of the date and time cannot be derived from the database alone, as addressed in the section *Generating MyRubberbandsML.*

```
<order_history customer_id="1">
   <order id="1">
       <customer_address   address_type="Ship To Address"
        customer_id="1"/>
```

```
            <order_date sayas="May 18, 2001 at 16 17 hours">
              2001-05-18T16:17:16
            </order_date>
            <order_status>Processing</order_status>
            <tax>0.09</tax>
            <shipping_charge>0.4</shipping_charge>
            <total_charge>2.48</total_charge>
            <product id="1" quantity="3"/>
            <product id="3" quantity="1"/>
        </order>
    </order_history>
```

Finally, to provide the user with detailed order information, the full product name and description must be available. This will also allow the user to ask for a product list, and eventually we can perhaps extend the interface to enable products to be ordered by voice. Note that the `<product_list>` is not associated with any particular `<customer_record>`.

Also note that, ideally, the `<product_list>` wouldn't actually be in the same document as the customer data. However, we'll keep everything in one file here to avoid the issue of linking between documents. It might amuse us to picture the harried developers reaching the same conclusion to save time and give themselves some chance of meeting their beloved boss's deadline. Later on, they will no doubt want to refine the process and generate smaller XML documents that can be processed more quickly.

```
    </customer_record>
    <product_list>
      <product id="1" name="MIXED1000" price="1.99">
     Mixed Bag of 1000 Rubber Bands</product>
      <product id="2" name="MIXED5000" price="4.09">
     Mixed Bag of 5000 Rubber Bands</product>
      <product id="3" name="RED1000" price="2.19">
     Bag of 1000 Red Rubber Bands</product>
      <product id="4" name="RED10000" price="17.49">
     Bag of 10000 Red Rubber Bands</product>
      <product id="5" name="BLUE1000" price="0.99">
     Bag of 1000 Blue Rubber Bands</product>
      <product id="6" name="BLUE10000" price="8.99">
     Bag of 10000 Blue Rubber Bands</product>
    </product_list>
  </myrubberbands>
```

This example is formatted to fit the space above, and for readability, adds quite a bit of whitespace between `<product></product>` tags that would probably not occur in a real document.

From XML Document to XML Schema

Because this markup language is for internal consumption only, the developers could probably stop here without fully documenting their design with a DTD or XML Schema. An XML Schema fulfills the same purpose as a DTD, specifying the content and rules of an XML vocabulary, but is itself written as an XML document. Now that the XML Schema specification is complete, it will no doubt gain in popularity and overtake the DTD as the preferred means of XML definition.

So, for those of us wary of the old programmer's caveat that code easy to understand now will look like a foreign language in a month, a schema will be written down, to provide a Rosetta Stone for developers yet to come. Let's look at a snippet of it to see the relationship between schema and our actual document.

As XML, the first thing to define is the top-level element, which, for a schema, is a complex type. This can contain zero or more customer records (themselves represented by a complex type) and an optional product list.

```
<xsd:element   name="myrubberbands" type="MyRubberbandsType"/>

<xsd:complexType name="MyRubberbandsType">
  <xsd:sequence>
    <xsd:element name="customer_record" type="CustomerRecordType"
     minOccurs="0" maxOccurs="unbounded"/>
    <xsd:element name="product_list" type="ProductListType"
     minOccurs="0" maxOccurs="1"/>
  </xsd:sequence>

  <xsd:attribute  name="export_type" type="ExportTypeEnumerationType"/>
</xsd:complexType>
```

The customer record definition is given in the example below. The `id` attribute of `<customer>` elements is defined as a key by the `<xsd:key>` construct, which means it must be unique, and can be referenced elsewhere in the schema, similar to the `FOREIGN KEY` construct of SQL. The key definition uses XPath to specify its context.

```
<xsd:complexType name="CustomerRecordType">
  <xsd:sequence>
    <xsd:element name="customer" type="CustomerType" minOccurs="1"
     maxOccurs="1">
      <xsd:key name="KeyMainCustomerID">
        <xsd:selector xpath="/myrubberbands/customer_record/customer"/>
        <xsd:field xpath="@id"/>
      </xsd:key>
    </xsd:element>
    <xsd:element name="order_history" type="OrderHistoryType" minOccurs="0"
     maxOccurs="1"/>
  </xsd:sequence>
</xsd:complexType>
```

The remainder of the schema follows the pattern of the above example, and the full schema to define this XML vocabulary is available for download along with the rest of the example code.

Generating MyRubberbandsML

Now that the markup language has been defined, documents need to be generated for the users. In a true production environment, both the generation of the XML and the XSL transformation of the XML document would take place on the fly using JSP or some similar technology. However, to save time, the developers decide to generate the XML from the database in a batch process, and then convert to static VoiceXML, WML, and HTML files using XSLT in a similar manner. Perl is an ideal language for an application like this, using the Data Base Interface (DBI) module to connect to our RDBMS. The Perl script called `export_myrubberbands.pl` generates the source XML and transforms it to the target language and is provided with the code download. The XSL transformation of the examples was done with Michael Kay's Instant Saxon program, although there are Perl APIs available, such as XML::Sablotron, that could perform the transform directly without external software.

VoiceXML by XSLT

So far, we have examined the existing database, outlined a suitable voice interface for it, and defined our source markup language and the method for generating it. Now, we are ready to create a stylesheet to convert it to a VoiceXML form implementing the design we decided on in the previous section *Designing A Voice Interface.* This stylesheet, `myrubberbands2vxml.xsl`, is quite lengthy, and can be found in its entirety in the code download. Here, I shall pick out just the important points in the code for discussion; including the dynamic generation of grammars, some VoiceXML features worthy of particular attention, and fundamental XSL concepts used.

VoiceXML Stylesheet

Note that the stylesheet is designed to produce a single VoiceXML document containing just one user's data. So, its top-level template only matches documents where the top-level attribute `export_type` is set to `single`. The `indent` attribute on the <xsl:output> tag will produce a well-formatted result document that will be easier for a human brain to examine.

```
<?xml version = "1.0"?>
<xsl:stylesheet  xmlns:xsl="http://www.w3.org/1999/XSL/Transform" version="1.0">

<xsl:output method="xml" encoding="ISO-8859-1" indent="yes"/>

<xsl:template match="myrubberbands[@export_type='single']/customer_record">
<vxml version="1.0">

<meta name="author" content="Underpaid Myrubberbands Engineer"/>
<meta name="copyright" content="Copyright (C) 2001 Myrubberbands.com"/>
```

The next block illustrates one way XSL can generate elements with an attribute having dynamic content: the <xsl:element> construct.

```
<xsl:element name="meta">
  <xsl:attribute name="name">description</xsl:attribute>
  <xsl:attribute name="content">Voice Interface for #<xsl:value-of
select="customer/@id"/>
  </xsl:attribute>
</xsl:element>
```

We will need to set up some variables for use in the VoiceXML document. First off, we grab the user's Automatic Number Identification (ANI) and Dialed Number Identification Service (DNIS) for later use. These correspond to the phone number that originated the call (analogous, but not identical to, the consumer caller ID service) and the number that the user dialed. The implementation of these is system dependent, and the data may not be available for all calls in any case. They are included here mainly for illustration. In a real application, the ANI can be used for auto-identification of the user.

The `form_pointer` variable will be used for navigation later.

```
<var name="customer_ani" expr="session.telephone.ani"/>
<var name="customer_dnis" expr="session.telephone.dnis"/>
<var name="session_error_count" expr="0"/>
<var name="form_pointer" expr="'mainMenu'"/>
<var name="user_command" expr="''"/>
```

Next come the form-level help dialogs, which here attempt to mimic typical responses likely from a real-life call center, contrary to the advice of Chapter 6:

```
<help count="1">
  What seems to be the trouble?
  <reprompt/>
</help>
<help count="2">
  Come on - isn't this easy enough to understand?
  <reprompt/>
</help>
<help count="3">
  Hey <xsl:value-of select="customer/firstname"/>, are you stupid or something?
  <reprompt/>
</help>
```

The design specifies that the main menu command is always available. We can implement that with a global VoiceXML `<link>` element:

```
<link next="#mainMenu">
  <grammar type="application/x-jsgf"> main menu </grammar>
</link>
```

Again, we use the information from the XML file to customize the prompts for the user. This form `welcomeMessage` corresponds to the "welcome message" box in the interface design diagram earlier.

```
<form id="welcomeMessage">
  <block>
    <prompt bargein="false" timeout="0.1s">
      Hello, <xsl:value-of select="customer/firstname"/>.
      Welcome to the my rubber bands dot com voice order status system.
    </prompt>
    <goto next="#mainMenu"/>
  </block>
</form>
```

Next, we come to the `mainMenu` form, the primary form of the voice application. There is a form-level `<nomatch>` element here to transfer control flow to the `errorHandler` form when an utterance doesn't match the grammar. This form is used for most no-match events throughout the application, to keep track of the total number of such errors that have occurred this session. The `<noinput>` handler here ensures the main menu is repeated when the user doesn't respond to the prompt. In a future version of the product, the designers may implement some kind of timeout to restrict the number of loops, and disconnect the user if there is no response for a long time, but this issue need not concern us now.

```
<form id="mainMenu">

  <nomatch>
    <goto next="#errorHandler"/>
  </nomatch>

  <noinput>
    <goto next="#mainMenu"/>
  </noinput>

  <block>
    <assign name="form_pointer" expr="'mainMenu'"/>
  </block>
```

```
    <field name="userSaid">

      <prompt bargein="true" timeout="3s">
        This is the main menu.
        <break msecs="500"/>
        You can say product list to hear a list of products.
        <break msecs="500"/>
        You can say order status to check your order status.
        <break msecs="500"/>
        You can say frequently asked questions to get more
        information.
        <break msecs="500"/>
        You can always say main menu to return to this
        menu, or help for additional help.
      </prompt>

      <grammar type="application/x-jsgf">
        list
        product list |
        more information |
        frequently asked questions |
        questions |
        order status
      </grammar>
```

In order to keep track of the currently active form, the global variable `form_pointer` is set. This could be used to implement specific navigation logic, for example, by changing the behavior of a command slightly depending on where the command originated. Once the prompt has been played, and the user has responded with an utterance matching the inline grammar, the <filled> handler for this <field> is entered. This copies the value returned by the grammar to the global variable `user_command`, which is used by the `navigator` form to direct control flow to the required form. We could also use <subdialog> and pass a parameter, but this is simpler, and sufficient for this application.

```
      <filled>
        <assign name="user_command" expr="userSaid"/>
        <goto next="#navigator"/>
      </filled>
    </field>
  </form>
```

Now our main menu form is finished, we can start to implement the dialogs that provide the application's basic functionality. First up is the `orderStatus` form that makes the most extensive use of dynamic content generation:

```
  <form id="orderStatus">
    <noinput>
      <assign name="user_command" expr="'main menu'"/>
      <goto next="#navigator"/>
    </noinput>

    <nomatch>
      <goto next="#errorHandler"/>
    </nomatch>

    <field name="userSaid">
```

We need a test here to check that the customer does indeed have outstanding orders, and play a message to that effect:

```
      <prompt bargein="true" timeout="1s">
  <xsl:if test="count(/myrubberbands/customer_record/order_history/order) != 0">
        This is a list of all your orders.
  </xsl:if>
  <xsl:if test="count(/myrubberbands/customer_record/order_history/order) = 0">
        You have not placed any orders within the last thirty days.
  </xsl:if>
        <break msecs="500"/>
```

The next block creates a prompt for each order that was in the source XML document by using the XSLT element <xsl:for-each> to select XML elements that match the XPath in its attribute. The sayas attribute from the <order_date> element in our XML file is used here to provide an audio cue to identify the order to the user.

```
  <xsl:for-each select="order_history/order">
        <sayas class="date">
        <xsl:value-of select="order_date/@sayas"/>,
        </sayas>
        you placed an order. Say order number
        <xsl:value-of select="position()"/>
        to hear more about it.
        <break msecs="500"/>
  </xsl:for-each>
      </prompt>

      <grammar type="application/x-jsgf">
        list |
        product list |
        more information |
        frequently asked questions |
        questions |
        order status |
```

The grammar also includes an option dynamically generated by the XSLT code. The user can say, "order number one" to access data on the first order in their list. This JSGF could be improved to accept shorter instructions, such as "order one", or even "one", but be aware that using "order number" followed by the number will help the ASR system correctly identify the user utterance, and will probably improve application performance in this situation.

In this chapter, all the grammars are inline, but XSLT could just as easily be used to create standalone external grammars in separate files, or to generate grammars in multiple formats (GSL, JSGF, XML) from a common data source, by the application of different stylesheets.

```
  <xsl:for-each select="order_history/order">
        order number <xsl:value-of select="position()"/> |
  </xsl:for-each>
        buy me
      </grammar>

      <filled>
        <assign name="form_pointer" expr="'productList'"/>
        <assign name="user_command" expr="userSaid"/>
        <goto next="#navigator"/>
      </filled>

    </field>
  </form>
```

Just as we iterated over the order_history/order node-set to create grammars with options for all the orders of a customer, we must now iterate over these nodes again to create individual forms containing the details for each order. If there were consistently a very large number of orders per user, we might look at generating the order details on the fly using JSP or PHP to create a separate VoiceXML document.

```
<xsl:for-each select="order_history/order">
<xsl:variable name="order_detail_counter" select="position()"/>
<form id="order_{$order_detail_counter}">
```

The block above illustrates the other way XSLT offers for including dynamic content in an attribute value, this time through the <xsl:variable> element, the value of which can be output by preceding the identifier with the dollar sign, $. This technique is used several times when creating the VoiceXML forms for each order.

```
  <noinput>
    <!-- This falls through to order status top level -->
    <assign name="user_command" expr="'order status'"/>
    <goto next="#navigator"/>
  </noinput>

  <nomatch>
    <goto next="#errorHandler"/>
  </nomatch>

  <block>
   <assign name="form_pointer" expr="'order_{$order_detail_counter}'"/>
  </block>

  <field name="userSaid">
```

The following code generates the prompt to announce the order detail:

```
    <prompt bargein="true" timeout="1s">
      This order was placed on <sayas class="date">
      <xsl:value-of select="order_date/@sayas"/></sayas>.
      <break msecs="500"/>
      The order consisted of
<xsl:for-each select="product">
      quantity <xsl:value-of select="./@quantity"/> of product
```

The <xsl:value-of> element below retrieves the name of the product with an XPath expression that selects products from the XML product_list section where the id attribute matches the id attribute of the current order. This is analogous to a SQL join between the customer_order and customer_order_product tables from relational schema. Note that XPath denotes an attribute with use of the at symbol, @.

```
      <xsl:value-of
select="/myrubberbands/product_list/product[@id=current()/@id]"/>
      <break msecs="500"/>
</xsl:for-each>
      The total of the order was
```

Next, we see the VoiceXML <sayas> element put to use. Whether or not this causes the contents to be rendered correctly as currency depends on the TTS engine used, and its support for pronunciation markup. The rest of the block repeats the previous technique to add order options to the inline <grammar> element.

```
        <sayas class="currency">
        $<xsl:value-of select="total_charge"/></sayas>.
        The status of this order is
        <xsl:value-of select="order_status"/>.
      </prompt>

      <grammar type="application/x-jsgf">
        list |
        product list |
        more information |
        frequently asked questions |
        questions |
        order status |
        <xsl:for-each select="/myrubberbands/customer_record/order_history/order">
          order number <xsl:value-of select="position()"/> |
        </xsl:for-each>
        buy me
      </grammar>

      <filled>
        <assign name="form_pointer" expr="'productList'"/>
        <assign name="user_command" expr="userSaid"/>
        <goto next="#navigator"/>
      </filled>

    </field>
  </form>
  </xsl:for-each>
```

At this point we'll skip over the product list option, because it doesn't illustrate anything we haven't already seen. However, the product listing prompt offers the user the option to say, "Buy me", in which case their call is transferred to the MyRubberbands.com's telephone service center by the `placeOrder` form below. This is the quickest way for the company to add some commerce capability to the voice system, but note that the VoiceXML `<transfer>` element is not implemented by all platforms. When the user returns from the call, they are unconditionally sent to the main menu by the subsequent `<goto>` element.

```
  <form id="placeOrder">
    <block>
      <prompt bargein="false" timeout="1s">
        Transferring your call to customer service.
      </prompt>
    </block>
    <transfer name="callSales" dest="MYRUBBERBND" connecttimeout="30s"
     bridge="true"/>
    <block>
      <goto next="#mainMenu"/>
    </block>
  </form>
```

We can also skip over the frequently asked questions option, since it contains only static VoiceXML code. We are now almost at the end of our stylesheet, where the `navigator` form is located, holding the navigation logic for many of the state transitions in our interface design.

It consists simply of an if-else construct that expresses the state transitions on the diagram of the user interface earlier. If more commands, states, or transitions were to be added to the design, the complexity of the interface might exceed the limitations of this method of implementation.

```
<form id="navigator">
  <block>
    <if cond="user_command == 'product list' || user_command == 'list'">
      <goto next="#productList"/>
    <elseif cond="user_command  == 'questions' ||
          user_command == 'frequently asked questions' ||
          user_command == 'more information'"/>
      <goto next="#FAQ"/>
    <elseif cond="user_command == 'order status'"/>
      <goto next="#orderStatus"/>
    <elseif cond="user_command == 'buy me'"/>
      <goto next="#placeOrder"/>
```

The stylesheet drives the rest of the navigation engine by creating forms for each individual order in this customer's order history. It does this by means of the following `<xsl:for-each>` construct:

```
<xsl:for-each select="order_history/order">
<xsl:variable name="order_counter" select="position()"/>
    <elseif cond="user_command == 'order number {$order_counter}'"/>
      <goto next="#order_{$order_counter}"/>
</xsl:for-each>
    <else/>
      <goto next="#mainMenu"/>
    </if>
  </block>
</form>
```

Finally, we come to the `errorHandler` form that is used by most of the `<nomatch>` handlers in the dialog. This error handler keeps a running count of the number of errors, and when four errors have occurred, it will apologize and disconnect the user. This isn't the friendliest way of handling errors, and is not suitable for a long-range solution that would more likely transfer the user to a human operator at this point. Not only that, but we'd probably want more sophisticated logic for processing errors, maybe using ECMAScript to vary the response according to the time elapsed since the last error.

```
<form id="errorHandler">
  <block>
    <assign name="session_error_count"
          expr="session_error_count + 1"/>

    <if cond="session_error_count &lt; 4">
      <prompt bargein="false" timeout="0.1s">
        I'm sorry, but I'm unable to understand you.
      </prompt>
      <if cond="session_error_count &gt; 2">
        <prompt bargein="false" timeout="0.1s">
          It seems I am having trouble.
        </prompt>
      </if>

      <goto next="#navigator"/>
    <else/>
      <prompt bargein="false" timeout="0.1s">
        I'm sorry, but I'm having a lot of difficulty understanding you. If you
        are currently in a noisy environment, please call back later.
      </prompt>
      <exit/>
    </if>
  </block>
</form>
```

All that needs to be done now is to close the document, after including an empty template matching standalone `<product_list>` elements, to suppress any output from them. Without this, default XSLT templates would be applied that output text children of any elements that aren't explicitly matched by a template already.

```
</vxml>
</xsl:template>
<xsl:template match="product_list"/>
</xsl:stylesheet>
```

That brings us to the end of our VoiceXML stylesheet.

Running the Stylesheet

Now it is time to run the stylesheet transform, and produce a complete VoiceXML document for one of our users. This can be done with the next command if you are using Saxon:

```
C:\>saxon customer_1.xml myrubberbands2vxml.xsl > customer_1.vxml
```

The next screenshot shows the structure of the generated VoiceXML document if viewed in Microsoft Internet Explorer. The form nodes have been collapsed to fit the whole document into the window. Note that the only significant variation in documents for different customers will be in the number of order detail forms produced. Now, all that is lacking is a platform to try out our dialog.

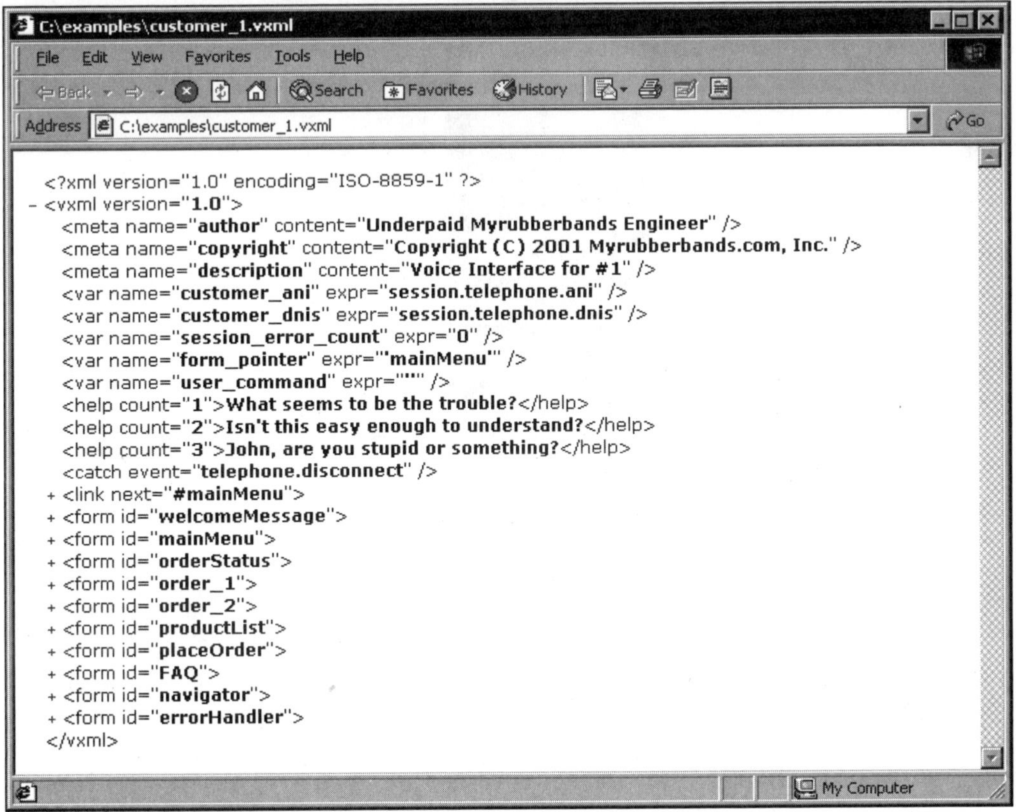

Executing the VoiceXML Dialog

At this point, I shall introduce the Motorola Mobile Application Development Kit (MADK) version 2.0, as it is a powerful tool for testing and debugging VoiceXML code. It provides a complete Integrated Development Environment (IDE) that allows the development and simulation of both VoiceXML and WML without the need for picking up a phone. It includes a syntax-checking mechanism that validates the source file against the target language's DTD.

The following image shows our VoiceXML document created by the stylesheet executing in the simulator. The simulator uses the Microsoft Agent software to vocalize audio output, through the Office Assistant character. User response can be either by voice or by typing responses into the box at the bottom of the phone image. A transcript of the session is displayed in the main IDE window.

Of course, when the time comes to launch the system, the application will need to be completely tested on the host platform, but this tool offers a more traditional environment for developing VoiceXML that many developers may prefer to the online IDEs provided by the main voice platforms.

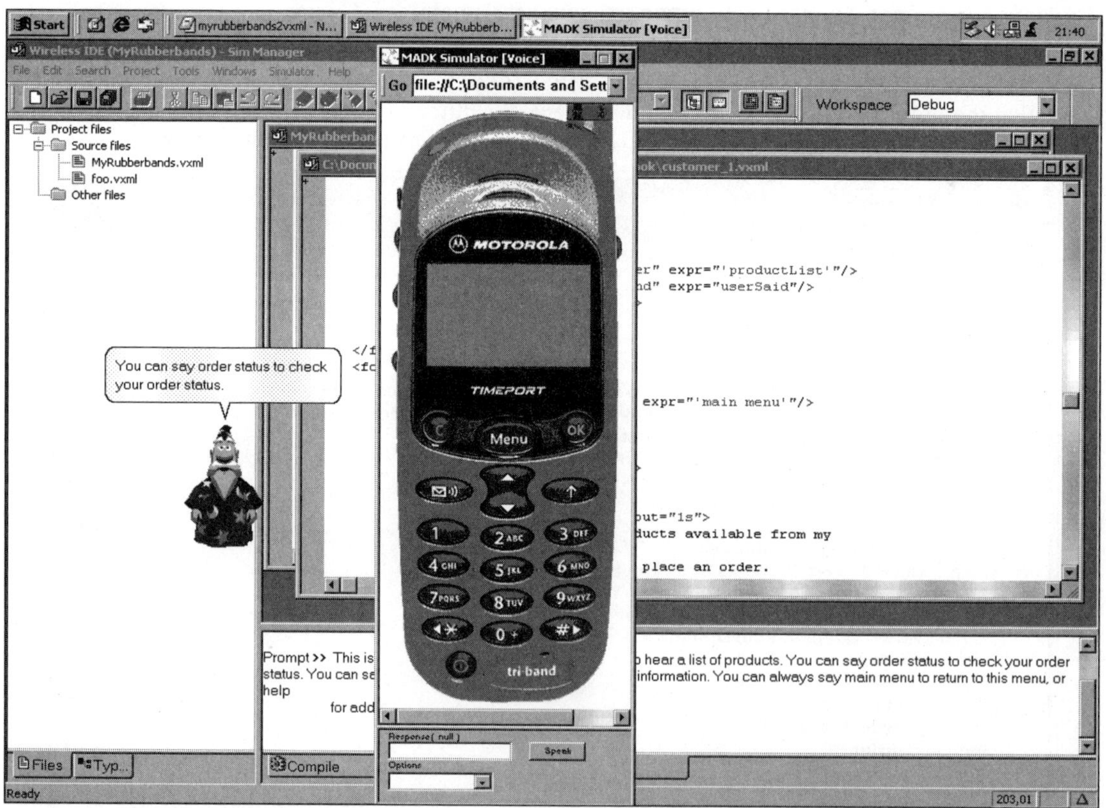

That's as far as we will be going in our discussion of the VoiceXML interface for the MyRubberBands site. I will now briefly look at how XSLT can generate documents in other markup languages from the same XML source data.

WML with XSLT

Let's suppose that the director is over the moon with the response generated by the voice access system, and our development team now have the task of rolling out a Wireless Markup Language (WML) interface to complement it. Although the display and input methods of WAP devices severely limit their utility, I intend to show how a simple WML interface is practically "free" after the effort we have already invested in developing an XML representation of our data.

All that this interface will do is allow the viewing of a small subset of the data contained in the original document, in the same categories as the voice application. These include order status, product list, frequently asked questions, and one additional category, a brief summary of the user's registered profile. This application is one way only. The user can only view data, and cannot change anything from the WAP device. Like the VoiceXML example, the entire application is contained in one document – that is, a single "deck" of WML "cards". This example is for illustration only, and lacks fundamental necessities such as login/access control. Anything more complex than this "read-only" application will require significant server-side logic, whether or not the output is generated with XSLT.

This stylesheet, `myrubberbands2wml.xsl`, is fairly small, and can be found with the rest of the example code for download. It is also replicated here, but there are few annotations, as it does not introduce any significant concepts that weren't also used in the VoiceXML stylesheet.

WML Stylesheet

The stylesheet for WML output is very similar to the VoiceXML template. There are only a few differences of any significance.

```
<?xml version = "1.0"?>
<xsl:stylesheet xmlns:xsl=http://www.w3.org/1999/XSL/Transform version="1.0">

<xsl:output method="xml" encoding="ISO-8859-1"
  doctype-public="-//WAPFORUM//DTD WML 1.1//EN"
  doctype-system="http://www.wapforum.com/DTD/wml_1.1.xml"  indent="yes"/>

<xsl:template match="myrubberbands/customer_record">
  <xsl:variable name="firstname" select="customer/firstname"/>

<wml>

  <!-- Main Menu -->

  <card id="main_menu" title="{$firstname}'s MyRubberBands">
    <p mode="wrap">
      <a href="#my_profile">My Profile</a><br/>
      <a href="#order_status">Order Status</a><br/>
      <a href="#product_list">Product List</a><br/>
      <a href="#faq">FAQ</a><br/>
      <!-- Link out of this XML-generated document -->
    </p>
  </card>
```

The profile summary illustrates a common "beginner" problem for XSLT: how to format whitespace in the finished result. Using the literal value ` ` to denote a hard-coded space in the target character set is often the simplest way to do it.

```
<card id="my_profile" title="{$firstname}'s Profile">
  <p mode="wrap">
    <xsl:value-of select="customer/firstname"/><br/>
    <xsl:value-of select="customer/lastname"/><br/>
    <xsl:value-of select="customer/username_or_email"/><br/>
    <xsl:value-of select="count(customer_address)"/> 
    <xsl:if test="count(customer_address) == 1">Address </xsl:if>
    <xsl:if test="count(customer_address) != 1">Addresses </xsl:if>
    On File<br/>
    <a href="#main_menu">Main Menu</a><br/>
  </p>
</card>
```

For simplicity, the `order_status` card will contain all the data, rather than linking to submenus:

```
  <card id="order_status" title="{$firstname}'s Orders">
    <p mode="wrap">
    <xsl:if test="count(order_history/order) = 0">
    There are no orders on file.<br/>
    </xsl:if>
<xsl:for-each select="order_history/order">
      Order #<xsl:value-of select="position()"/><br/>
      <xsl:value-of select="order_date"/><br/>
      <xsl:value-of select="total_charge"/><br/>
      <xsl:value-of select="order_status"/><br/>
      =========
      <br/><br/>
</xsl:for-each>
      <a href="#main_menu">Main Menu</a><br/>
    </p>
  </card>
```

We'll skip the product list and frequently asked questions cards as they are completely static pages, although the code download contains the full file content. Now we can apply the WML stylesheet to our XML source in just the same way as we did for the VoiceXML stylesheet:

```
C:\>saxon customer_1.xml myrubberbands2wml.xsl > customer_1.wml
```

Like the VoiceXML example, it probably makes sense to script an automatic batch generation of these documents. It is also possible that the login sequence can use the customer's login attempt as an event to request the transform, or we can apply stylesheets dynamically from within ASP or JSP.

Executing the Generated WML Deck

The next images show the simulator executing the customer's WML order status document. This simulator can load configurations for different phones to aid testing.

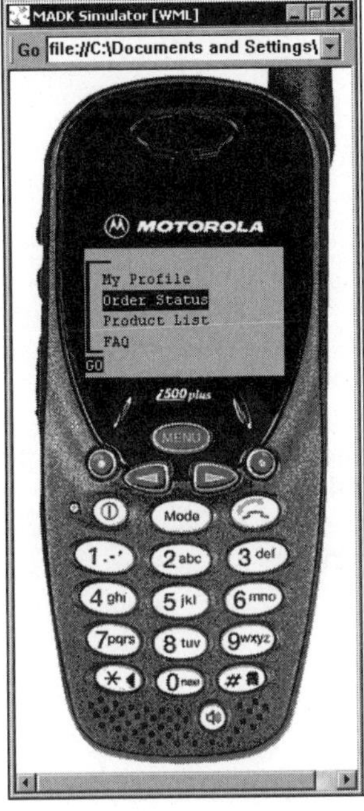

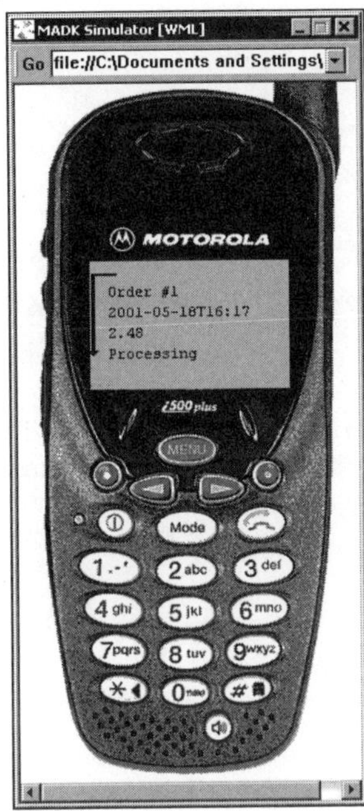

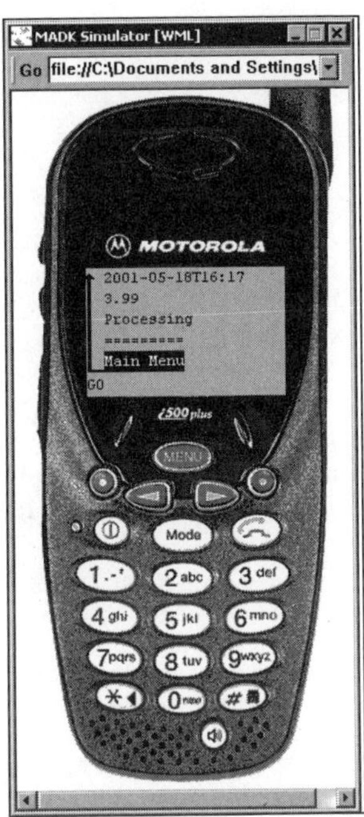

HTML with XSLT

The WML project was so successful that the director is now beside himself with joy, and, quite smitten with XSLT, he has decided that our team should now develop a stylesheet to generate part of the existing HTML site from the XML data. The beauty of using XSLT is that there can be as many interface look-and-feel designs as needed.

The stylesheet, named `myrubberbands2html.xsl`, is significantly smaller than the VoiceXML template, mainly as it produces only simple HTML pages. You may wish to experiment by having the stylesheet create more sophisticated HTML to get a feel for using XSLT in this way.

HTML Stylesheet

The HTML stylesheet is very similar to the VoiceXML and WML stylesheets, and the subject matter is probably a little more familiar as well. Notice that commonly "unclosed" HTML tags, such as <hr> and <p>, have to be written as properly formed XML and closed correctly, as in <hr/>, otherwise the XSLT processor will complain that the stylesheet is not well-formed. To support some browsers, such as Netscape Navigator, it may be necessary to insert a space between the tag name, and the closing / of an empty element. For example, the <hr/> should be <hr />.

```
<?xml version = "1.0"?>
<xsl:stylesheet xmlns:xsl="http://www.w3.org/1999/XSL/Transform" version="1.0">
<xsl:output method="html" encoding="ISO-8859-1" indent="yes"/>

<xsl:template match="myrubberbands/customer_record">
<html>
  <head>
```

```
    <title>
  Customer Profile: <xsl:value-of select="customer/username_or_email"/>
    </title>
  </head>
  <body>
  <h2>
  Customer Profile For:
  <xsl:value-of select="customer/lastname"/>,
  <xsl:value-of select="customer/firstname"/>
  (<xsl:value-of select="customer/username_or_email"/>)
  </h2>
  <hr/>
```

To display the user's addresses, we use `<xsl:call-template>`. This is similar to a function or subroutine call, letting us keep the logic for formatting addresses in one place, and also letting us pass parameters. The address template itself comes towards the end of the stylesheet.

```
  <h2>Registered Addresses</h2>
  <table border="1">
  <tr valign="top">
  <xsl:for-each select="customer_address">

    <td>
    <h4><xsl:value-of select="@address_type"/></h4>
    <xsl:call-template name="formatAddressTemplate"/>
     </td>
  </xsl:for-each>
  </tr>
  </table>
    <hr/>

  <!--
    Display all the user's order history.
  -->
  <xsl:for-each select="order_history">
  <table border="1">
    <tr>
    <td>Date</td>
    <td>Status</td>
    <td>Summary</td>
    <td>Ship To</td>
    <td>Total</td>
    </tr>
    <xsl:for-each select="order">

    <tr>
    <td><xsl:value-of select="order_date"/></td>
    <td><xsl:value-of select="order_status"/></td>
    <td><table>
    <xsl:for-each select="product">
```

Again we use an XPath expression similar to a SQL `JOIN` in order to retrieve the ship-to address with the fairly complex `select` attribute below:

```
      <tr>
        <td>(<xsl:value-of select="@quantity"/>) <xsl:value-of
       select="//product_list/product[@id=current()/@id]"/></td>
      </tr>
    </xsl:for-each>
```

```
      </table>
      <td>

         <xsl:for-each select="//customer_record/customer_address[
        @address_type=current()/customer_address/@address_type
          and
                 @customer_id=current()/customer_address/@customer_id]">
        <xsl:call-template name="formatAddressTemplate"/>
         </xsl:for-each>
      </td>
      </td>
      <td halign="right">$<xsl:value-of select="total_charge"/>
      </td>
      </tr>
      </xsl:for-each>
    </table>
    </xsl:for-each>

    <hr/>
    Copyright 2001, MyRubberbands.com, Inc. All Rights Reserved.
    </body>
  </html>
  </xsl:template>
```

Once again, we mustn't forget the blank template to suppress unwanted output for unmatched items.

```
  <xsl:template match="product_list"/>
```

Finally, this is the named template for formatting address information. Notice that it assumes that the current node is a <customer_address>. Therefore, before using <xsl:call-template>, the stylesheet must use an <xsl:for-each> or similar method to ensure the context is at the desired node.

```
  <xsl:template name="formatAddressTemplate">

    <xsl:value-of select="address1"/><br/>
    <xsl:if test="address2 != ''">
      <xsl:value-of select="address2"/><br/>
    </xsl:if>

    <xsl:if test="city != '' and state_or_prov != ''">
      <xsl:value-of select="city"/>,
      <xsl:value-of select="state_or_prov"/> 
      <xsl:value-of select="postalcode"/><br/>
    </xsl:if>
```

Phone numbers from the database are the unformatted, ten-digit US style.

```
    <xsl:if test="phone != ''">
        (<xsl:value-of select="substring(phone, 1, 3)"/>)
        <xsl:value-of select="substring(phone, 4, 3)"/>-
        <xsl:value-of select="substring(phone, 7, 4)"/><br/>
    </xsl:if>

    <xsl:if test="email != ''">
      <xsl:element name="a">
       <xsl:attribute name="href">mailto:<xsl:value-of select="email"/>
       </xsl:attribute>
       <xsl:value-of select="email"/>
      </xsl:element>
```

```
      <br/>
    </xsl:if>
  </xsl:template>
  </xsl:stylesheet>
```

The next image shows a typical HTML page created by this template. Spicing this up is a job for one of MyRubberBands' web designers or graphics artists. That brings to a conclusion our third XSL-generated view of our XML data format.

Incorporating this HTML output in the company's existing web site could be accomplished in a number of ways. Someday, when the majority of web clients support client-side XSLT transformation, we could send raw XML to the client for them to render with the appropriate stylesheet already cached on their browser. In the meantime, some sort of server application will be necessary to both implement access control and actually perform the transformations when required.

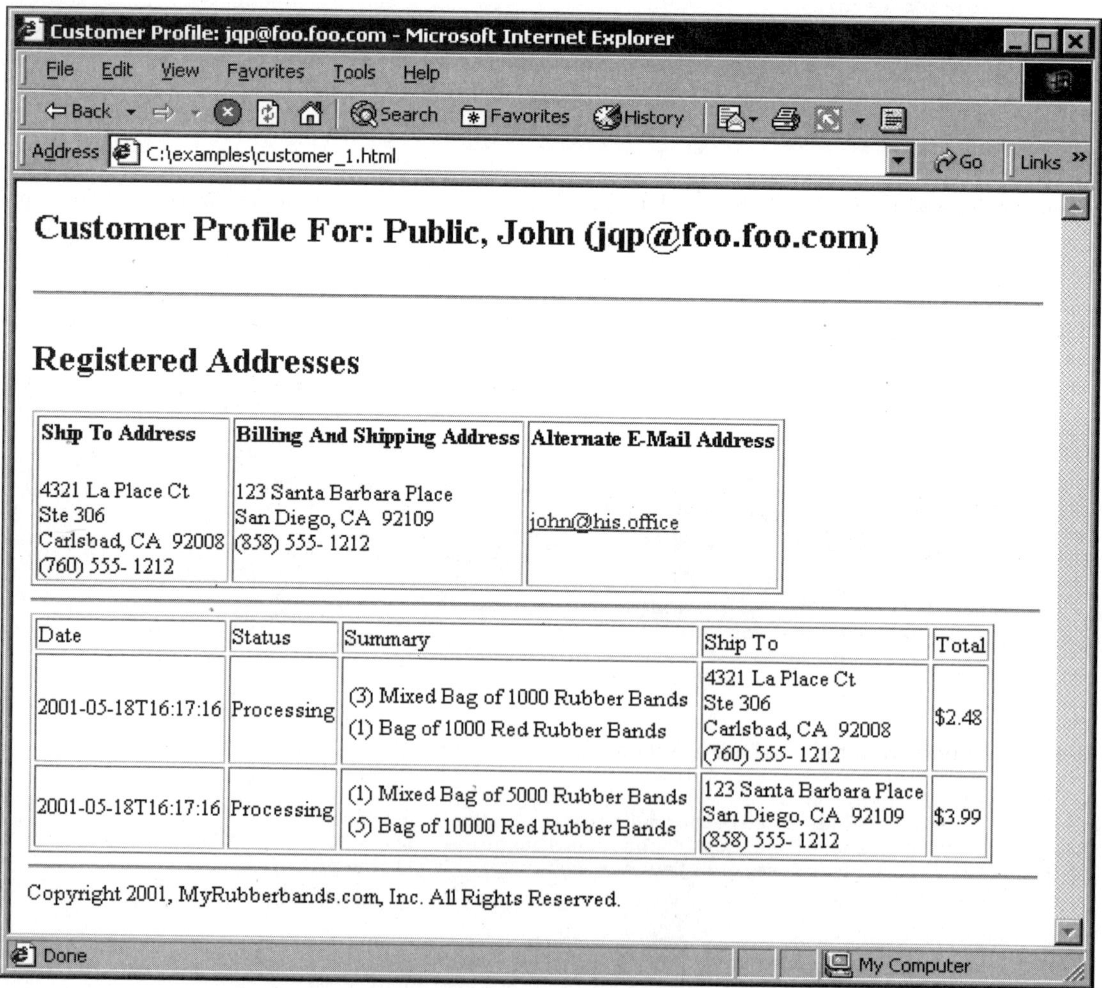

Customer Profile For: Public, John (jqp@foo.foo.com)

Registered Addresses

Ship To Address	Billing And Shipping Address	Alternate E-Mail Address
4321 La Place Ct Ste 306 Carlsbad, CA 92008 (760) 555- 1212	123 Santa Barbara Place San Diego, CA 92109 (858) 555- 1212	john@his.office

Date	Status	Summary	Ship To	Total
2001-05-18T16:17:16	Processing	(3) Mixed Bag of 1000 Rubber Bands (1) Bag of 1000 Red Rubber Bands	4321 La Place Ct Ste 306 Carlsbad, CA 92008 (760) 555- 1212	$2.48
2001-05-18T16:17:16	Processing	(1) Mixed Bag of 5000 Rubber Bands (5) Bag of 10000 Red Rubber Bands	123 Santa Barbara Place San Diego, CA 92109 (858) 555- 1212	$3.99

Copyright 2001, MyRubberbands.com, Inc. All Rights Reserved.

Summary

In this chapter we explored the process of using XSLT to provide the user with multiple interfaces to data in a legacy database, that does not provide native XML access to data. We defined a set of requirements for a voice interface based on some business needs. We designed an XML format to mark up the legacy data, and documented it with an XML Schema. We created XSL templates to produce a VoiceXML interface, ran the VoiceXML inside a simulator, and also looked at stylesheets to produce WML and HTML documents.

```
<?xml version="1.0"?>
<vxml version="1.0">
<form id="foo">
<block>
<prompt>
Hi. My name is Bob
</prompt>
</block>
</form>
</vxml>
```

8

Adding VoiceXML to an Existing Web Site

In this chapter, we will add a VoiceXML interface to an existing web site powered by a relational database. As you may expect, extending an existing database-based site to offer VoiceXML functionality alongside the HTML interface is a relatively straightforward task. Our phone site will use primarily text-to-speech output: although current text-to-speech algorithms are just about good enough to be used in this way, a simple method of reducing errors in pronunciation is discussed. We shall also look at how audio content in a format such as MP3 can be converted to the phone-optimized format required in order for it to be made available over the phone.

Our phone site has been developed for the Tellme platform, and it can be accessed by dialing 1-800-555-TELL (8355), waiting for the main menu, and then dialing 1-TAPIR (1-82747).

The web site that we shall voice-enable, the Tompkins County Green Party at http://www.tcgreens.org, features a mix of news stories, articles, and information about upcoming events. There is a problem, however, in that many of the potential audience, people interested in alternative politics, don't own a computer: maybe they don't have the money, or maybe they simply don't want one. Either way, VoiceXML can extend the reach of the site to people like these, and also provide an acceptable interface for remote access by all.

With a site targeted at a geographical area with a population of 100,000, the addition of a voice interface that can be accessed over regular telephones opens up the site to a far more general audience.

As the existing web application generates HTML, making it generate VoiceXML as well isn't too difficult, and is similar to adding a PDF, Flash, or WML (for WAP) front-end. A new interface in one of these formats can be considered either an application on its own, or a part of the existing application. As VoiceXML catches on, we'll see more and more web applications with both HTML and VoiceXML interfaces. Currently, I've chosen to put the VoiceXML portion of the site under the directory http://www.tcgreens.org/vxml/, and treat the VoiceXML pages as a single application. This is convenient, because it bundles all the VoiceXML files in one place, and because all hits to the VoiceXML interface will be logged under a single directory. An alternative hierarchy I considered would have divided the application into three, with a main menu at /vxml/, and sub-applications under /gl/vxml/ and /radio/vxml/, to keep the VoiceXML news section with the HTML news section, and the phone-enabled sound files with the HTML sound files in http://www.tcgreens.org/radio.

There is of course the possibility of setting up a separate web server, say http://vxml.tcgreens.org/. One advantage is that it would completely separate logs of VoiceXML traffic from other activity on the site, simplifying the job of making separate web usage reports for VoiceXML and conventional web activity. It's maybe an exaggeration to call this a separate web server, as a single instance of Apache can be configured to create any number of "virtual servers" on the same IP address. Configuring a separate web server, however, involves changing Apache's configuration files to add a DNS entry for the new name – this is something I expect to do in the near future. Fortunately, the inconvenience of changing the URL of a VoiceXML site is currently less than for an HTML-based site because your users access it through a central hosting service, and because VoiceXML sites are usually less interlinked than HTML sites.

Web Site Overview

Our site shares a dual processor Pentium machine with several other web sites, managed by the popular Apache web server from http://www.apache.org. Dynamic portions of our site are written in PHP, a web scripting language that resembles ASP and JSP in that code enclosed in tags, `<?php` and `?>`, can be embedded inside HTML or XML documents. The PHP code so delimited consists of instructions for the server to execute before sending the page to the client. PHP is open source software that you can freely download and use from http://www.php.net/. It's easy to install and easy to learn, and runs on many forms of UNIX, as well as Windows. It is compatible with many servers including the popular Apache and Microsoft IIS, as well as more obscure varieties like AOLServer and Roxen. Queries on our database are made using SQL statements inside embedded PHP code, so inserting the results of the query into the output page.

Adding a Voice Interface

As ours is a database-backed site, we're lucky in that the new interface can be little more than a new page that retrieves the information, and outputs it in VoiceXML. In general though, we'd have a much harder time translating a site that stores its content in static HTML files, essentially because HTML doesn't contain a whole lot of information about the structure of a document. Unless you've imposed a specific structure on your documents, perhaps in conjunction with Cascading Style Sheets, it's difficult to devise software to break an HTML document into its key elements, discarding or replacing parts to generate well-formed and functional VoiceXML documents. If, on the other hand, the HTML content on your site is automatically generated from XML files, say, such as the site at http://www.honeylocust.com/limon/, you could replace your HTML generator script with one to generate VoiceXML, as in Chapter 7. Audio content, in a format such as `.wav` or `.mp3`, needs to be translated in to a more suitable format, although this is a straightforward task, because there is no conceptual difference between listening to audio on the phone or on a computer.

Cookies and Logging

Most voice platforms, such Tellme, BeVocal, and VoiceGenie don't support cookies. Although it wouldn't be difficult for voice platforms to support short-duration session cookies, it's not clear how voice platforms could support persistent long-duration ones. A VoiceXML browser built into a car, an advanced mobile telephone, or running on a PC, could store cookies in the same way a PC-based web browser does. At best, a phone gateway could associate cookies with particular calling phone numbers, or particular users once they have authenticated themselves. Either case introduces concerns about security and privacy, further discouraging gateway manufacturers from implementing cookies.

However, VoiceXML's session variables can be used as a substitute for session cookies to provide temporary information storage, and we can make a substitute for persistent cookies, to track users between visits, with the `session.telephone.ani` variable. By determining the telephone number of a caller, it's possible to bind information to particular telephones. A further security check can be carried out if desired, perhaps even based on the voice print of the caller. Unfortunately, the `session.telephone.ani` variable is not available on many platforms, including Tellme, and you should also to be prepared for malicious callers who might try to obscure or falsify ANI (Automatic Number Identification) information.

Some web environments, such as JSP, do allow objects to remain in RAM on the web server between requests. In fact, some application servers are specifically designed to tie a persistent thread to a particular web session – allowing web applications to be written in a style close to that of GUI applications. Although such programming models can be flexible, it's difficult to build applications that scale well if you overuse such features.

In the case of PHP, however, no variables survive from one request to the next: applications are stateless. If a PHP application is to have any memory that persists between requests, it needs to store information outside the web server: in the database, in the web browser (encoded in a URL, in form variables, or in a cookie), or through a combination of the two.

It's common practice to assign an identifier to a single user session consisting of a sequence of web requests, and because of the stateless environment, this session identifier must be stored on the web browser. A single such identifier provides the key to a potentially unlimited amount of information stored on the server. Cookies are the most convenient way to link a particular browser with a particular session on the web. However, some applications store session information by including it in the URLs they generate, like so:

```
http://www.somesite.com/apage.html?session_id=481f7-212a
```

Although it would be possible to encode session information in URLs inside VoiceXML documents, it's not possible with current platforms to use cookies, as we said above. Fortunately, VoiceXML supports application-scope variables, stored on the VoiceXML platform for the duration of the call. As we'll see later in this chapter, application scope variables can be declared using the `<var>` element, given a value by the VoiceXML `<assign>` element, and transmitted back to the server as either `GET` or `POST` variables by specifying them in the `namelist` attribute of the `<submit>` element.

Because VoiceXML interacts with a web server through the same HTTP protocol used with HTML, it leaves a similar record in the server logs, including the IP address of the voice platform, the time, and URL requested. Like web browsers, VoiceXML platforms transmit user-agent strings that differentiate one platform from another, and VoiceXML interactions from interactions with conventional web browsers.

Differences between VoiceXML and HTML

When developing a VoiceXML application based on an HTML site, we need to consider the differences between VoiceXML and HTML as application platforms and communication media, so our interface will be effective in the new medium.

VoiceXML, fortunately for us, lacks the equivalent of a back button, which, although a valuable feature that makes users feel secure by providing a consistent way to back out of any situation, can make life difficult for web developers. In particular, the back button can cause users to submit pages in an incorrect order, or submit pages more than once, confusing an interactive application. The back button can introduce an unexpected schism between the state of a page and the state of an application. A twofold approach to preventing problems with the back button is required: designing applications firstly so users don't feel tempted to use the back button, and secondly so that a form submitted out of order doesn't cause confusion.

There is currently a lot of disparity between how VoiceXML is implemented on different platforms. Those who are developing applications that are intended to be reusable may feel pressure to develop applications that work on multiple voice portals: one strategy is to stick to a subset of features that will work across a range of voice portals, while another is to use the `USER_AGENT` strings transmitted by the voice portals to determine what voice portal is being used and make changes in the output document accordingly.

So what's the difference between effective VoiceXML and HTML design? Marshall McLuhan, famous for the aphorism "The medium is the message", declared that when we "change the sensory balance of man, ... man changes". With radio, television and HTML, we only succeeded in discovering the most effective ways of using each medium through experience. Unlike HTML, VoiceXML is oriented in time, rather than in space – this is why VoiceXML is more like a programming language than a page description language. As we saw in Chapter 6, *Good Application Design*, unlike a visual pages which a reader can scan, VoiceXML users are limited by the human ability to hold at most 3 to 7 pieces of information in short term memory at any one time. This has a raft of implications for the developer, essentially meaning that a VoiceXML site can't offer as much information per interaction "node" as an HTML site. A phone site needs to be more focused, and possibly that's a good thing, because the scale and the richness of the Web invites us to divide our attention and be scatterbrained.

Implementation choices

One HTML document corresponds to one page; in other languages, such as WML, more than one page or "card" can be stored in a single document, along with instructions as to which card to display depending on the user's actions. If a "node" represents the concept of a page in both voice and visual platforms, then VoiceXML is like WML in that multiple interaction nodes can be stored in a single document. Specifically, different dialog elements (`<form>` and `<menu>`) can represent different nodes, and we can navigate between them using `<goto>`. While developing a headline-reading application, I saw two choices open to me:

1. A main index document listing stories by their title, and providing links to documents that read more detailed information on a particular story

2. A single document containing both an index and additional nodes with more details on the particular stories

By putting multiple nodes in a document, we reduce the number of round trips between client and server, but increase the amount of information transferred per trip. In practice, the VoiceXML platform, the Internet, and my server application, together, interact fast enough so the difference between these choices is inconsequential for this application: network performance is less of a concern than it is for users of WAP or the Web over slow connections. Although the second option more closely resembles the main HTML page at tcgreens.org, I chose option 1 for the headline reader application because the additional round trips to the server means that we will have a record in our server logs of which stories people are listening to over the Web. For developing a menu for a list of songs, later in the chapter, I tried option 2.

VoiceXML developers face a similar choice when it comes to deciding how much processing to do on the server and how much to do on the VoiceXML platform. Because it needs to coordinate transitions between interaction nodes, VoiceXML has much of the functionality of a programming language, which is fortified by close integration with JavaScript. Much of the work that's done with the `<if>` element, for instance, could be done on the server, both in the case of deciding what to read to a user at a given point, and in the case of deciding what page to load from the server depending on what a user chose. If we don't need to work closely with a database or other information resources, we can write elaborate applications that run on the voice platform with few or no round trips. Having the voice platform do processing can take load off your server, and, properly used, can enable a clean design where the server is passed the exact amount of information that it needs to process a page for each round-trip. However, applications get more complicated and harder to debug the more languages are involved, and the harder you push the envelope of the voice platform, the more likely you are to encounter platform incompatibilities.

Tailoring Content for TTS

The first time I accessed my VoiceXML application from my telephone, I felt an incredible thrill, much like the thrill I felt when I used the Web for the first time, or when I developed my first database-backed web application. However, the thrill faded just a bit when my application pronounced "Vieques" (Vee Eck Hays) as "Veeks" and "7-11" as "seven to eleven." We need to work around the limitations of VoiceXML if we want to develop effective applications.

Some limitations come from the nature of speech communication, aggravated by the telephone. Some words sound alike, to both humans and computers. The telephone makes things worse because it cuts off frequencies above 3000 Hz, so that it's actually impossible to distinguish plosive consonants at the beginnings of words. It's difficult to spell words by reading letters over the phone, because some letters sound the same ("D" and "T"), although you can always resort to a system such as the international phonetic alphabet ("Alpha", "Bravo" and so on) or similar, as covered in Chapter 10, *Nuance SpeechObjects.*

In practice, people rarely notice the limitations of telephone speech because, in most contexts, only one interpretation makes sense. This is why VoiceXML supports grammars – by restricting the range of possible interpretations, we reduce the possibility for error. The technology is impressive: both Tellme and BeVocal, for instance, allow the retrieval of stock quotes for the 9,000-odd corporations listed on American stock markets. They understand alternative pronunciations, such as "Disney", "Walt Disney" and "The Walt Disney Corporation" and can even recognize obscure companies such as "The Finger Lakes Bank Corporation". Even so, it's easy to select prompts that encourage confusion: when I was developing my headline reader, I discovered that Tellme has a hard time distinguishing "next" from the number "six", so I decided to use the word "older" rather than "next" to have the system read a list of older headlines.

The bottom line is, there is probably no algorithm that could be designed to read arbitrary text such as e-mail addresses well enough so that human listeners could correctly distinguish them all. If it's important that people understand a particular phrase or URL, you should tweak the spelling so that the TTS pronounces it in a way that people will understand. Generally, when choosing e-mail support addresses and such like, it's wise to make sure that they can be easily pronounced and remembered. In any case, users of a phone site may not own a computer, so it would be preferable to provide phone numbers for contact information rather than, or in addition to, e-mail addresses.

The text-to-speech algorithms used by VoiceXML platforms are surprisingly good – good enough to read text intelligibly from the database over the phone – but they do make mistakes at a disturbing rate. Text-to-speech systems perform best with common words, but will inevitably make mistakes with unfamiliar words with nonstandard pronunciations: acronyms, foreign words (such as place names), and people's names all cause problems. The most difficult to handle are words that can have multiple pronunciations (and meanings) but just a single spelling, such as "to *lead* a horse" versus "*lead* paint", and "*live* broadcast" versus "*live* in peace".

Practically, the particular errors that crop up will depend on your site. Every site will specialize on some particular topics, and will have a certain set of unusual words that will be used again and again. Although I suspect that it's impossible to attain perfect pronunciation without a human actually listening to the output of the site and correcting it by hand, there is a simple technique to make a phone site much easier to understand. The basic idea is to replace words that are mispronounced with something that is more pronounceable for the system. Static content could be adjusted by hand, but for sites of any size or sites with dynamic content, an automated approach is called for. The technique uses a substitution table to replace commonly mispronounced words with phonetic spellings. The function `fix_tts()`, contained in the file `vxml-common.php`, shows how simple this can be in PHP. This file can then be included in any other PHP files that need it by the line:

```
require "vxml-common.php";
```

It draws on another file, `vxml-substitions.php` that contains the actual list of substitutions. Here's `vxml-common.php` now:

```
<?php

  require "vxml-substitutions.php";

  function fix_tts($string) {
      global $vxml_subs;

      foreach($vxml_subs as $from=>$to) {
         $string=str_replace($from,$to,$string);
      };

      return $string;
   };

?>
```

I chose to hardcode the list of substitutions in their own PHP file for simplicity, and because the list won't change that often. Here's that file, `vxml-substitutions.php`:

```
<?php

    $vxml_subs=array(
        "FTAA"=>"F T A A",
        "ASGP"=>"A S G P",
        "Houle"=>"Hool",
        "7-11"=>"7 11",
        "Vieques"=>"Vee Eck Hays",
        "NYS"=>"New York State",
        "HWS"=>"Hobart William Smith"
    );

?>
```

This does have the disadvantage of requiring somebody to edit the file every time they want to add a substitution. It would be possible, and in some ways desirable, to store the substitution table in the database, so that users could add and change substitutions via a web interface. If reading this table creates too much load on the database, we could automatically generate a file similar to `vxml-substitions.php` outside of the database each time the substitutions change. (With a stock PHP installation, we would still have the overhead of parsing PHP code, but add-ons such as Zend Cache http://www.zend.com or APC http://apc.communityconnect.com, would allow the table to stay in RAM between hits.)

Text-to-speech accuracy could be improved by semantic markup, adding additional computer-readable information. For instance, HTML 4.0 contains the `<acronym>` element, which we could use in conjunction with a function like `fix_tts()` to spell an acronym out. Even so, our system still needs knowledge of the irrational particulars of such things if it's going to be as accurate as a knowledgeable human: "FBI" is spelled out, while "NASA" is spelled phonetically, and "NYS" is often pronounced "New York State".

Then there are heteronyms: words with multiple pronunciations. Simple substitution tables won't work in this case. In the long term, it's likely that text-to-speech software will get smarter about this, and make a guess by examining the syntax of a sentence. For instance, in "*live* broadcast", live is an adjective, while in "I *live* upstairs", live is a verb. Text-to-speech software could also employ a **semantic concordance** – a table that distinguishes different meanings (or senses) of words, and contains statistics for how often a certain sense is meant if another word is contained in the same sentence. Information about Wordnet, a dictionary of word senses that can be used with a semantic concordance, can be found at the following URL: http://www.cogsci.princeton.edu/~wn/.

The VoiceXML standard contains the `<sayas>` element for giving the text-to-speech system pronunciation hints. One use of `<sayas>` gives the text-to-speech algorithm a phonetic spelling, while still retaining the correct spelling in the document, which would be useful for search engines, editors, and other programs that might benefit from the correct spelling:

```
<sayas sub="vee eck hays">Vieques</sayas>
```

Unfortunately, Tellme doesn't currently support the `<sayas>` element, and other platforms (such as BeVocal) support it incompletely, not supporting the `phon` attribute that would make it possible to specify the pronunciation of words with the International Phonetic Alphabet (IPA.) The planned VoiceXML 2.0 may support SSML (the Speech Synthesis Markup Language), offering improved control over text-to-speech. In the meantime, developers should be aware that different VoiceXML platforms are likely to use different Text-to-Speech engines, which will pronounce words in different ways.

Of course, the imperfections of text-to-speech may not be acceptable for your application, in which case you will have to record human voices for prompts and content. You can achieve a professional sound just by recording speech with a good quality microphone and editing it with software such as CoolEdit, available as shareware from http://www.cooledit.com/.

Writing for Phone and Web

Writing for the HTML Web is different from writing for print, because it's harder to read on a computer screen than it is on paper, and users are accustomed to using the web in a different way from magazines and books. Typically, writing for the Web has to be about 50% shorter than writing for print. In most cases, writing for the phone Web will need to be even more concise: VoiceXML platforms read text at about 150 words per minute, which is close to the rate of speakers on radio and television. There's nothing technical to stop people listening to long programs over VoiceXML, but would they really want to spend half an hour listening to the phone? Extensions of VoiceXML to non-phone platforms, such as automobiles, or the use of headphones and speakerphones could change this for some users.

The content on tcgreens.org is particularly appropriate for the telephone for two reasons. First, we take special care that our headlines are concise. We get many of our stories from e-mail messages and other web sites, but we nearly always rewrite headlines to make them more succinct – to make sure that readers see (or hear) the headline and immediately understand what the story is about. (It's especially important to avoid cute or clever headlines that aren't descriptive.) Secondly, our stories are divided into two sections, an introduction and a body. We try to write stories in the *inverted pyramid* style of journalism, where the first paragraph summarizes the story. Succeeding paragraphs develop the story in more detail in such a way that a reader who stops halfway would have learned the most important details of the story. As a result, readers who scan the top page of our HTML site get a survey of the site's content, and can easily decide which stories they'd like to read in detail. Our weekly e-mail to people registered on the site is popular with people because it contains titles and summaries that make it easy to keep up to date without getting an e-mail box plugged with mail or spending hours reading. This same style is effective on the phone.

The Back End

Our site uses the MySQL relational database interface for storage management. In addition to handling the details of inserting and deleting information, relational databases automatically handle concurrent reads and updates, and provide locking mechanisms to avoid any remaining problem areas. There are several databases behind our site, such as the database of news stories, `geeklog_stories`.

The PHP pages to generate VoiceXML include simple SQL SELECT statements, to select certain rows and columns from a database. For instance, the following query:

```
SELECT sid,uid,title,date,introtext FROM geeklog_stories WHERE uid=28;
```

would return a table like this one, where `sid`, `uid`, `title`, `date`, and `introtext` are the names of fields of `geeklog_stories`:

sid	uid	title	date	introtext
20010222121400668	28	About Tompkins County	2001-02-22	Tompkins County is located in Central New York State, about 220 miles...
2001022511520036	28	Proud to live in a Progressive City	2001-02-25	Ithaca was declared America's most "enlightened" city by the <a href=...

Most sites will need a certain amount of custom software, but we can save time by incorporating software already available, be it open source or proprietary. Care is then needed to make the site appear as a seamless whole, but this still saves us development costs overall. We'll have to modify applications to make their appearance and behavior consistent with the rest of the site, and also so that they access any common user databases. In the case of tcgreens.org, we combined our user management system with a weblog application, Geeklog (http://www.geeklog.org) and the popular discussion group software Phorum (http://www.phorum.org/).

Perhaps the signature characteristic differentiating simple and sophisticated web sites is the provision of a site-wide user management system that authenticates users and tracks session information. A user management system is necessary if we want a user's interaction with a site to continue from session to session over a long period of time – and if we want to restrict certain functions of the site to only those users with administrative privileges. For some sites, such as intranet sites, a user management system might only need to provide an interface for adding users by hand, but many Internet-based sites will require a means for users to create their own accounts automatically. A user management system should also provide ways to contact users by e-mail, and a good user interface for administrators to view and edit users. One could spend a lot of time developing a user management system before attending to the interesting parts of building a site. For these reasons, we created our own user management system, the Tapir User Manager, designed especially to be integrated with existing sites and web applications: tcgreens.org is just one of many sites using TUM, others have tens of thousands of registered users. You can get a copy of Tapir User Manager, as well as other software used on tcgreens.org by visiting http://www.tcgreens.org/software/.

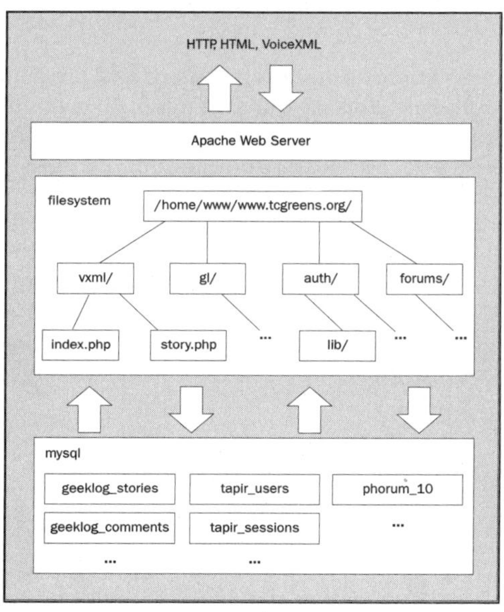

The Voice-Enabled News Interface

The main voice interface to tcgreens.org lets people hear headlines and the introductions of stories over the phone. Much like the interface of search engines, users navigate through a linear list of choices with a fixed number of choices per interaction node. Users move between nodes by saying "older" or "newer", or can hear details, including the title, contributor, date, and introduction on a story by saying or dialing a digit. The call begins at the document `index.php`. The first time that `index.php` is loaded, it plays a banner message and instructions, which is suppressed when reloaded. Users can stop listening to a story by saying "stop", and when they return to `index.php`, the application remembers their position in the index.

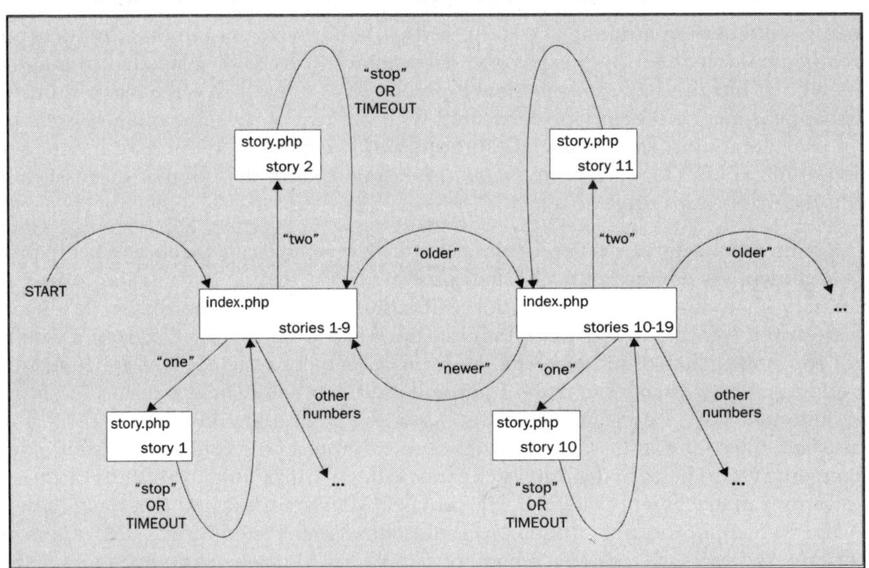

Code Organization

Our application uses a simple system for separating content and presentation that we use elsewhere on the site. For a document titled `index.php` we put SQL queries, user authentication, and other elaborate PHP code in a file titled `index-head.php` in the directory code/ beneath the directory that `index.php` resides in. `index-head.php` loads information into variables, which are then substituted into `index.php`. There is a similar set-up for `story.php` and `story-head.php`. Unlike more elaborate template systems, this doesn't allow HTML authors to be entirely ignorant of programming, but it does allow them to do 90% of their work knowing only 10% of PHP. Although this system does not perfectly separate presentation from content, it places few limitations on the behavior and performance of the site. Another advantage of this organization is that certain operations, such as setting cookies, HTTP headers, or redirecting to another page can only be done before we output data. By doing computations early in the processing of a page, we have the largest number of options open.

The Header File: vxml-header.php

VoiceXML pages on our site are built using a PHP header file containing the information needed at the start of all our VoiceXML documents. It sets the MIME type to `text/xml`, adds the standard XML declaration, and the Tellme DTD. Neither BeVocal nor Tellme require these formalities, but they are required by the specification. Not only that, but including them makes it possible to validate your document with external XML validators, which often produce more useful error messages than do the VoiceXML platforms (one such validator lives at http://www.hcrc.ed.ac.uk/~richard/xml-check.html). Our header also specifies the application root document to be `root.php`, and enables the new Tellme scoping behavior that follows the VoiceXML 1.0 specification.

```
<?php header("Content-Type: text/xml");
      echo '<?xml version="1.0"?>' ?>

      if(substr($REQUEST_URI,-8,8)=="root.php") {
         $application='';
      } else {
         $application=' application="root.php"';
      };

      echo '<?xml version="1.0"?>' ?>
<!DOCTYPE vxml PUBLIC
     "-//Tellme Networks//Voice Markup Language 1.0//EN"
     "http://resources.Tellme.com/toolbox/vxml-Tellme.dtd">
<vxml<?php echo $application?>>
   <meta name="scoping" content="new"/>
```

An important detail is that we check `$REQUEST_URI` to make sure that the application root document, `root.php`, doesn't begin with the line:

```
<vxml application="root.php">
```

but rather, this one:

```
<vxml>
```

This is important, because although some platforms may tolerate self-referential application root documents (as Tellme did when I started developing my application), others, such as BeVocal, will terminate with an error message, or go into an infinite loop (as Tellme does now).

Storing state

Our application stores two pieces of state information:

- How many times the visitor has visited (`visit_count`)
- The user's position in the index (`start`)

Because Tellme doesn't support cookies, we have to find another way of holding state. One of them is to shuttle variables back and forth between the client and server, encoding them in the URL. Another is to store them in application-scope variables, variables defined in the application root document that persist for the duration of a call. We shall take the latter path in this case, using the file `root.php`.

root.php: The Application Root Document

```
<?php require("vxml-header.php") ?>
   <var name="visit_count" expr="0"/>
   <var name="start" expr="0"/>
</vxml>
```

The application root document is loaded once, initializing the variables to zero when the application starts. Although definitions in the application root document are visible in all of the documents that make up an application, the root document does not reset the values of variables when a new document is loaded. Like cookies without an expiration date, application root variables persist between documents for the duration of a telephone call.

The server can set application-scope variables while generating any document by inserting an `<assign>` element into the document:

```
<assign name="myvariable" expr="7"/>
```

where the value of `expr` is a JavaScript (strictly speaking, it's ECMAScript) expression. Don't forget that strings need to be enclosed in single quotes inside the double quotes. Another thing to watch out for when using application-scope variables is accidentally setting them with `<var>` in a given document, rather than with `<assign>`. By using `<var>`, you tell the platform to create a new variable with document, form, or field scope that 'shadows', sometimes temporarily, the application scope variable with results that are infuriatingly difficult to debug. See Chapter 5, for more on variables.

Unlike cookies, application-scope variables are not automatically available to our web server. In some cases, they don't need to be, for instance `visit_count` is used solely on the voice platform. In other cases though, we need to share an application-scope variable with our server, and we must name it specifically in the `namelist` element of the `<submit>` element. Thus, it's not possible to pass variables if we are using the `<goto>` element to link to other forms on our server.

Security

One thing to be careful about: variables that are passed between client and server can be tampered with. For instance, a user could possibly impersonate a VoiceXML browser with a tool like curl, available from http://curl.haxx.se. This isn't much of a problem for our application, but it could be if we were using the information, say, to authenticate a user. There are principally two dangers here.

Firstly, we can be sent a web request that contains toxic information – information that will cause our software to misbehave in a way that causes a security problem. One example of this is the "buffer overflow" problem that occurs in applications in C, and another occurs in powerful interpreted languages like SQL. If we incorporate information from form variables into a SQL query, there's some risk that a user will be able to execute SQL code that does something that we don't want. One way to prevent this is to make sure that we only substitute information from form variables into single quotes, and that we pass variables through a function like PHP's `addslashes()`, which prefixes quote characters with slashes, to prevent malicious users from ending the quote in the SQL statement.

Another risk is that information can be falsified. For instance, by altering a session identifier or a user identifier, a user could gain excessive privileges on the system. PHP can prevent unauthorized users tampering with data on the client with the technique of digital signing. One popular method uses the standard MD5 checksum, available in most environments. In PHP, we can sign the variable `$var` with the MD5 algorithm, protected by secret information in `$secret` as follows:

```
$hash=md5sum("$secret-$var");
$signed_var="$var-$hash";
```

When this information is returned from the client, we can check it like this:

```
list($var,$hash)=explode("-",$signed_var);
$new_hash=md5sum("$secret-$var");
if ($new_hash != $hash) {
   /* terminate with error message */
};
```

index.php

`index.php` is the initial document that a user visits at the beginning of the call. It reads out a list of up to nine headlines, letting a user select stories they'd like to get details on. It starts by including the `index-head.php` file, so we'll take a look at that first.

index-head.php

The `index-head.php` file acts as a reusable module, and contains the SQL code to populate our PHP variables, such as `$stories` and `$count`, so they can be used throughout the application.

```
<?php
  require "tapir-sql.php";
  require "vxml-common.php";

  $conn=tapir_connect_ro();
```

Variables encoded by the `GET` (that is, encoded in the URL query string) or `POST` methods are visible in PHP. At the beginning of the call, `$start` will be undefined. If it's not defined, we set it to zero. Note that we abort the script if the contents of `$start` is not numeric, to prevent a malicious person from causing our script to generate incorrect SQL.

```
  if (!isset($start)) {
    $start=0;
  };

  # make sure it's a number
  if (!is_numeric($start))
    die("non numeric \$start='$start'");
```

We create a `WHERE` clause to select stories that are both ready for public viewing, and meant to be seen on the top page. These stories are then ordered using the `ORDER BY` clause to put 'featured' articles at the beginning, sorting articles of equal priority by date. The `LIMIT` clause makes the database start by returning result number `$start`, and limits the maximum number of results to nine.

The result of the query is fetched by `fetch_objects()`, which returns an array called `$stories`. Like many languages, PHP indices start from zero, so `$stories[0]` is the first row, and `$stories[8]` is the ninth row. Fields can be accessed with the `->` operator: `$stories[3]->sid` retrieves a story identifier, and `$stories[5]->title` retrieves a title.

```
$where_clause="WHERE workflow_status>127 AND flag_visible_on_top=1";
  $r=$conn->query("SELECT sid,title FROM geeklog_stories $where_clause ORDER BY
featured DESC,date DESC LIMIT $start,9");
  $stories=$r->fetch_objects();
```

We need to have a count of the total number of stories so that we can determine if there are any more for the user to hear:

```
  $r=$conn->query("SELECT COUNT(*) FROM geeklog_stories $where_clause");
  $count=$r->fetch_scalar();
```

The interface between `index-head.php` and `index.php` is a set of variables defined in `index-head.php`, including `$stories` and `$count`, as well as `$older` and `$newer`, two Boolean values that determine if we need links to older and newer headlines. In larger projects, with multiple developers, it's wise to document these interfaces in the template documents (`index.php` in this case).

```
  # These Boolean variables denote the existence of older/newer stories

  $older=(($start+9)<$count);
  $newer=($start>0);

?>
```

Back to index.php

As we said above, `index.php` starts by including the `index-head.php` file just described, and also the application-wide header file, `vxml-header.php`, that we saw earlier.

```
<?php require("index-head.php") ?>
<?php require("vxml-header.php") ?>
```

Following the order of execution, we'll turn our attention to `index-head.php`. The `index-head.php` file loads the database access library, and then obtains a read-only connection to the database. Tapir User Manager has a built-in object-oriented wrapper for MySQL to automate error handling and file locking.

The document that we generate consists of a single form, which contains a single field, `sid`, corresponding to the database identifier of a selected story. Note that the `<vxml>` tag is produced by `vxml-header.php`.

```
  <form
    <field name="sid">
```

By looping through `$stories`, we dynamically generate a grammar that links digits (spoken and dialed) to story IDs. If older or newer stories exist, we also generate corresponding `<option>`s. Note that PHP loops and if statements can contain sections of non-PHP code.

```
      <grammar><![CDATA[ [
        <?php
          for($i=1;$i<=count($stories);$i++) {
            echo "[$i dtmf-$i] {<option \"".$stories[$i-1]->sid."\">}";
          };
        ?>
      <?php if($older) { ?> [older] {<option "older">} <?php } ?>
```

```
            <?php if($newer) { ?> [newer] {<option "newer">} <?php } ?>
            [music songs] {<option "music">}
            ] ]]></grammar>
```

The generated grammar, which is active for the entire time the user is at the index page, looks like this:

```
[
 [1 dtmf-1] {<option"2001051610080367">}
 [2 dtmf-2] {<option"20010514130133707">}
 [3 dtmf-3] {<option "20010514123936213">}
 [4 dtmf-4] {<option "20010510184347253">}
 [5 dtmf-5] {<option "20010510182709750">}
 [6 dtmf-6] {<option "2001050814142020">}
 [7 dtmf-7] {<option "20010507064331228">}
 [8 dtmf-8] {<option "20010507063301573">}
 [9 dtmf-9] {<option "20010507061741777">}
 [older] {<option "older">}
 [music songs] {<option "music">} ]
```

All of the speech in this document is contained in one <prompt> element. First we check if this is the user's first visit to this page during this call. Next, we play a welcome message. We then increment visit_count. This simple interactivity happens entirely on the VoiceXML platform, without PHP needing to become involved.

```
        <prompt>
            <if cond="visit_count==0">
               <audio>Tompkins County Green Party.</audio>
            </if>
            <assign name="visit_count" expr="visit_count+1"/>
```

The VoiceXML platform decides what message to send next, depending on the value of start. When index.php executes for the first time, the variable start is initialized to zero by the application root document, almost as soon as the PHP script sends the document to the voice platform. PHP scriptlets fill in the position and the story count for the audio announcement:

```
            <if cond="start==0">
               <audio>Here are the most recent headlines.</audio>
            <else/>
               <audio>Here are headlines <?php echo $start+1 ?> through <?php echo
 $start+count($stories) ?> of <?php echo $count?>. </audio>
            </if>
```

Next, we loop through $stories to output the headlines, passing them through fix_tts() to improve pronunciation:

```
      <audio>Speak or press the number to hear the summary of a story or say music
 to hear a list of songs</audio>
      <?php for($i=0;$i<count($stories);$i++) { ?>
               <audio><?php echo ($i+1) ?></audio>
               <pause>300</pause>
               <audio><?php echo fix_tts($stories[$i]->title) ?></audio>
            <?php } ?>
```

The output will look something like this:

```
<audio>1</audio>
<pause>300</pause>
<audio>Greens oppose National Missile Defense and militarization of space</audio>
<audio>2</audio>
<pause>300</pause>
<audio>Bush's new Social Security commission</audio>
<audio>3</audio>
<pause>300</pause>
<audio>Shut down Nine Mile Point!</audio>
<audio>4</audio>
<pause>300</pause>
<audio>Volunteers wanted</audio>
<audio>5</audio>
<pause>300</pause>
<audio>TC Greens join Living Wage Coalition</audio>
<audio>6</audio>
<pause>300</pause>
<audio>The battle for Vee Eck Hays</audio>
<audio>7</audio>
<pause>300</pause>
<audio>Bush Administration pursues self-serving and dangerous energy plan</audio>
<audio>8</audio>
<pause>300</pause>
<audio>Bush: the first hundred days</audio>
<audio>9</audio>
<pause>300</pause>
<audio>Why Greens Have No Regrets</audio>
```

Note that at the time of writing, Tellme doesn't support the VoiceXML 1.0 standard <break> element, so we must use the proprietary <pause> element to introduce a delay into spoken text. If older or newer headlines exist, we generate an appropriate message:

```
         <?php if ($older) { ?>
            <audio>say older to hear older headlines</audio>
         <?php } ?>
         <?php if ($older && $newer) { ?>
            <audio>or</audio>
         <?php } ?>
         <?php if ($newer) { ?>
            <audio>say newer to hear more recent headlines</audio>
         <?php } ?>
      </prompt>
```

If the voice platform recognizes a phrase from the grammar, execution passes to the <filled> element. The variable `sid` will contain the value that was specified in the `{<option>}` of the grammar. If it is either `older` or `newer`, we add or subtract nine from `start`, and pass the result to `index.php`. The VoiceXML platform remembers the new value of `start`, so it will persist when `index.php` is executed again; however, we need to put `start` in the `namelist` attribute to make it available to the PHP script. When the <submit> executes, it will generate a URL like this:

```
http://www.tcgreens.org/vxml/index.php?start=9
```

Note that the PHP script doesn't have to check whether the `$older` or `$newer` conditions are valid because `older` or `newer` will only appear in the grammar when older or newer stories actually exist. If `sid` isn't `'older'` or `'newer'`, then it's a story identifier, and we pass it back to the server as:

```
http://www.tcgreens.org/vxml/story.php?sid=20010514123936213
```

```
          <filled>
             <if cond="sid=='older'">
                <assign name="start" expr="'<?php echo $start+9 ?>'"/>
                <submit next="index.php" namelist="start" method="get"/>
             <elseif cond="sid=='newer'"/>
                <assign name="start" expr="'<?php echo $start-9 ?>'"/>
                <submit next="index.php" namelist="start" method="get"/>
             <elseif cond="sid=='music'"/>
                <goto next="music.php"/>
             <else/>
             <else/>
                <submit next="story.php" namelist="sid" method="get"/>
             </if>
          </filled>
       </field>
    </form>
</vxml>
```

story.php

`story.php` reads the details for a particular story, including the title, date, contributor, and introduction. Similar to `index.php`, it includes `code/story-head.php`, which initializes a database connection.

story-head.php

```
<?php
  require "tapir-sql.php";
  require "vxml-common.php";

  $conn=tapir_connect_ro();
  $_sid=addslashes($sid);
```

Although `sid` is supposed to be a number, any HTTP client could pass our application any variable value it wants! This could be a problem if someone deliberately made up a string that would make our database misbehave. For example, in the following query:

```
      $r=$conn->query("SELECT title,introtext,UNIX_TIMESTAMP(date)     AS
date,CONCAT(first_name,' ',last_name) AS name,bodytext FROM
geeklog_stories,tapir_users WHERE sid='$_sid' AND workflow_status>127 AND
tapir_users.user_id=geeklog_stories.uid");
  $story=$r->fetch_object();
```

we could get in trouble if `$_sid` contained a single quote. Potentially, a malicious user could insert unwanted SQL code into the statement that would alter the query. Some databases will even allow multiple queries, separated by semicolons, to be grouped into a single batch, so if we had opened a read-write connection, someone malicious could alter or even entirely erase our database. To head off poison SQL attacks, we pass `$sid` through `addslashes()` which replaces `'` with `\'`.

The query above is a join query between geeklog_stories and tapir_users that takes advantage of the ability of SQL to perform computations in a query by converting a date into a UNIX timestamp given in seconds since midnight, January 1, 2001, and concatenating the author's first and last names to form a full name.

Because Geeklog escapes quotes inside the database (for instance, ' is encoded as \'), and also allows certain HTML tags such as <P> and <B> inside stories (which aren't valid VoiceXML), we next process introtext to eliminate redundant HTML tags and remove gratuitous backslashes. We then format the date in Month, Day, and Year format, as in May 5, 1998. I have tried Tellme's date output subdialog, but I felt that the recorded human voice clashed with the text-to-speech voice used by the rest of the site. Finally, the script computes the word count of the story's body.

```
        $_introtext=stripslashes(strip_tags($story->introtext));
        $_date=date("l F j",$story->date);
        $_name=$story->name;
        if(strlen($story->bodytext)>0) {
              $_words=sizeof(explode(" ",$story->bodytext));
        } else
              $_words=0;

   ?>
```

Back to story.php

Also similar to index.php, story.php contains just one form, one field, and one grammar.

```
   <?php require("story-head.php") ?>
   <?php require("vxml-header.php") ?>
      <form id="main">
         <field name="input" timeout="2">
            <grammar><![CDATA[ [
               [stop dtmf-0] {<option "stop">}
            ] ]]></grammar>
```

story.php simply substitutes in the variables defined in story-head.php, and passes them through the fix_tts() function:

```
            <prompt>
               <audio>Say stop to return to the headline list</audio>
               <audio><?php echo fix_tts($story->title) ?></audio>
               <audio><?php echo $_date ?></audio>
               <audio>Contributed by <?php echo fix_tts($_name) ?></audio>
               <audio><?php echo fix_tts($_introtext) ?></audio>
```

If the word count of the body isn't zero (some stories don't have a body), we refer people to the web site, which, naturally, requires special spelling:

```
               <?php if ($_words>0) { ?>
                  <audio>For the complete story, an additional <?php echo $_words ?>
   words visit our web site at w w w dot t c greens dot org</audio>
               <?php } ?>
            </prompt>
```

If the user says "stop" or if the dialog times out, we go back to the index, passing the application-scope variable `start` back to the server, so it can remember the user's position in the index.

```
            <noinput>
               <submit next="index.php" namelist="start" method="get"/>
            </noinput>
            <filled>
               <submit next="index.php" namelist="start" method="get"/>
            </filled>
         </field>
      </form>
   </vxml>
```

Delivering Audio to the Telephone

Streaming audio and video are exciting areas for growth on the Web. Improvements in players, encoders, and server software are making multimedia content more appealing than ever. Because audio content can be easily repurposed for the telephone, VoiceXML offers a special opportunity to expand the audience of audio-based sites.

The most important task in converting web audio for the telephone is **transcoding**; converting audio from the archival format used on the site into something that VoiceXML platforms can play. The VoiceXML specification doesn't require that platforms support any particular audio formats, however, it suggests that VoiceXML platforms support raw audio data without headers and `.wav` format files with an 8 kHz sample rate and 8-bit mu-law encoded data. This format has a long history, as it has been used for digital transmission of telephone calls since the 1970s – with a bandwidth requirement of 56 Kbit/sec, this much data can't be streamed down a dialup connection, but can be easily streamed from most web servers to a voice platform. This format is appealing because it provides a lossless path from the web server, through the long distance network, until the call hits the customer's copper loop for landline phones, or the wireless network for cell phones.

Another digital format exists that has a special relationship to the wireless network. Worldwide, the dominant cell system is GSM, which encodes audio at 2.4 kbit/sec using code-excited linear prediction (CELP.) Although current VoiceXML platforms don't support GSM encoding for audio, GSM carries audible signals at very low bandwidth and would be the format of choice for possible VoiceXML interpreters running on advanced cellular phones.

For the web and other multimedia platforms, we need to distinguish between archival and distribution formats. Real Audio and Windows Media are good for transmitting audio to clients, but, being proprietary, lossy, and often granulated coarsely in time, they're not good for archiving, editing or storage. Uncompressed formats, such as `.wav` are suitable for archival purposes. However, uncompressed files are unreasonably large to transmit over a network and unwieldy to handle even on a hard disk. Two forms of lossy compression are in common use. Transform encoding, which breaks up an audio signal into its component frequencies and uses a psychoacoustic model to remove frequencies that are inaudible or (relatively) unimportant is used by MP3 and proprietary systems at bit rates greater than about 16 kbps. CELP-related encoders, on the other hand, are used by proprietary systems at lower bitrates (less than 7 kbps), and are particularly useful for encoding soundtracks to videos aimed at dialup users.

When we started publishing audio on tcgreens.org, we decided to publish audio in both Real Audio and Windows Media formats, thinking that this would be the best way to reach a large audience. Recent developments, however, have convinced us that MP3 is now the leading technology for web audio. MP3 good enough for archiving, and although close listening can reveal artifacts in music files encoded at 128kbps, most listeners wouldn't notice the difference making it great for commercial applications. Newer encoders (such as LAME, available from http://www.sulaco.org/mp3/) are able to encode tolerable voice and music in the range of 16-24 kbps. MP3 can be used for download and a pseudo-streaming mode, where we download into a buffer, and start play as soon as we have enough data to play a file without interruptions. It is also suitable for live streaming broadcasts with software like Shoutcast (http://www.shoutcast.com/) and Icecast (http://www.icecast.com/). In addition, it's possible to use open source tools for everything from encoding to playback, and MP3 is supported by all the major commercial media players, making MP3 available to the majority of web users without a need to download further software.

Although the VoiceXML platforms are all promising to support more audio formats, uncompressed data at 8000 Hz in mu-law format with a `.wav` header is the most widely accepted format at this time. Uncompressed telephone audio is lossless and consumes 56 kbps of bandwidth at the server, or about 20 simultaneous streams over a T-1 connection. There's little motivation to use formats that consume more bandwidth – the only motivation, other than sheer convenience, for using a different format would be to reduce bandwidth demand on the server. Because tcgreens.org uses MP3 as an archival format, our strategy for publishing audio on the phone is to convert MP3 files to 8000 Hz/mu-law `.wav` files with a shell script, `phone-convert`, with the help of the tools mpg123 (http://www.mpg123.de/) and sox:

```
#!/bin/sh

mpg123 -r 44100 -m -s $1.mp3 | sox -r 44100 -t .raw -w -s - -r 8000 -b -U $1-
phone.wav
```

After compiling `phone-convert` and installing it in your PATH, converting MP3 files to phone audio files is simple. To convert `Countdown.mp3` to `Countdown-phone.wav`, for instance, type:

```
$ phone-convert Countdown
```

User interface

So now we can have a look at the VoiceXML form that provides the interface to our streaming media. Unlike for the headline form, here we shall put the `<audio>` for the choices in the same file as the index: one form, but four fields:

```
<vxml>
  <form>
    <field name="main">
      <grammar>
      <![CDATA[
        [
        [dtmf-1 1] {<option "1">}
        [dtmf-2 2] {<option "2">}
        [dtmf-3 3] {<option "3">}
        [headlines] {<option "headlines">}
        ]
      ]]>
      </grammar>
      <prompt>
```

```
        <audio>Speak or say the number to hear a song, or say headlines
          to return to the index</audio>
        <pause>400</pause>
        <audio>1 Playing with our Toys, by Sheryl and Ashleigh Udoh</audio>
        <pause>400</pause>
        <audio>2 No Respect for the Process, with Hal Wilner and Jim
          Hightower</audio>
        <pause>400</pause>
        <audio>3 The Countdown, featuring Adam Horowitz and Ralph Nader</audio>
      </prompt>
      <filled>
        <if cond="main=='headlines'">
          <goto next="index.php"/>
        <else/>
          <goto expritem="'song'+main"/>
        </if>
      </filled>
    </field>
```

The field for a single song is:

```
    <field name="song1">
      <grammar><![CDATA[ [
       [stop dtmf-0] {<option "stop">}
      ] ]]></grammar>
      <prompt>
        <audio>Say stop to return to the list of songs</audio>
        <audio src="media/Countdown-phone.wav"/>
      </prompt>
      <noinput>
        <goto expritem="'main'"/>
      </noinput>
      <filled>
        <goto expritem="'main'"/>
      </filled>
    </field>
```

Three behaviors are defined for how a VoiceXML platform loads audio: these can be specified in the `fetchhint` attribute of `<audio>`, as well as with the `<property>` element. These are `prefetch`, which loads the audio clip when the document loads, `safe`, which loads the audio clip just before it is played, and `stream`, which plays the audio immediately, requiring the platform be able to download it fast enough from the server. Support for these options is platform-dependent, and it's necessary to specify that you want streaming behavior from BeVocal, whereas Tellme seems to stream large audio files by default.

To continue with the fields for the remaining songs:

```
    <field name="song2">
      <grammar><![CDATA[ [
           [stop dtmf-0] {<option "stop">}
         ] ]]></grammar>
      <prompt>
        <audio>Say stop to return to the list of songs</audio>
        <audio src="media/NoRespectfortheProcess-phone.wav"/>
      </prompt>
```

```
        <noinput>
          <goto expritem="'main'"/>
        </noinput>
        <filled>
          <goto expritem="'main'"/>
        </filled>
      </field>
      <field name="song3">
        <grammar><![CDATA[ [
          [stop dtmf-0] {<option "stop">}
        ] ]]></grammar>
        <prompt>
          <audio>Say stop to return to the list of songs</audio>
          <audio src="media/whatside-phone.wav"/>
        </prompt>
        <noinput>
          <goto expritem="'main'"/>
        </noinput>
        <filled>
          <goto expritem="'main'"/>
        </filled>
      </field>
    </form>
  </vxml>
```

Summary

In this chapter we've had the chance to discuss the architecture of database-backed sites, and addressed some of the issues involved in making both database and audio content available on the telephone via VoiceXML. In addition to developing an application for reading news stories from tcgreens.org and for playing audio files, we have discussed workarounds for the limitations of text-to-speech conversion, and how to produce content that works well on both web and phone.

As VoiceXML is such a new technology, we've only had time to scratch the surface. The next phase of integrating such sites with VoiceXML would be to introduce more sophisticated interactivity, principally by letting users make changes in a database rather than just being able to listen to information. A system for user authentication and registration would be essential: certainly it would be possible for users to log in with a numeric identifier and PIN, but it could be possible to use voice recognition to single out a user by asking a series of questions such as name, zip code, etc., and verify their identity by voice-print recognition rather than password. Nuance's software supports this, and BeVocal supplies an interface. Rather than using cookies, unavailable on most current platforms, application-scope variables can be used to track session identifiers.

Adding information to a database poses its own challenges. Compared to a mouse and keyboard, the telephone keypad and voice recognition grammars are a limited means of input. Because error rates would be high, it would be essential to verify all user inputs. Fortunately, we can learn from the large base of existing interactive voice response (IVR) systems that are already in use.

This chapter has concerned itself with the task of adding VoiceXML functionality to existing sites, be they informational sites like tcgreens.org, or sites that are primarily business applications. The same web and database technology can be applied to creating a generation of applications specific to VoiceXML, that make heavy use of audio recording and playback – the potential of interactive sites that use VoiceXML in this way is very exciting, and many are sure to emerge as the technology matures.

```
<?xml version="1.0"?>
<vxml version="1.0">
<form id="foo">
<block>
<prompt>
Hi. My name is Bob
</prompt>
</block>
</form>
</vxml>
```

9

Dynamic VoiceXML with ASP

In this chapter, we will look at how VoiceXML can be used to extend existing enterprise applications by voice-enabling Microsoft's Outlook, including the address book and calendar functions. The application will allow a user to call in to check e-mails and appointments, forward, compose, or reply to e-mails, and schedule new appointments, all from a regular phone. I'll also talk about how to implement an outbound-call service to notify you when you have a new e-mail. Some general VoiceXML design principles will be implemented that are applicable to many other applications you may devise, although I believe you'll find this example to be worthwhile in itself.

In addressing the problem of voice-enabling Outlook, I have followed the strategy outlined by George Polya in his book *How to Solve It*. Fans of Polya may recognize the headings I've used as reflecting this approach.

Understanding the Problem

Employee access to corporate information systems, including e-mail, scheduling, and calendaring, when out of the office is a prospect that offers many advantages: a host of roles can benefit enormously from easy access to key corporate information anywhere and at any time. The majority of solutions that have become available to fulfill this demand center on devices with wireless Internet access, such as wireless Palm devices and web phones. However, there are so many different types of devices, with different features offered by their tiny screens and keypads, developers have their work cut out trying to cater for each type of device. For users, it'll never be easy to enter characters using miniscule keypads, not even mentioning those situations where it's just not possible for people to type, like while driving or walking.

Enter voice, the natural way to communicate. Voice provides a more convenient way to access and manage information for people on the move than cute little gadgets. Of course, there are environments and situations where talking out loud will not be appropriate, and other types of mobile access may be preferred, but in general, voice access will be the superior choice.

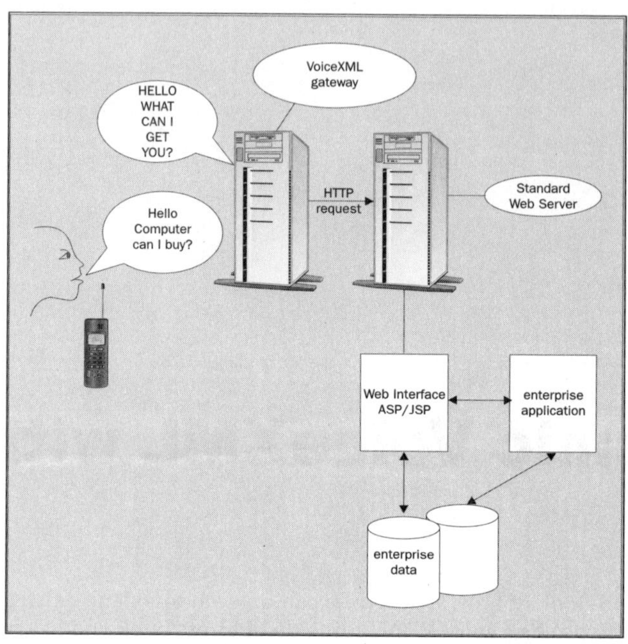

IVR (Interactive Voice Response) applications have been around for a long time, providing services such as bank or credit card information over any standard phone. But traditional IVR solutions typically use only one-way voice communication – from the application to the user, whose interaction with the system is limited to touch-tone key presses or a small selection of 'hot words'. Imagine having to grapple with such an interface when trying to find an e-mail from a particular colleague. Also, IVR applications generally require users to work their way through a long sequence of menus to achieve something that would be simple using voice commands directly.

Simple IVR of this type is far from dead, despite the hype coming from companies pushing ASR (Automatic Speech Recognition) and their own VoiceXML platforms. IVR still provides an economical way to handle many problems. A commercial ASR engine can cost $1,000 or more per line, and even if you use a hosting service to deploy your application, each minute can cost $0.15 or more. For simpler tasks where user interaction doesn't require complicated commands, IVR still offers a very cost-effective approach. But for those applications requiring more sophisticated interactivity, ASR and VoiceXML may provide the answers.

Now we've discussed some of the background to voice applications, we can move on to look at corporate information systems, using Microsoft Exchange/Outlook as a focus, and what voice-enabling Outlook will involve.

Corporate Information Systems

There is a plethora of corporate information solutions on the market today, from CRM (Customer Relationship Management) systems to Order Management systems. But just about every business needs some type of e-mail and calendar software to facilitate people working together – so-called groupware applications. Microsoft Exchange/Outlook and Lotus Domino/Notes dominate the groupware market, with about 70% of market share between them. That's probably why wireless-enabling Outlook or Notes has been one of the first things that wireless solution providers have aimed to do.

Both Outlook and Notes offer extensive, and similar, features for sharing and managing corporate and personal information. For example, Outlook has many standard folders – Inbox, Outbox, Calendar, Contacts, Tasks, and Notes, to which your own can easily be added. In a corporate environment, by default, all the information in both standard folders and custom folders for a user are stored in a 'profile' saved on the Exchange server.

Our problem requires programmatic control over Outlook. Not surprisingly, the means to do this is almost the same as for any other of the modern software applications from Microsoft: we use COM (Component Object Model). COM is the standard way for Microsoft applications to communicate with each other. Outlook itself has more than one object model so that user applications in Visual C++, Visual Basic, or VBScript can control it. So what will be the use cases for our voice-enabled Outlook application? Once these are determined, we can examine these Outlook object models and find out which one is the best for our application.

Voice-enabling Outlook

When users call up our future voice-enabled Outlook service, what should they expect? Let's summarize the use cases we'll handle now:

- Read out new e-mails one by one
- Read out e-mails filtered by sender or level of importance
- Forward or reply to a received e-mail
- Compose a new e-mail to someone in the address book
- Check for appointments at specified dates and read them out
- Schedule new appointments
- Notify the user by phone when new e-mails that meet specific conditions arrive

So our application will let us call in and say something like "check new e-mails from Amanda", "check all the important e-mails", "send an e-mail to Amanda", "check my appointments for next week", "schedule a new appointment on May 30, 2001 from 10:30 am to 12 noon", and so on. New messages will be recorded and sent as an attachment when replying, forwarding, or composing e-mails. We'll also allow the user to spell out words to enter a brief subject and descriptive text when scheduling new appointments.

Devising a Plan

The pretty sophisticated goals we've outlined now require a plan so we can set about achieving them.

Generating Dynamic VoiceXML Using ASP

We could choose to use other web server technologies such as Java Server Pages (JSP) and Java Servlets, but as we're voice-enabling Microsoft Outlook, it makes sense to use Microsoft Internet Information Server (IIS) and Active Server Page (ASP). For those of you who really want to use Java technologies with Outlook, there's good news and bad news. The good news is that yes, you can do that. The bad news is that you're still going to have to understand the object model of Outlook and know how to perform COM client programming in Java. A good book I can recommend for this is *Inside Distributed COM* by Guy Eddon and Henry Eddon, published by Microsoft Press. If, however, you want to use JSP or servlets with another e-mail system such as Yahoo Internet e-mail, you are able to sidestep COM by simply using the JavaMail API, available for download from http://java.sun.com/products/javamail.

While developing our dynamic VoiceXML ASP application, a priority is to minimize round trips to the web server. In other words, we want to invoke a new ASP only when we need to run some server-side script code to get new information or handle new data such as uploading a recorded message. This means we will use client-side scripting (that is, script executed by the voice interpreter) within `<script>` elements to save and process information obtained by the ASP. Doing this will allow us to use client-side script to quickly access any further information when requested by the user. The standard script language in VoiceXML is ECMAScript, a standardized form of JavaScript, and so we embed ECMAScript code in our ASP applications to send to the voice interpreter.

In general, it's pretty easy to repurpose your existing knowledge of ASP applications for creating VoiceXML-based services, although clearly you will need to familiarize yourself with the VoiceXML language. This chapter contains plenty of practical, working code that illustrates the power of the VoiceXML language and by the end you should be in a position to extend our Outlook voice service or create new VoiceXML applications using ASP should you need to.

Programming Outlook

Microsoft offers a variety of messaging technologies for developers to use with Outlook, such as Simple MAPI (Messaging API), Extended MAPI, MAPI ActiveX Controls, the Outlook Object Model, and Collaboration Data Objects (CDO). Each technology is suitable for different types of applications. Because we will be generating VoiceXML dynamically with ASP, and as VBScript is the standard scripting language for ASP, an object model is most appropriate. Anyone familiar with ASP and VBScript knows how easy it is to draw on functionality published by an automation server or object model.

The two main object models from Microsoft – the Outlook Object Model and CDO – both provide an automation wrapper for MAPI. For client applications, there may not be a clear choice. But for an application designed to be run as a server application, like our ASP application that will run under IIS, the Outlook Object Model is not appropriate. For those interested, the detailed reasons for this are covered in a Microsoft article available at
http://support.microsoft.com/support/kb/articles/Q237/9/13.asp.

So we are left with one single object model for our ASP applications: CDO. CDO contains 23 classes, among them are `Session`, `Folders`, `Folder`, `Messages`, `MessageFilter`, `Message`, `Attachments`, `AddressLists`, and `AddressEntry`. For detailed information on these, either look at the CDO object model references online at http://msdn.microsoft.com, or buy one of the many books available, such as Wrox's *Professional Outlook 2000 Programming, Outlook 2000 VBA Programmer's Reference*, or *Professional ADSI CDO Programming with ASP*. In the remainder of the chapter, you'll see how easy it is to use CDO in ASP. Now, we're almost ready to start writing some dynamic VoiceXML code.

Setting up the Development Environment

Below are listed the system requirements for the voice-enabled Outlook application:

- Microsoft Windows NT 4 Workstation/Server or Windows 2000
- Microsoft Outlook 2000 client software – you can use it either in the corporate environment with Microsoft Exchange or at home without Exchange
- Access to a VoiceXML hosting platform. BeVocal was used for this chapter
- Microsoft web server IIS 4.0 or above that runs on the same machine as your Outlook client
- Access to your Outlook and IIS machine from the Internet outside
- JDK 1.2 and JavaServer Web Development Kit (JSWDK) 1.0. The reason for this is that I am using a JSP-based application to upload recorded messages

Even if you're not using such a system, by following the source code in the chapter you can still walk through the development process and gain a taste of VoiceXML development.

Outlook 2000

To use CDO, you need to have the runtime DLL `cdo.dll` on your system. Normally it's located in `C:\program files\Common Files\System\Mapi\1033\NT`. If it's not there and you can't find it anywhere on your machine with Search | For Files or Folders, it means that CDO is not installed yet. To install it, all you need do is launch Outlook 2000 setup, and check the CDO box.

If you use Outlook at work, your Outlook client probably talks to Exchange Server without you even realizing it. If Outlook is set up to connect to Microsoft Exchange, which is most likely, then you don't need to change any settings on your Outlook for the sample application. If your system is not set up for Exchange, then some instructions to help you configure it correctly can be found in the `readme.txt` file in this chapter's download. You will also need to ensure IIS is installed on your machine and that your mail server can be visited from the Internet.

IIS and ASP

ASP is included in IIS 3.0 or above. You don't need to change any settings after you install IIS 4.0 on NT 4 or IIS 5.0 on Windows 2000. The following lines can be placed in an ASP file (don't forget to insert the profile name your Outlook uses when starting; find it from Control Panel | Mail | Show Profiles...) to test your setup:

```
<%
set Session("objsession") = Server.CreateObject("MAPI.Session")

rem there are two ways to test CDO with IIS/ASP - both use the CDO Logon method.
rem On NT 4, either method will work fine; on Win2K, only the 2nd method works.

rem first, use a profile name with the Logon method
Session("objsession").Logon("your default profile")

rem if the above line doesn't work, comment it and uncomment the following:
rem Session("objsession").Logon "", "", False, True, 0, True,
rem "exchangeServerName" & vbLF & "exchangeE-MailName"
%>
```

If this runs without error, then great, your system is correctly configured for running ASP/CDO applications. If however, it doesn't work as it should, choose View Source in your browser, and if the above lines have generated the error Collaboration Data Objects – [MAPI_E_LOGON_FAILED (80040111)], then it indicates you're dealing with a tricky beast: IIS authentication failure. To resolve this issue, you have to set the Anonymous User on IIS to your Outlook machine's logon name. For example, if you use the user name Administrator to log on to your NT/Outlook/IIS machine, then open the IIS Internet Service Manager. Go to Default Web Site Properties | Directory Security | Anonymous Access and Authentication Control | Edit. In the Authentication Methods dialog box, the Allow Anonymous Access option should be enabled. Click on the Edit button beside it, change the Anonymous Username to the built-in Guest account of your login domain – or if you use Outlook at home and don't have a domain, you'll have to use your logon name. Now when you run the above ASP code, you shouldn't see any error messages.

VoiceXML Platform

Currently at least five voice startups provide VoiceXML platforms that allow developers to freely register and test VoiceXML applications: BeVocal, VoiceGenie, Voxeo, Tellme, and HeyAnita. Some, but not all, also provide a hosting service for commercially deploying your applications. Some other big players such as IBM and Motorola also offer VoiceXML tools and platforms for developers to use. Personally, I favor BeVocal, although any reasonably compliant platform should suffice equally well. See Chapter 2 for an in-depth comparison of the major platforms, along with setup instructions.

JSP

I've not found ASP-based code to be well suited to uploading recorded messages, so I have used JSP code for this part of the application. Setting up a test Java web server is not too difficult and the effort required is worthwhile in the long run. I use Sun's JavaServer, although there are alternatives around that you could use. There are a few guidelines to help you set up JavaServer in the `readme.txt` file found in the download for this chapter. Once this is done, we're finally ready to begin looking at the code for our short case study.

Carrying Out the Plan

All the code in this section has been tested and works well on the BeVocal platform. However, I haven't used any BeVocal-specific features, although sometimes there are benefits to be had by making use of such extras for a given platform. All the code here is VoiceXML 1.0 compliant, except the use of the `<log>` element, which is likely to be included in VoiceXML 2.0. BeVocal uses `<log>` to generate debug messages to view later in the Log Browser. VoiceXML 1.0 doesn't specify a particular grammar format, so I have chosen the Nuance Grammar Specification Language (GSL) as it is the most widely supported format across current VoiceXML platforms.

In the code, you'll see references to http://www.openland.com, which is my own test server. After you have set up your own server, replace www.openland.com with your own URL, and place all the ASP files in an IIS virtual directory called `wrox`.

Getting Started

First, we create a root document that will be included in all other VoiceXML documents with the application attribute of the <vxml> element. In the root document, typically named root.vxml, we put global settings and global event handlers. In the file root.vxml below, we specify the maintainer's e-mail address and the application name. You could choose to put these and other <meta> settings in every VoiceXML document in the application. Also, we have a global property setting for fetchaudio that specifies the URI of an audio file to play while waiting for a document to be fetched with <goto>, <submit>, or <subdialog>. VoiceXML 1.0 defines many possible <property> settings. As they're platform-related, you need to check with your VoiceXML platform's documentation to see which are supported and to what extent. Finally we have a global handler for the telephone hang up event: whenever you hang up the phone, a cleanup ASP will be called, which simply calls the CDO Session.Logoff method.

Note that you may want to put convenient global variables in root.vxml and have one VoiceXML document communicate with a called <subdialog> via such global variables. However, you may be surprised by the behavior when documents A and B both use global variables declared in a root document. For instance, let's say that some of these variables declared in root.vxml are assigned in document A, and A then calls document B using <subdialog>. In B, we will find that the values just assigned to those root-level variables are missing! This is in fact a direct result of following the VoiceXML 1.0 specification, which states that when a <subdialog> is invoked, all variables and state information for the calling dialog, including the application root document if present, must be reinitialized. The correct way to pass variables to <subdialog> is in fact with parameters, as shown later. If you really need global variables, the right place to set them is not in the common root document, but in the starting VoiceXML page that contains the main application loop.

So, as you see, our root.vxml document doesn't declare any variables:

```
<?xml version="1.0"?>

<vxml version="1.0">
  <meta name="maintainer" content="jtang@openland.com" />
  <meta name="application" content="email and calendar" />

  <property name="fetchaudio" value="http://www.openland.com/wrox/waiting.wav"/>

  <catch event="telephone.disconnect.hangup">
    <log> Entering catch event hangup </log>
    <goto next="http://www.openland.com/wrox/end.asp"/>
    <log> Exiting catch event hangup </log>
  </catch>
</vxml>
```

Shown below is end.asp, containing the simple code for logging out of Outlook. We use a session variable objsession to store the CDO session created during startup. That way, we can refer to it from any ASP file in our application.

```
<?xml version="1.0"?>

<%Session("objsession").Logoff%>
```

```
<vxml version="1.0">
  <form>
    <block>
      <log> Inside end.asp </log>
    </block>
  </form>
</vxml>
```

The overall hierarchy of the ASPs that make up this application is shown in the figure below:

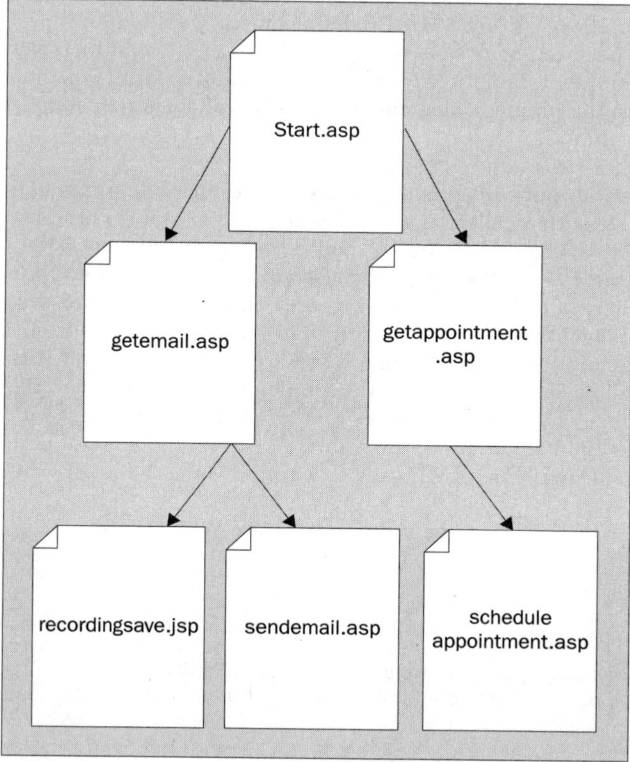

Now we come to the initial document for the application, `start.asp`. This is where any global variables, were any to be used, would be placed. The full URL for this start page – here I am using http://www.openland.com/wrox/start.asp – should be specified as the active URL in the Remote URL Based Application Development box in your BeVocal café environment.

What actually happens after you call in to start this application is that the ASP server code below initiates a CDO session by calling `Server.CreateObject("MAPI.Session")`. Then we call the CDO session's `Logon` method with our Outlook profile name. After this initialization, the first VoiceXML form is entered which asks whether the user wishes to check e-mail or their calendar.

```
<?xml version="1.0"?>

<%
set Session("objsession") = Server.CreateObject("MAPI.Session")
```

```
Session("objsession").Logon("Jeff Tang")
%>

<vxml version="1.0" application="root.vxml">

<form id="start">
  <field name="service">
    <grammar>
    <![CDATA[
    [
      (?check ?my [email messages]) {<service email>}
      (?check ?my [calendar appointments diary schedule]) {<service calendar>}
    ]
    ]]>
    </grammar>
      <prompt>
        Welcome to Jeff's Voice Email. Which service do you require?
      </prompt>
    <help>
      You can check your email or calendar.
    </help>
    <filled>
      <if cond="service == 'email'">
        <goto next="#email"/>
      <else/> <!-- service is calendar -->
        <goto next="#calendar"/>
      </if>
    </filled>
  </field>
</form>
```

The VoiceXML embedded in this ASP consists of the <form> named `start` with a single <field> called `service`. The VoiceXML interpreter enters this field and won't exit it until it has obtained a suitable value for the variable, according to the specified grammar. Here, we are using an inline grammar, declared at the start of the <field> element. Next, we tell the interpreter the message we want the caller to be greeted with, plus a message to replay for user utterances in the standard help grammar. When the field has been filled, we can transfer control to the appropriate form according to the value of `service`. These forms come next, still in `start.asp`. The `email` form is shown below, asking whether to check all the e-mails or just new e-mails. At this point, you can still change your mind and check your calendar instead.

```
<form id="email">
  <field name="emailtype">
    <grammar>
    <![CDATA[
    [
      (?only new [emails email]) {<emailtype newemail>}
      (all ?the [email emails]) {<emailtype allemail>}
      calendar {<emailtype calendar>}
    ]
    ]]>
    </grammar>
      <prompt>
        Do you want to check only new emails or all the emails?
```

```
      </prompt>
    <help>
      You can say new emails or all emails.
    </help>
    <filled>
      <if cond="emailtype == 'calendar'">
        <goto next="#calendar"/>
      </if>
    </filled>
  </field>
```

The only way out at this stage is when the user selects calendar, otherwise we remain in the form, entering the next <field> element shown below. Here the user may select a filter to select "important" e-mails, or e-mail from a particular person in their address book. Incidentally, a good way to play around with all those CDO objects and methods is to use Visual Basic. After you've got the CDO code to do what you want with Visual Basic, you can easily copy it over to the VBScript in an ASP.

Note that we need `lcase(addentry.name)` in the for-loop of the <grammar> element. This is because in GSL, all the grammar word names (**slot names**) have to be in lowercase. If you don't convert with a function like VBScript's `lcase()`, you'll get run time errors in the VoiceXML application. The `For Each`-loop itself runs through all the entries in your Outlook Address Book, and creates a GSL grammar line for each entry. For example, if you have the entry John Doe in your address book, the following GSL output will be generated: `(?email from john doe) {<emailfilter "john doe">}`.

We also add the two slot names `none` and `toplevel` to give the option of not specifying any filters and going back to the top-level form.

```
  <field name="emailfilter">
    <grammar>
        <![CDATA[
    [
      (important ?[email emails]) {<emailfilter important>}
      [no (all ?the ?new [email emails])] {<emailfilter none>}
      [main home (top level)] {<emailfilter toplevel>}
      <%
      For Each addentry In Session("objSession").AddressLists.Item(1)
       .AddressEntries
        response.write("(?email from " & lcase(addentry.name)  & ")
         {<emailfilter """ & addentry.name & """>}")
      Next
      %>
    ]
    ]]>
    </grammar>
      <prompt>
        Do you want to only check important emails or emails from someone?
    </prompt>
    <help>
      You can say important emails or email from someone in your address book.
    </help>
    <filled>
      <if cond="emailfilter == 'toplevel'">
        <goto next="#start"/>
      </if>
```

```
      Please wait while I get your email information.
    </filled>
  </field>
```

So after this filtering query is finished, we're ready to get our Outlook e-mails by a new round trip to the Exchange server. New VoiceXML developers who haven't realized the power and neatness of the <subdialog> element who are used to traditional web development, might think of using <goto> or <submit> immediately. However, the unique beauty of <subdialog> is that, just like a function call, it allows control to be returned to the calling code. The function is one of those things that you don't realize the usefulness of – until you start to deal with a language that doesn't support them. <subdialog> provides the navigation functionality, which otherwise would have to come from <goto> or <submit>, with the consequent loss of control over the current document.

So, the following <subdialog> call allows us to save our current context, and transfer control to the external ASP as specified in the src attribute. After a <return> is met in the VoiceXML document generated by this ASP, control is returned to start.asp and execution continues at <filled> in the <subdialog> – in this case, a <clear> call resets all field variables in the form to undefined, thus causing execution of the current form to repeat when the form's closing tag is encountered.

```
    <subdialog name="getemail" method="get" namelist="emailtype emailfilter"
     src="http://www.openland.com/wrox/getemail.asp">
      <filled>
        <clear/>
      </filled>
    </subdialog>

  </form>
```

The last and longest of the three VoiceXML forms in start.asp begins with the primary <field> named caltype that determines whether the user wishes to check appointments for a specific day, week, or month. Also, as shortcuts, the user can view appointments for today, yesterday, and tomorrow, or for this week, last week, or next week. Then come three further fields, each using the cond attribute. This attribute lets us apply a test before entering a particular field. Lastly, we use a similar <subdialog> to pass the collected information to another ASP file.

```
  <form id="calendar">
    <var name="caltime" expr="'default'"/>

    <field name="caltype">
      <grammar>
      <![CDATA[
      [
        (?[on a specific] day) {<caltype day>}
        (?[on a specific] week) {<caltype week>}
        (?[on a specific] month) {<caltype month>}

        today {<caltype today>}
        yesterday {<caltype yesterday>}
        tomorrow {<caltype tomorrow>}

        (this week) {<caltype thisweek>}
        (last week) {<caltype lastweek>}
        (next week) {<caltype nextweek>}
```

```
        (top level) {<caltype toplevel>}
      ]
      ]]>
      </grammar>

      <prompt>
        How do you want to check your appointments?
      </prompt>
      <help>
        You can say a specific day, week, month, or today, yesterday, tomorrow,
        or this week, last week, or next week.
      </help>

      <filled>
        <if cond="caltype == 'toplevel'">
          <goto next="#start"/>
        </if>
      </filled>
    </field>


    <field name="calday" type="date" cond="caltype == 'day'">
      <prompt>
        For which day do you want to check the appointments?
      </prompt>
      <help>
        Please say month, day, and year.
      </help>
      <filled>
        <assign name="caltime" expr="calday"/>
      </filled>
    </field>

    <field name="calweek" type="date" cond="caltype == 'week'">
      <prompt>
        For which week do you want to check the appointments? Please give the
         date of that Monday.
      </prompt>
      <help>
        Please say any date of some day of the week.
      </help>
      <filled>
        <assign name="caltime" expr="calweek"/>
      </filled>
    </field>

    <field name="calmonth" cond="caltype == 'month'">
      <grammar>
      [january february march april may june july august september October
       november december]
      </grammar>
      <prompt>
        For which month do you want to check appointments?
      </prompt>
      <filled>
        <assign name="caltime" expr="calmonth"/>
```

```
      </filled>
    </field>

    <subdialog name="getappnt" method="get" namelist="caltype caltime"
src="http://www.openland.com/wrox/getappointment.asp">
      <filled>
        <clear/>
      </filled>
    </subdialog>

  </form>

</vxml>
```

Retrieving E-Mail

The next ASP file, getemail.asp, contains server-side VBScript code and CDO to get hold of the requested messages.

```
<?xml version="1.0"?>

<vxml version="1.0" application="root.vxml">

  <var name="docEmailNum" expr="1"/>
  <var name="docEmailCount"/>
  <var name="docEmailMsgs"/>

  <form id="start">
    <block>
      <prompt>
<%
  set objInbox = Session("objsession").Inbox
  If objInbox Is Nothing Then
    Response.Write("You have no emails in your inbox")
  else
    set objMsgs = objInbox.Messages
    if Request.QueryString("emailtype") = "newemail" then
      objMsgs.Filter.Unread = True
    end if
    if Request.QueryString("emailfilter") = "important" then
      objMsgs.Filter.Importance = 2
    elseif not Request.QueryString("emailfilter") = "none" then
      objMsgs.Filter.Sender = Request.QueryString("emailfilter")
    end if
    response.write("You have " & objMsgs.Count & " emails that match your
     request.")
  end if
  %>
      </prompt>
```

In the following code, we save the messages' From, Subject, TimeReceived, and Text properties to a JavaScript array, along with each e-mail's unique ID to use later when forwarding or replying to an e-mail. The use of VoiceXML client-side JavaScript saves round trip calls to the server. An alternative to using JavaScript would be to simply pass a list of e-mail IDs and when you want to get detailed information on an e-mail, call a server ASP.

A `Replace()` function call gets rid of any illegal characters in a message's subject or body. Also for simplicity, we use the VB function `Left()` to read only the first 200 characters of each e-mail message.

```
<script>
  docEmailCount = <%=objMsgs.Count%>;
  docEmailMsgs = new Array();
  <%  for i=1 to objMsgs.Count
    set objMsg = objMsgs.Item(i)
  %>
    var msg = new Object();
    msg["ID"] = "<%=objMsg.ID%>";
    msg["From"] = "<%=objMsg.Sender%>";
    msg["Subject"] = "<%=Replace(objMsg.Subject, "&", " ")%>"
    msg["TimeReceived"] = "<%=objMsg.TimeReceived%>";
    msg["Text"] = "<%=Replace(Replace(Replace(Left(objMsg.Text, 200),
     vbNewLine, " "), "<", ""), ">", "")%>";

    docEmailMsgs[<%=i%>] = msg;
  <% next%>
</script>

    <if cond="docEmailCount == 0">
      <return/>
    </if>
  </block>

  <field name="action">
    <grammar>
     <![CDATA[
    [
      ([list read] ?them) {<action read>}
      [nothing quit] {<action quit>}
      (check ?other ?[email emails]) {<action check>}
    ]
    ]]>
    </grammar>

    <prompt>
      What do you want to do with those emails?
    </prompt>

  <filled>
    <if cond="action == 'quit'">
      <prompt>
        Thank you for using our service. Good bye.
      </prompt>
      <disconnect/>
    <elseif cond="action == 'check'"/>
      <return/>
    <!--if user says "read", nothing will happen in the <filled> here. But
        in the next <field>, the email content is read as a prompt -->
    </if>
  </filled>
</field>
```

Because we have saved all the e-mail information in a form-level variable, we can use it within the next field to playback the currently selected e-mail, and allow the user to browse the e-mail list by the keywords "previous", "next", "first", and "last".

```
    <field name="nextaction">
      <grammar>
      [previous next first last reply forward compose toplevel check quit]
      </grammar>

      <prompt>
        email number <value expr="docEmailNum"/>.
        From <value expr="docEmailMsgs[docEmailNum][&quot;From&quot;]"/>,
        Subject is <value expr="docEmailMsgs[docEmailNum][&quot;Subject&quot;]"/>,
          Received time is <value expr="docEmailMsgs[docEmailNum]
           [&quot;TimeReceived&quot;]"/>,
          Content is <value expr="docEmailMsgs[docEmailNum][&quot;Text&quot;]"/>.
        What do you want to do next?
      </prompt>
      <help>
        You can say previous, next, first or last to listen to another email.
        Or say reply, forward, or compose.
      </help>

      <filled>
        <if cond="nextaction == 'toplevel'">
          <goto next="http://www.openland.com/wrox/start.asp"/>
        <elseif cond="nextaction == 'previous'"/>
          <script>
              <![CDATA[
            docEmailNum = docEmailNum - 1;
            if (docEmailNum < 1)
              docEmailNum = 1;
          ]]>
          </script>
          <clear namelist="nextaction"/>
        <elseif cond="nextaction == 'next'"/>
          <script>
            docEmailNum = docEmailNum + 1;
            if (docEmailNum > docEmailCount)
              docEmailNum = docEmailCount;
          </script>
          <clear namelist="nextaction"/>
        <elseif cond="nextaction == 'first'"/>
          <script>
            docEmailNum = 1;
          </script>
          <clear namelist="nextaction"/>
        <elseif cond="nextaction == 'last'"/>
          <script>
            docEmailNum = docEmailCount;
          </script>
          <clear namelist="nextaction"/>
        <elseif cond="nextaction == 'check'"/>
          <return/>
        <elseif cond="nextaction == 'quit'"/>
          <prompt>
```

```
          Thank you for using our service. Goodbye.
        </prompt>
        <disconnect/>
      </if>
    </filled>
  </field>
```

Next there is a slightly different use of <subdialog>. Instead of calling another document, we call another form elsewhere in this same document. When you call another document, if the document is an ASP file, you can use a method attribute of get or post, passing parameters via the namelist attribute. The ASP file can thus get the values of those parameters using Request.QueryString or Request.Form. But if the called document is a plain VoiceXML document, you use <param> to pass information to the document, and the same applies when calling a <form>.

We make use of the cond attribute to select which <subdialog> should be called. Remember that the <subdialog> elements here act as function calls, so when each returns, we continue in the main processing loop.

```
    <subdialog name="replyemail" cond="nextaction == 'reply'"
               src="#replyemail">
      <param name="emailid"
        expr="docEmailMsgs[docEmailNum][&quot;ID&quot;]"/>
      <param name="recepient"
        expr="docEmailMsgs[docEmailNum][&quot;From&quot;]"/>
      <filled>
        <clear namelist="nextaction replyemail"/>
      </filled>
    </subdialog>

    <subdialog name="forwardemail" cond="nextaction == 'forward'"
               src="#forwardemail">
      <param name="emailid"
        expr="docEmailMsgs[docEmailNum][&quot;ID&quot;]"/>
      <filled>
        <clear namelist="nextaction forwardemail"/>
      </filled>
    </subdialog>

    <subdialog name="composeemail" cond="nextaction == 'compose'"
               src="#composeemail">
      <filled>
        <clear namelist="nextaction composeemail"/>
      </filled>
    </subdialog>
  </form>
```

Just as you can call functions inside other functions, so can you nest <subdialog> calls inside forms or documents called by a new <subdialog>. The replyemail <form> breaks the task into two further <subdialog> calls, the first to record the user's message, and the next to send it.

```
  <form id="replyemail">
    <var name="emailid"/>
    <var name="recepient"/>
    <var name="uri"/>
```

```
    <subdialog name="recordandupload" src="#recordandupload">
      <param name="emailid" expr="emailid"/>
    </subdialog>

    <subdialog name="sendemail" src="#sendemail">
      <param name="emailid" expr="emailid"/>
      <param name="recepient" expr="recepient"/>
      <param name="withattachment"
        expr="recordandupload.ifrecord"/>
      <param name="sendtype" value="reply"/>
    </subdialog>

    <block>
      <prompt cond="sendemail.result == 'success'">
        Your email has been sent.
      </prompt>
      <prompt cond="sendemail.result == 'failure'">
        There was a problem sending your email. Your email has not been sent.
      </prompt>
      <return/>
    </block>
  </form>
```

When forwarding e-mail the main change is that we need to ask to whom the e-mail should be sent. We're limiting this to one of the names in the user's address book. So we use the same CDO code as in the <grammar> element of the emailfilter <field> in email.asp earlier.

```
  <form id="forwardemail">
    <var name="emailid"/>
    <var name="uri"/>
    <var name="recepient"/>

    <field name="towhom">
      <grammar>
      <![CDATA[
      [
      <%
        For Each addentry In Session("objSession").AddressLists.Item(1)
         .AddressEntries
          response.write("(?to " & lcase(addentry.name) & ") {<towhom """ &
            addentry.name & """>}")
        Next
      %>
      ]
      ]]>
      </grammar>

      <prompt>
        To whom do you want to forward this email?
      </prompt>
      <help>
        Please say a name in your address book to forward this email to.
      </help>
    </field>
```

```
<subdialog name="recordandupload" src="#recordandupload">
  <param name="emailid" expr="emailid"/>
</subdialog>

  <subdialog name="sendemail" src="#sendemail">
    <param name="emailid" expr="emailid"/>
    <param name="recepient" expr="towhom"/>
    <param name="withattachment" expr="recordandupload.ifrecord"/>
    <param name="sendtype" value="forward"/>
  </subdialog>

  <block>
    <prompt cond="sendemail.result == 'success'">
      Your email has been sent.
    </prompt>
    <return/>
  </block>
</form>
```

When composing a new e-mail, we won't have a pre-saved email ID, and as we are using the e-mail ID as the filename for temporarily saving the recording, we set it to the arbitrary value `1234567890`.

```
<form id="composeemail">
  <var name="uri"/>
  <var name="recepient"/>

  <field name="towhom">
    <grammar>
    <![CDATA[
    [
      <%
      For Each addentry In Session("objSession").AddressLists.Item(1)
       .AddressEntries
        response.write("(?to " & lcase(addentry.name) & ") {<towhom """ &
          addentry.name & """>}")
      Next
      %>
    ]
    ]]>
    </grammar>

    <prompt>
      To whom do you want to compose a new email?
    </prompt>
    <help>
      Please say a name in your address book you want to send a new email to.
    </help>
  </field>

  <subdialog name="recordandupload" src="#recordandupload">
    <param name="emailid" value="1234567890"/>
  </subdialog>

  <subdialog name="sendemail" src="#sendemail">
```

```
    <param name="emailid" value="1234567890"/>
    <param name="recepient" expr="towhom"/>
    <param name="withattachment" expr="recordandupload.ifrecord"/>
    <param name="sendtype" value="compose"/>
  </subdialog>

  <block>
    <prompt cond="sendemail.result == 'success'">
      Your email has been sent.
    </prompt>

    <return/>
  </block>
</form>
```

In the following form, after a recording is made and confirmed, we use yet another `<subdialog>` to upload the recorded message to your web server. This is where JSP is used. Notice that this time, we set the `method` attribute to `post` and pass both the user's recording `emailmsg` and the e-mail ID in `namelist`.

```
<form id="recordandupload">
  <var name="emailid"/>

  <field name="ifrecord" type="boolean">
    <prompt>
      Would you like to record a message as an attachment of this email?
    </prompt>
    <filled>
      <if cond="ifrecord == false">
        <!-- if user doesn't want to record, return immediately -->
        <return namelist="ifrecord"/>
      </if>
    </filled>
  </field>

  <!-- otherwise do the recording and uploading -->
  <record name="emailmsg" beep="true" maxtime="30s" finalsilence="2000ms">
    <prompt>
      Please record your message after the tone.
    </prompt>
    <noinput>
      Sorry I did not hear anything.
      <reprompt/>
    </noinput>
  </record>

  <field name="confirm" type="boolean">
    <prompt>
      Your message is <value expr="emailmsg"/>. Do you want to keep this
      message?
    </prompt>
    <filled>
      <if cond="confirm">
        <prompt>
          OK, please wait while I save your message.
        </prompt>
```

```
          <else/>
            <prompt> OK, let's try again.</prompt>
            <clear namelist="emailmsg confirm"/>
          </if>
        </filled>
      </field>


    <subdialog name="upload" method="post" namelist="emailmsg emailid"
               enctype="multipart/form-data"
               src="http://www.openland.com:6666/voice/recordingsave.jsp">
      <param name="emailid" expr="emailid"/>
    </subdialog>


    <block>
      <return namelist="ifrecord"/>
    </block>
  </form>
```

The `sendemail` form confirms that you want to send the message, and then calls an ASP file to send it.

```
  <form id="sendemail">
    <var name="emailid"/>
    <var name="recepient"/>
    <var name="withattachment"/>
    <var name="sendtype"/>
    <var name="result" expr="'failure'"/>

    <field name="sendconfirm" type="boolean">
      <prompt>
        Do you wish to send this message to <value expr="recepient"/>?
      </prompt>

      <filled>
        <if cond="sendconfirm">
          <prompt>
            Please wait while I deliver your message.
          </prompt>
        <else/>
          <prompt>
            Your message has been discarded.
          </prompt>
          <assign name="result" value="'discarded'"/>
          <return namelist="result"/>
        </if>
      </filled>
    </field>

    <subdialog name="sendemailasp" cond="sendconfirm" method="get"
               namelist="recepient emailid withattachment sendtype"
               src="http://www.openland.com/wrox/sendemail.asp">
      <filled>
        <assign name="result" expr="sendemailasp.result"/>
      </filled>
```

```
  </subdialog>

  <block>
    <return namelist="result"/>
  </block>

</form>
</vxml>
```

Sending E-Mail

Here's the JSP file `recordingsave.jsp` that saves the recording so it may then be uploaded to the server. For simplicity, we save the message to your C: drive under the name of the e-mail ID passed as a parameter.

```
<?xml version="1.0"?>

<vxml version="1.0" application="root.vxml">
<form>
  <var name="emailid"/>
  <!-- this variable gets passed as a param in the subdialog -->
        <%@ page import="java.io.*" %>
        <%@ page import="java.util.*" %>

  <block>
    <log>
      emailid=<value expr="emailid"/>.
    </log>

        <%
          ServletInputStream myIn = request.getInputStream();
          int reqLength = request.getContentLength();
          System.out.println("In the JSP!");
          System.out.println("request class is " + request.getClass());
          System.out.println("request length is " + reqLength);

          String val = request.getParameter("emailmsg");
          String emailid = request.getParameter("emailid");
          System.out.println("emailid = " + emailid);

          //long l = System.currentTimeMillis();
          //String filename ="c:/" + l +".wav";
          String filename ="c:/" + emailid +".wav";
          System.out.println("filename=" + filename);
          OutputStream myout = new FileOutputStream(new File(filename));

          myout.write(val.getBytes());
          myout.close();
        %>

    <prompt>
      Your message has been saved.
    </prompt>
    <return/>
  </block>
```

```
</form>
</vxml>
```

Up next is the ASP file `sendemail.asp` that uses CDO to send e-mail. The CDO code for compose, reply, and forward does differ slightly, but they're all pretty straightforward for you to follow.

```
<?xml version="1.0"?>
<vxml version="1.0" application="root.vxml">

<form id="start">
  <var name="result"/>

  <block>
    <%
    if Request.QueryString("sendtype") = "compose" then
      set objMsg = Session("objSession").Outbox.Messages.Add

    elseif Request.QueryString("sendtype") = "reply" then
      set objMsgOrig = Session("objsession").GetMessage(Request.QueryString
        ("emailid"))
      set objMsg = objMsgOrig.Reply()

    elseif Request.QueryString("sendtype") = "forward" then
      set objMsgOrig = Session("objsession").GetMessage(Request.QueryString
        ("emailid"))
      set objMsg = objMsgOrig.Forward()
    end if

    if Request.QueryString("withattachment") = "true" then
      set objAtt = objMsg.Attachments.Add
      objAtt.Name = "MessageFromJeffTang.wav"
      objAtt.ReadFromFile("c:\" & Request.QueryString("emailid") & ".wav")
    end if

    ' create the recipient - if this is a reply, then no need to set recipient
    if Not Request.QueryString("sendtype") = "reply" then
      Set objOneRecip = objMsg.Recipients.Add
      objOneRecip.Name =  Request.QueryString("recepient")
      objOneRecip.Resolve
    end if

    objMsg.Update
    objMsg.Send
    %>

    <assign name="result" expr="'success'"/>
    <return namelist="result"/>
  </block>
</form>
</vxml>
```

Retrieving Appointments

The CDO code in `getappointment.asp` uses the default calendar folder to retrieve appointments based on specified times. The values &H00600040 and &H00610040 are used for the start date and end date. In CDO, the start date means the time on or before, and the end date means the time on or after. So to get all of today's appointments, we set the start date to midnight today, and the end date to midnight yesterday.

It's true the code contains some tedious details. But these details allow users of our service to easily get appointments for today, tomorrow, this week, next week, and so on. The full code is given here so you can see for yourself what it takes to build such an appointment service.

```
<?xml version="1.0"?>

<vxml version="1.0" application="root.vxml">

  <var name="docAppntNum" expr="1"/>
  <var name="docAppntCount"/>
  <var name="docAppnts"/>

  <form id="start">
    <block>
      <prompt>
      <!-- caltype can be day, week, or month -->
      <!-- time can be 20010301, or CURRENT (for today or this week or this
           month), or one of the 12 months -->

      <%
      set objCalFold = Session("objsession").GetDefaultFolder
       (CdoDefaultFolderCalendar)
      set collAppointments = objCalFold.Messages
      set msgFilter = collAppointments.Filter
      set mfFields = msgFilter.Fields

      rem &00600040 means start date, &H00610040 means end date.
      if Request.QueryString("caltype") = "today" then
        call mfFields.Add(&H00600040, date+1)
        call mfFields.Add(&H00610040, date)
      elseif Request.QueryString("caltype") = "yesterday" then
        call mfFields.Add(&H00600040, date)
        call mfFields.Add(&H00610040, date-1)
      elseif Request.QueryString("caltype") = "tomorrow" then
        call mfFields.Add(&H00600040, date+2)
        call mfFields.Add(&H00610040, date+1)
      elseif Request.QueryString("caltype") = "day" then
        ayear = Left(Request.QueryString("caltime"), 4)
        amonth = Mid(Request.QueryString("caltime"), 5, 2)
        aday = Right(Request.QueryString("caltime"), 2)

        call mfFields.Add(&H00600040, CDate(amonth & "/" & aday & "/" &
         ayear)+1)
        call mfFields.Add(&H00610040, CDate(amonth & "/" & aday & "/" & ayear))

      elseif Request.QueryString("caltype") = "thisweek" then
        if weekday(date) = 1 then
```

```
        ' today is sunday - this week means this past week
          call mfFields.Add(&H00600040, date + 1)
          call mfFields.Add(&H00610040, date - 6)
        else ' sunday - saturday: 1 - 7
          call mfFields.Add(&H00600040, date + 9 - weekday(date))
          call mfFields.Add(&H00610040, date + 2 - weekday(date))
        end if

      elseif Request.QueryString("caltype") = "lastweek" then
        if weekday(date) = 1 then
          call mfFields.Add(&H00600040, date + 1)
          call mfFields.Add(&H00610040, date - 6)
        else
          call mfFields.Add(&H00600040, date + 2 - weekday(date))
          call mfFields.Add(&H00610040, date - 7 - weekday(date))
        end if

      elseif Request.QueryString("caltype") = "nextweek" then
        if weekday(date) = 1 then
          call mfFields.Add(&H00600040, date + 8)
          call mfFields.Add(&H00610040, date + 1)
        else
          call mfFields.Add(&H00600040, date + 16 - weekday(date))
          call mfFields.Add(&H00610040, date + 9 - weekday(date))
        end if

  elseif Request.QueryString("caltype") = "week" then
    ayear = Left(Request.QueryString("caltime"), 4)
    amonth = Mid(Request.QueryString("caltime"), 5, 2)
    aday = Right(Request.QueryString("caltime"), 2)
    wd = Weekday(CDate(amonth & "/" & aday & "/" & ayear))

    if wd = 1 then ' it's sunday
      call mfFields.Add(&H00600040, CDate(amonth & "/" & aday & "/" & ayear)+ 8)
      call mfFields.Add(&H00610040, CDate(amonth & "/" & aday & "/" & ayear)+ 1)

    else ' sunday - saturday: 1 - 7
      call mfFields.Add(&H00600040, CDate(amonth & "/" & aday & "/" & ayear)+ 9
        - wd)
      call mfFields.Add(&H00610040, CDate(amonth & "/" & aday & "/" & ayear)+ 2
        - wd)
    end if

  elseif Request.QueryString("caltype") = "month" then
    amonth = Request.QueryString("caltime")

    if amonth="january" then
      call mfFields.Add(&H00600040, #1/31/2001 11:59:59 PM#)
      call mfFields.Add(&H00610040, #1/1/2001 12:00:00 AM#)
    elseif amonth="february" then
      call mfFields.Add(&H00600040, #2/28/2001 11:59:59 PM#)
      call mfFields.Add(&H00610040, #2/1/2001 12:00:00 AM#)
    elseif amonth="march" then
      call mfFields.Add(&H00600040, #3/31/2001 11:59:59 PM#)
      call mfFields.Add(&H00610040, #3/1/2001 12:00:00 AM#)
    elseif amonth="april" then
```

```
      call mfFields.Add(&H00600040, #4/30/2001 11:59:59 PM#)
      call mfFields.Add(&H00610040, #4/1/2001 12:00:00 AM#)
    elseif amonth="may" then
      call mfFields.Add(&H00600040, #5/31/2001 11:59:59 PM#)
      call mfFields.Add(&H00610040, #5/1/2001 12:00:00 AM#)
    elseif amonth="june" then
      call mfFields.Add(&H00600040, #6/30/2001 11:59:59 PM#)
      call mfFields.Add(&H00610040, #6/1/2001 12:00:00 AM#)
    elseif amonth="july" then
      call mfFields.Add(&H00600040, #7/31/2001 11:59:59 PM#)
      call mfFields.Add(&H00610040, #7/1/2001 12:00:00 AM#)
    elseif amonth="august" then
      call mfFields.Add(&H00600040, #8/31/2001 11:59:59 PM#)
      call mfFields.Add(&H00610040, #8/1/2001 12:00:00 AM#)
    elseif amonth="september" then
      call mfFields.Add(&H00600040, #9/30/2001 11:59:59 PM#)
      call mfFields.Add(&H00610040, #9/1/2001 12:00:00 AM#)
    elseif amonth="october" then
      call mfFields.Add(&H00600040, #10/31/2001 11:59:59 PM#)
      call mfFields.Add(&H00610040, #10/1/2001 12:00:00 AM#)
    elseif amonth="november" then
      call mfFields.Add(&H00600040, #11/30/2001 11:59:59 PM#)
      call mfFields.Add(&H00610040, #11/1/2001 12:00:00 AM#)
    elseif amonth="december" then
      call mfFields.Add(&H00600040, #12/31/2001 11:59:59 PM#)
      call mfFields.Add(&H00610040, #12/1/2001 12:00:00 AM#)
    end if

  end if

  nCount = 0
  For Each objItem In collAppointments
    Count = nCount + 1
  Next

    response.write("You have " & nCount & " appointments that match your
     request.")
%>
      </prompt>
```

After getting the appointment collection, we use the same technique as for e-mail, of saving the details in a VoiceXML JavaScript array, reading out the current appointment, and browsing as requested.

```
  <script>
    docAppntCount = <%=nCount%>;
    docAppnts = new Array();
    <%
    i = 0
    For Each objItem In collAppointments
      i = i + 1
    %>
      var appnt = new Object();
      appnt["StartTime"] = "<%=objItem.StartTime%>";
      appnt["EndTime"] = "<%=objItem.EndTime%>";
```

```
        appnt["Subject"] = "<%=Replace(objItem.Subject, "&", " ")%>";
        appnt["Text"] = "<%=objItem.Text%>";
        docAppnts[<%=i%>] = appnt;
      <% next%>
    </script>

    <if cond="docAppntCount == 0">
      <goto next="http://www.openland.com/wrox/start.asp"/>
    </if>
  </block>

  <field name="action">
    <grammar>
    [previous next first last forward schedule new check toplevel quit]
    </grammar>

    <prompt>
      Appointment number <value expr="docAppntNum"/>.
      Start time <value expr="docAppnts[docAppntNum][&quot;StartTime&quot;]"/>,
      End time is <value expr="docAppnts[docAppntNum][&quot;EndTime&quot;]"/>,
      Subject is <value expr="docAppnts[docAppntNum][&quot;Subject&quot;]"/>,
      Text is <value expr="docAppnts[docAppntNum][&quot;Text&quot;]"/>,
      What do you want to do next?
    </prompt>

    <help>
      You can say previous, next, first or last to listen to another appointment.
    </help>

    <filled>
      <if cond="action == 'toplevel'">
        <goto next="http://www.openland.com/wrox/start.asp"/>
      <elseif cond="action == 'previous'"/>
        <script>
        <![CDATA[
          docAppntNum = docAppntNum - 1;
          if (docAppntNum < 1)
            docAppntNum = 1;
        ]]>
        </script>
        <clear namelist="action"/>
      <elseif cond="action == 'next'"/>
        <script>
          docAppntNum = docAppntNum + 1;
          if (docAppntNum > docAppntCount)
            docAppntNum = docAppntCount;
        </script>
        <clear namelist="action"/>
      <elseif cond="action == 'first'"/>
        <script>
          docAppntNum = 1;
        </script>
        <clear namelist="action"/>
      <elseif cond="action == 'last'"/>
        <script>
          docAppntNum = docAppntCount;
```

```
      </script>
      <clear namelist="action"/>
    <elseif cond="action == 'schedule' || action == 'new'"/>
      <goto next="#newappnt"/>
    <elseif cond="action == 'check'"/>
      <return/>
    <elseif cond="action == 'quit'"/>
        <prompt>
          Thank you for using our service. Good bye.
        </prompt>
        <disconnect/>
      </if>
    </filled>
  </field>
</form>
```

To schedule a new appointment, we first need to collect six pieces of information: the start date, start time, end date, end time, subject, and descriptive text. The first four pieces of information are easy to get, using the built-in grammar types `date` and `time`. To allow users to enter free-form text is pretty difficult at present. Because of the limitations of current speech recognition engines, there's no way to recognize a text without using some kind of grammar. One method is to allow users to spell the text based on a grammar of all the 26 English letters. To indicate that spelling has finished, the slot name `finished` is added, along with `space` to enter a space between spelled words. So, for example, if prompted to enter a subject or text, you could say "S-E-E space D-O-C-T-O-R finished". You could enhance this however by writing a more comprehensive grammar and using the N-Best post-processing, as covered in detail in Chapter 10, *Nuance SpeechObjects*.

Once all the information has been obtained, we call another ASP, `scheduleappointment.asp`, and pass it all the collected data.

```
  <form id="newappnt">
    <var name="subjectinput" expr="''"/>
    <var name="textinput" expr="''"/>

    <field name="startdate" type="date">
      <prompt>
        What's the start date of your new appointment?
      </prompt>
    </field>

    <field name="starttime" type="time">
      <prompt>
        What's the start time of your new appointment?
      </prompt>
    </field>

    <field name="enddate" type="date">
      <prompt>
        What's the end date of your new appointment?
      </prompt>
    </field>

    <field name="endtime" type="time">
      <prompt>
```

```
      What's the end time of your new appointment?
    </prompt>
  </field>

  <field name="subject">
    <grammar>
    [a b c d e f g h i j k l m n o p q r s t u v w x y z space finished]
    </grammar>

    <prompt cond="subjectinput == ''">
      Please spell your subject now. After you're done, say finished.
    </prompt>

    <filled>
      <if cond="subject == 'finished'">
        <prompt>subject is <value expr="subjectinput"/></prompt>
        <assign name="subject" expr="subjectinput"/>
      <elseif cond="subject == 'space'"/>
        <assign name="subjectinput" expr="subjectinput + ' '"/>
        <clear namelist="subject"/>
      <else/>
        <assign name="subjectinput" expr="subjectinput + subject"/>
        <prompt><value expr="subject"/></prompt>
        <clear namelist="subject"/>
      </if>
    </filled>
  </field>

  <field name="text">
    <grammar>
    [a b c d e f g h i j k l m n o p q r s t u v w x y z space finished]
    </grammar>

    <prompt cond="textinput == ''">
      Please spell your text now. After you're done, say finished.
    </prompt>

    <filled>
      <if cond="text == 'finished'">
        <prompt>subject is <value expr="textinput"/></prompt>
        <assign name="text" expr="textinput"/>
      <elseif cond="text == 'space'"/>
        <assign name="textinput" expr="textinput + ' '"/>
        <clear namelist="text"/>
      <else/>
        <assign name="textinput" expr="textinput + text"/>
        <prompt><value expr="text"/></prompt>
        <clear namelist="text"/>
      </if>
    </filled>
  </field>

  <block>
    <log>startdate=<value expr="startdate"/>, starttime=<value
     expr="starttime"/>, enddate=<value expr="enddate"/>, endtime=<value
     expr="endtime"/>.
```

```
      </log>
    </block>

    <subdialog name="scheduleappntasp" method="get"
       namelist="startdate starttime enddate endtime subject text"
       src="http://www.openland.com/wrox/scheduleappointment.asp"/>

    <field name="another" type="boolean">
      <prompt>
        Do you want to schedule another appointment?
      </prompt>
      <filled>
        <if cond="another">
          <clear/>
        <else/>
          <return/>
        </if>
      </filled>
    </field>
  </form>
</vxml>
```

Scheduling Appointments

In the ASP file `scheduleappointment.asp`, we use CDO to let us create a new appointment. Afterwards comes the `<return>` element to allow another appointment to be scheduled if desired.

```
<?xml version="1.0"?>
<vxml version="1.0" application="root.vxml">

  <form id="start">
    <block>
  <%
    set objCalFold = Session("objsession").GetDefaultFolder
     (CdoDefaultFolderCalendar)
    set collAppointments = objCalFold.Messages
    set appntItem = collAppointments.Add

    rem the following code to add an attachment can be uncommented if you like
    rem set objAtt = appntItem.Attachments.Add
    rem objAtt.Name = "MessageFromJeffTang.wav"
    rem objAtt.ReadFromFile("c:\1234567890.wav")

    startdate = Request.QueryString("startdate")
    starttime = Request.QueryString("starttime")
    enddate = Request.QueryString("enddate")
    endtime = Request.QueryString("endtime")

    startyear = Left(startdate, 4)
    startmonth = Mid(startdate, 5, 2)
    startday = Right(startdate, 2)
    starthour = Left(starttime, 2)
    startmin = Mid(starttime, 3, 2)

    if Right(starttime, 1) = "a" then
```

```
      startampm = "AM"
    else
      startampm = "PM"
    end if

    endyear = Left(enddate, 4)
    endmonth = Mid(enddate, 5, 2)
    endday = Right(enddate, 2)
    endhour = Left(endtime, 2)
    endmin = Mid(endtime, 3, 2)
    if Right(endtime, 1) = "a" then
      endampm = "AM"
    else
      endampm = "PM"
    end if

    appntItem.StartTime = CDate(startmonth & "/" & startday & "/" & startyear &
     " " & starthour & ":" & startmin & ":" & "00 " & startampm)
    appntItem.EndTime = CDate(endmonth & "/" & endday & "/" & endyear & " " &
     endhour & ":" & endmin & ":" & "00 " & endampm)
    appntItem.Subject = Request.QueryString("subject")
    appntItem.Text = Request.QueryString("text")
    appntItem.Update

    response.write("Your new appointment has been scheduled.")
  %>
      <return/>
    </block>
  </form>
</vxml>
```

This completes our application to provide Outlook functionality over a regular phone. But what about if you want to sit back and relax, knowing you will be notified by phone as soon as that important e-mail you've been waiting for comes in? Well, go ahead and sit back and relax, because we can do that too.

Notification of New E-Mails

All the VoiceXML platform providers offer automated notification calls, but only to paying customers, presumably to avoid abuse. So here I won't tell go into any platform-specific details of how to make such calls, but I will show you exactly what it takes from a development standpoint to make it happen. You'll need to contact individual VoiceXML service providers for detailed pricing information.

In fact, it's actually a pretty simple task from the developer's point of view. You submit a URL request to a server made available to you by your service provider and typically pass the parameters including a phone number to dial, a user ID to identify yourself, the URL of the document to run when the call is answered, and an e-mail address to inform you of how the call went. Different companies may offer somewhat different parameters for you to use, but they are all in a similar vein. The following is a typical Java program that sends the URL request to an imaginary web server, and would be invoked when new e-mail arrives. We shall represent our imaginary web server with an ASP file you can put on your web server to simply output the information on new e-mails received that our Java application obtains. It would be a simple task to modify the Java program accordingly when you get the detailed server information and request parameters from your service provider. The reason I chose to use Java is its simplicity in doing network programming. You may use C/C++ to achieve the same result; but it may not be as easy as the Java code.

So here is the Java program, `NotifierRequest.java`:

```
import java.io.*;
import java.net.*;
import java.util.*;

public class NotifierRequest
{
    public static void main(String[] argv)
    {
    if (argv.length < 4)
    {
      System.out.println("Usage: java NotifierRequest <phone> <user_id>
        <notifier_url> <email>");
      System.exit(1);
    }
        try
        {
    URL u = new URL("http://www.openland.com/wrox/notifierrequest.asp?phone=" +
     argv[0] + "&UserID=" + argv[1] + "&NotifierURL=" + argv[2] + "&Email=" +
     argv[3]);
    BufferedReader br = new BufferedReader(new InputStreamReader
     (u.openStream()));

    String strLine;
    String strResult = "";
    while ((strLine = br.readLine()) != null)
    {
      strResult += strLine + "\n";
    }
    System.out.println(strResult);
        }
        catch (Exception e)
        {
          System.out.println("" + e);
        }
  }
}
```

Now you're perhaps wondering how we're going to trigger the Java application in the first place. We want to invoke the application whenever new e-mails meeting the specified criteria arrive. So the question is how to specify those criteria and how to hook the Java application up to an application that monitors new e-mails. Fortunately, Outlook provides a tool called Rules Wizard that lets us set up all this. You may choose to develop your own application to perform the monitoring task, but the Rules Wizard in Outlook is such a cool tool that I simply can't say no to it. To use it, go to Outlook Tools | Rules Wizard | New. In the next dialog box, select Check messages when they arrive as the type of rule you want to create, and click Next. Now you can specify the conditions you want to check, such as that overdue e-mail from your boss with the keyword "raise" or "promotion" in the e-mail subject or body. The list of conditions is so comprehensive that it's hard to imagine a condition not covered there.

Click Next again, and you now specify what to do when the conditions are met; in our case, run the Java program above. So here's the batch file you need to specify as the application to start: Check Start application and then select the filename of the following batch file, `NotifierRequest.bat`, as the application to execute. Complete the Rules Wizard, saving the new rule. It's that easy!

```
rem change classpath to include the path to the NotifierRequest.class file
set classpath=%classpath%;f:\jswdk-1.0.1\voice
java NotifierRequest <your-outbound-phone-number> <your-user-id>
     <your-notification-url> <your-email-address>
```

Finally, this ASP file, `NotifierRequest.asp`, can be put on your IIS machine to trap the notification request sent by the Java program:

```
<HTML>
<HEAD>
<TITLE>Request for Notifier</TITLE>
</HEAD>
<body>

<!--
http://www.openland.com/wrox/notifierrequest.asp?phone=4089728244&UserID=123456789
0&NotifierURL=http://www.openland.com/wrox/notifier.vxml&Email=jtang@openland.com
-->

Phone: <%=request.QueryString("Phone")%><br>
UserID: <%=request.QueryString("UserID")%><br>
NotifierURL: <%=request.QueryString("NotifierURL")%><br>
Email: <%=request.QueryString("Email")%><br>

</body>
</HTML>
```

Looking Back

In this case study of dynamic VoiceXML and ASP, we have seen how to integrate with and voice-enable a popular enterprise application, Microsoft Outlook. You've seen a lot of ASP code that generates VoiceXML documents containing JavaScript code inside `<script>` elements to handle the information saving and processing within the VoiceXML document. You've also seen the VoiceXML `<subdialog>` element in action, helping to make our VoiceXML application modular and robust. As your applications get more complicated, you definitely need to keep them maintainable and clean. Proper consideration of `<subdialog>` during the application design stage can be key. I hope I've successfully demonstrated the power of dynamically generating VoiceXML with traditional web server technologies, and you are now thinking about how VoiceXML can be used to dramatically increase the appeal of existing enterprise applications.

Of course, there are many improvements that can quite easily be made to the application we've looked at in this chapter. Here are a few that I can think of:

- Make grammars more complete: add more words to cover a greater range of user utterances
- Enhance e-mail functionality: read long e-mail messages in a more intelligent way; perhaps even read attachments if appropriate.
- Enhance calendar functionality: cancel and reschedule appointments, add an attachment when scheduling an appointment.
- Provide integration with other aspects of Outlook, such as Tasks and Notes.
- Error handling: more complete error handling and status reporting can be added inside each `<subdialog>`.

I'm sure there are many other things you can think of to improve on. The important thing to remember is that using dynamic VoiceXML to voice-enable enterprise applications can be both challenging and fun, and it makes excellent business sense in many situations.

```
<?xml version="1.0"?>
<vxml version="1.0">
<form id="foo">
<block>
<prompt>
Hi. My name is Bob
</prompt>
</block>
</form>
</vxml>
```

10

Nuance SpeechObjects

So far, we have seen various ways of creating our own VoiceXML documents filled with our own dialogs. Most of these have been fairly simple, but as you increase your skills, you will find that you will want more complex dialogs. How can you make this process simpler for yourself? One approach involves **reusable components**: dialogs that have already been created, which we can use time and time again. There are currently several companies that offer this kind of functionality, including IBM and Nuance.

IBM recently released a new set of tools called Reusable Dialog Components (RDC), available for download at http://www-4.ibm.com/software/speech/enterprise/wvs-rdc.html. RDC offers reusable components for basic dialogs such as obtaining credit card details, date and time information, or a user's telephone number. IBM's RDC are all implemented using VoiceXML subdialogs and grammars (JSGF), combined with JavaScript.

Nuance is one of the leading companies in the field of commercial Automatic Speech Recognition (ASR) engines. Many VoiceXML platforms currently support the Nuance ASR engine, or even base their platforms entirely on Nuance technologies. One of their most successful products is the SpeechObjects plug-in software component. SpeechObjects are reusable Java-based dialog modules that encapsulate aspects of conversational dialog, and incorporate some of the best practices in voice application design. The key here is reusability, which means fast time-to-market and added business value.

Although generally it may be a more straightforward task to use the IBM VoiceXML RDC – you can deploy and develop your own components from what you've learned so far – the extra effort needed to invoke Nuance SpeechObjects can give developers greater control over their applications. For example, SpeechObjects are capable of returning the list of N-best items for an utterance – that is the list of all possible recognition matches where the interpreter's confidence level is high enough for consideration. So, in this chapter we'll be looking at these objects in detail.

What makes Nuance SpeechObjects so interesting to us is the `<object>` element of the VoiceXML language, which allows us to embed Nuance SpeechObjects directly inside our applications. In this way, the `<object>` element is similar to the `<object>` or `<applet>` elements in HTML, that enable the use of powerful applet-based web applications. In VoiceXML, `<object>` bears many similarities to `<subdialog>`. Both encourage reusability, but the difference is that `<subdialog>` calls other static or dynamic pieces of VoiceXML code, while `<object>` calls a binary component that can be implemented in potentially any language.

A SpeechObject includes the prompts, grammar, and logic for a complete dialog, and returns a semantically meaningful result to the calling application. Nuance's **Foundation SpeechObjects** are a collection of SpeechObjects that provide support for a range of generalized dialogs for common situations, such as obtaining a user's credit card details or telephone number. For example, `SODate` is one of the Foundation SpeechObjects. When you invoke it, by default it plays an initial prompt asking "Which date do you want". Then, based on its built-in grammar, it recognizes a range of utterances such as "July 20, 2002", and returns the result in the form "07202002".

The Foundation SpeechObjects allow voice application developers to quickly assemble high-level reusable components to address many typical requirements of an application. You can also create your own specialized SpeechObjects from scratch if you wish, building on the core SpeechObjects framework, or of course make use of SpeechObjects designed by others.

It's true that not all VoiceXML platforms support SpeechObjects. So why should we still consider using SpeechObjects in VoiceXML? The VoiceXML 1.0 specification states that "While VoiceXML strives to accommodate the requirements of a majority of voice response services, services with stringent requirements may best be served by dedicated applications that employ a finer level of control". In other words, VoiceXML is a simple to use, high-level speech markup language aimed at a broad developer audience, and certain applications may not be suited to implementation in this language alone.

SpeechObjects, however, provide an inherently strong component model allowing for much more fine-grained control. Being a component model means we can parameterize behavior, and encapsulate code to hide complexity. The finer level of control includes being able to elicit multiple items of information, confirm and correct this information easily, and cope with the acoustic ambiguity that is inherent in human language, among other things. The term **acoustic ambiguity** describes the phenomenon of an utterance with an ambiguous interpretation – for example, to the question, "Do you think Lakers will win the series?", you could answer "I don't, no", or "I don't know", which would be hard to differentiate when heard. Often the best solution is to iterate through the list of N-Best possible matches returned by the recognition engine and prompt the user for clarification: this is not a feature that specification-compliant VoiceXML currently supports, but it can be provided through SpeechObjects.

SpeechObjects, which provide features such as skip lists, result filters, and a standard mechanism to iterate over multiple recognition matches from the recognition engine, are extremely good at coping with acoustic ambiguity. I'll show you a detailed example in the last section of this chapter. VoiceXML 1.0 doesn't yet provide for cycling through a list of multiple results, but some platforms such as BeVocal have added an extension to support N-Best items, and the upcoming VoiceXML 2.0 will likely include this facility. Even so, VoiceXML support for multiple results will probably never be able to reach the level of fine-grained control already offered by SpeechObjects.

To give you another example of a task that is only practicable to implement with Nuance SpeechObjects – that is, if you avoid VoiceXML proprietary extensions or waiting for the new specification of VoiceXML to arrive and become supported by service providers – consider speech verification. It is possible to create a SpeechObject that encapsulates the behavior required for speech verification, and can be employed directly from VoiceXML to perform voice-print security checking.

One other important benefit of SpeechObjects, deriving from its component model architecture, is that your source code is pre-compiled into a representation that affords a certain degree of intellectual property protection, as well as guarding against inadvertently modifying the source, none of which is possible with VoiceXML alone. For example, `<subdialog>`-based source-code-level dialog components will have to be loaded and interpreted at run time, while `<object>`-based SpeechObjects dialog components are pre-compiled to binary before loading.

Hopefully, you now have some idea of the unique benefits offered by SpeechObjects, and are keen to hear some more of the details. So, here's what I'll cover in this chapter: first I'll present a brief introduction to the theory behind SpeechObjects to give a better understanding of how they really work. Next, I'll illustrate how to use the existing Foundation SpeechObjects in your VoiceXML applications, moving on to show you how to create new reusable SpeechObjects of your own if you're still thirsty for advanced speech recognition features such as resolving ambiguity and filtering incorrect results. I will create a user-defined SpeechObject called `SOSpell` to this end that will enhance the spelling interface of the e-mail/calendar application from Chapter 9.

SpeechObjects Theory

First of all, we have the abstract interface called `SpeechObject`, which declares the primary method of any SpeechObject, `invoke()`. When you use a SpeechObject, you actually call this `invoke()` method. As `SpeechObject` is an abstract interface, there's also an abstract class called `NuanceSpeechObject` that implements the interface. `NuanceSpeechObject` serves as the abstract base class for all Foundation SpeechObjects. It provides several features common to all Foundation SpeechObjects along with utility member variables and methods for internationalization that allow for easy creation of locale-specific information. However, normally you won't need to worry about these; instead, you can just deal with `SODialog` and `SODialogManager`, the two primary framework Foundation SpeechObjects that both extend `NuanceSpeechObject`.

The following diagram summarizes the relationship above:

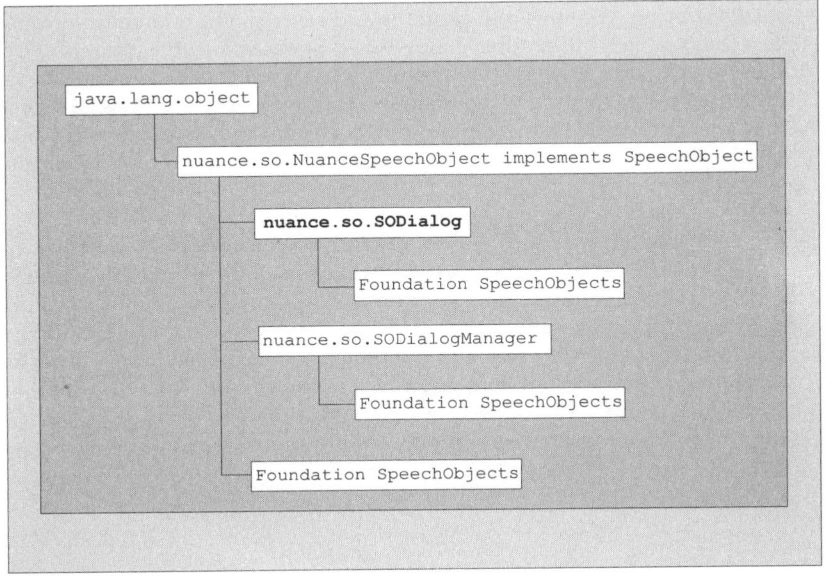

SODialog is the primary SpeechObject from which many of the Foundation SpeechObjects are derived. It adds behavior to the abstract class NuanceSpeechObject to help you build simple dialog units more easily. Its functionality includes:

- The invoke() method to execute a basic dialog. This includes playing the initial prompt, recognizing speech, and returning the results.
- Methods for managing the set of standard prompts in a dialog unit.
- Standard methods you can overload to convert raw recognition results into meaningful application data.
- Support for the "redo object" and DialogContext mechanisms implemented in NuanceSpeechObject.
- Mechanisms for tracking the number of times a SpeechObject is invoked and the maximum hit count before a dialog error is raised.
- Support for universal actions and standard error prompts.

While SODialog provides a framework for building a simple individual dialog unit, SODialogManager provides the generic framework for compound dialogs made of multiple dialog states, each of which can be a SODialog-derived dialog unit or another SODialogManager-derived compound dialog. A state table is used to define the logic for transitioning between dialog states. Typically you use SODialog as the base class for the individual dialog states invoked by an SODialogManager subclass.

SODialog is usable only as a base class for other dialog-based SpeechObjects. As it comes, SODialog itself is a skeleton dialog, containing null prompts and returning null recognition results. So to create a dialog SpeechObject of your own, you first declare a subclass of SODialog, provide default prompts for your dialog, extend the nested class SpeechObject.Result to define the format for the recognition results, and overload one or more of the SODialog result processing methods to examine raw recognition results and generate the final Result object. More on this in the section headed *Your Own SpeechObjects*.

Similarly, SODialogManager contains null prompts and returns null recognition results, and is usable only as a base class that you can build other dialog-based SpeechObjects on top of. You tailor SODialogManager to your own purposes by creating a SODialogManager subclass, implementing the SpeechObject to be used for each state in the dialog, creating a condition class corresponding to each type of transition in the dialog flow, building the state table for your dialog flow by adding each state and the entire set of possible state transitions, explicitly setting the initial dialog state, and finally returning the correct end result.

Besides SODialog and SODialogManager, two other useful framework Foundation SpeechObjects are SpeakerVerification and SOVoiceGrammarEnrollment. The former is a base class that extends NuanceSpeechObject with a generic framework for speaker verification and enrollment dialogs. SOVoiceGrammarEnrollment extends SODialogManager and can be used to add a phrase to a dynamic grammar for later use by the recognition engine. Normally you'll only need to deal with the eighteen concrete Foundation SpeechObjects described in the table in the following section, but there are many more available for more specialized purposes. Most are derived from SODialog or SODialogManager, although a few derive directly from NuanceSpeechObject for greater control.

Many of the Nuance Foundation SpeechObjects provide generic initial prompts that you should replace with specialized prompts for your own applications. Prompts and recognition grammars are both implemented by SpeechObjects as properties of an object, and there are two basic mechanisms for customization. Firstly, you can override these properties with values you specify by resetting those properties at run time, or alternatively you can create subclasses that set new properties on construction. Many SpeechObjects also have properties in addition to grammars and prompts that you can set. The `SODate` object, for example, lets you specify a range of acceptable dates. You can easily customize a SpeechObject at run time by setting its properties before each use, altering prompts, the recognition grammar, and any other properties provided by that SpeechObject.

Enough theory. Let's start to have some fun. If you just want to use the currently available Nuance Foundation SpeechObjects in VoiceXML, you may jump right into the next section. If you want to get a full understanding of SpeechObjects, Nuance provide excellent online documentation when you sign up for a free developer account:

http://extranet.nuance.com/developers/documentation/index.html#speech_objects

Foundation SpeechObjects in VoiceXML

The `<object>` element is used to call Nuance Foundation SpeechObjects from VoiceXML documents. According to the VoiceXML 1.0 specification, various objects may be accessed through the `<object>` element, as determined by the individual platform, and often include speaker-verification components and additional telephony functionality. Currently SpeechObjects are the only type of object with relatively wide support among the leading voice portals, but be aware that some do not support the `<object>` tag yet. Among those that do, in my opinion BeVocal is the best platform for deploying Foundation SpeechObjects.

Here's a summary of the 18 concrete Foundation SpeechObjects, with brief descriptions:

`SOAlphaDigitString`	Gets a sectioned alphanumeric string, for example,"C345-A68".
`SOBrowsableList`	Generates a dialog that plays items in a list and lets the caller navigate between the items.
`SOConfirm`	Provides a dialog asking whether to cancel or continue an operation.
`SOConfirmAndCorrect`	Provides a framework for a dialog to confirm and, if necessary, correct, recognition results returned from another SpeechObject-based dialog.
`SOCreditCardInfo`	Implements a dialog that gets credit card information, including card type, number, and expiration date.
`SODate`	Gets a date expression identifying a particular day, month, and year.
`SOImplicitConfirm`	Like `SOConfirmAndCorrect`, this allows the caller to cancel an operation, but interprets silence as implicit confirmation.
`SOMenu`	Generates a dialog that lets the caller select one item from a discrete list. Use this to create dialogs for selecting one or more items from a fixed set that is presented in sequence. Use `SOBrowsableList` if you want to allow the caller to navigate between list items or manipulate items.

SONATelephoneNumber	Gets a full telephone number in the U.S./Canadian 10-digit format.
SOQuantity	Gets a quantity, as an integer value between 0 and 99,999,999.
SORecord	Records an utterance after an optional initial prompt. This SpeechObject does not perform any recognition.
SOSectionedDigitString	Gets a sectioned digit string, for example, in an account number format such as "5454-5555-1234".
SOSimpleDigitString	Gets a digit string as a sequence of single integers.
SOSocialSecurityNumber	Gets a nine-digit string in the format "555-55-5555."
SOTime	Gets a time-of-day expression.
SOUSCurrency	Gets a currency amount in U.S. dollars.
SOUSZipCode	Gets a 5- or 9-digit U.S. postal code.
SOYesNo	Gets a yes or no response.

The only one of these that BeVocal doesn't support is `SORecord`. However, you can easily implement the recording feature using the VoiceXML `<record>` element, as in Chapter 9.

You may notice that there are built-in grammars available for the `<field>` element (see Chapter 3) which provide similar functionality to some of the SpeechObjects listed above, namely `SOConfirm`, `SODate`, `SOTime`, `SONATelephoneNumber`, `SOSimpleDigitString`, and `SOYesNo`. So when should you use the built-in VoiceXML grammar, and when should you turn to the corresponding Foundation SpeechObjects?

Normally, there's no real difference, except that built-in grammars may be more widely supported than SpeechObjects. However, SpeechObjects have convenient methods for you to easily access the recognized result. For example, `SODate` contains the methods `getDayOfWeek()`, `getDayOfMonth()`, `getMonth()`, and `getYear()` that you can use in date queries. Note that in the `<object>` element, you actually need to use the property corresponding to these methods, `DayOfWeek`, `DayOfMonth`, `Month`, or `Year`, because SpeechObjects are JavaBeans. Anyway, with the built-in grammar `date`, you'd have to parse the returned result to find these kinds of values. Also, SpeechObjects usually offer methods to let you more accurately control their behavior. `SODate`, for example, provides `setLowerDate()` and `setUpperDate()`, that you can use in the `<object>` element as shown to set the range of valid dates to between one year ago and one month in the future. Note that a negative number indicates the number of days before the current date:

```
<object classid="speechobject://nuance.so.SODate" name="thisdate">
  <param name="LowerDate" value="-365"/>
  <param name="UpperDate" value="30"/>
</object>
```

Generally speaking, Foundation SpeechObjects require that your voice portals work a little bit harder, but in return, they give greater flexibility than the comparable built-in grammars. The other Foundation SpeechObjects, where a corresponding VoiceXML counterpart is not available, simply provide us with a fast route to market, as they have typically done much of the grammar and logic work. If you take a look at the grammar that is built into `SOAlphaDigitString` for example, you'll see how much effort is required to write a comprehensive grammar, even for a relatively simple task like collecting letters and digits.

In the rest of the section, I'll show you some examples of Foundation SpeechObjects. There is a more complete list of examples by BeVocal, demonstrating all the Foundation SpeechObjects, available at the following location:

http://cafe.bevocal.com/docs/so_quick_reference/index.html

The first example utilizes `SOAlphaDigitString`, which provides a dialog interface for getting a sectioned alphanumeric string, such as xxxx-xx-xxxx. This can be useful in many situations, whenever spelling out a word or number is required, although specialized Foundation SpeechObjects exist for collecting a social security number, a telephone number, or a credit card number by imposing appropriate constraints. The usage of these objects is similar to SOAlphaDigitString, so this example will prepare you for all these other SpeechObjects too.

```
<?xml version="1.0"?>
<vxml version="1.0">

<form id="getAlphaDigitString">
  <object classid="speechobject://nuance.so.SOAlphaDigitString" name="rtnstr">
    <param name="initialPrompt" type="nuance.common.prompts.URLPrompt">
      <param name="URL" type="java.net.URL"
        expr="'http://www.openland.com/voicexml/verifyaccount.wav'"/>
    </param>
    <param name="format"
      type="array:nuance.so.sectioneddigitstring.WeightedFormat">
       <param index="0" type="nuance.so.sectioneddigitstring.WeightedFormat">
         <param name="prob" expr="'0.8'" />
         <param name="format" expr="'AAA-DD-DDD'" />
       </param>
       <param index="1" type="nuance.so.sectioneddigitstring.WeightedFormat">
         <param name="prob" expr="'0.2'" />
         <param name="format" expr="'DDD-AA-AAA'" />
       </param>
    </param>
  </object>
  <filled>
    <prompt>
      You said <value expr="rtnstr"/>
    </prompt>
  </filled>
  </form>

</vxml>
```

Running the above code on the BeVocal Café platform initiates the following sequence of events:

1. You first hear the custom prompt that asks for your account number, as set by the parameter `initialPrompt`. All the initialization and property customization for a SpeechObject occurs through such `<param>` elements. To provide your own `initialPrompt`, `recognitionErrorPrompt`, or `helpPrompt`, you set the `type` attribute to `nuance.common.prompts.URLPrompt`, then by means of a nested sub-`<param>`, specify the URL of the actual prompt. If you don't set these prompt properties, defaults are provided.

Each SpeechObject has its own properties, but all Foundation SpeechObjects share the following common properties that can be set using `<param>` elements inside the `<object>` element: `initialPrompt`, `recognitionErrorPrompt`, `helpPrompt`, `maxErrors`, `allowCancel`, and `exitOnHelp`.

2. The format parameter then tells the recognition engine what types of alphanumeric user input are acceptable. The format for SOAlphaDigitString is interpreted as an array of weighted formats, that is, possible formats each with a probability. A child parameter of each format parameter is required to specify the probability for that format in this way: `<param name="prob" expr="'0.8'"/>`. For each element in the array, an index parameter is used to describe the exact format. In the example here, two possible user input formats are defined, one is 'AAA-DD-DDD', meaning start with 3 letters, then 5 digits; the other is 'DDD-AA-AAA', meaning start with 3 digits, followed by 5 letters. A probability for the occurrence of each type is also specified: 1.0 (100%) for 'AAA-DD-DDD' and 0.2 (20%) for 'DDD-AA-AAA'.

3. So when the user utters a string such as "ABC45678" or "123ABCDE", the recognized result will be saved in the object name variable, alphanum. The SOAlphaDigitString also has a result property digitstring, which you can use to access the alphanumeric string returned like this: alphanum.digitstring. In the above example, using the unqualified object name is the same as using this longer format, as digitstring is the only property for the result.

In the next example, we'll see what to do when the returned result consists of several properties. We shall use SOCreditCardInfo, which provides a simple dialog for getting credit card-related information, including the type of card (American Express, Discover, Mastercard, Visa, and so on), card number, and expiration date. It's worth pointing out at this point that SOCreditCardInfo, unlike most other Foundation SpeechObjects, is not directly derived from SODialog, but from SODialogManager. This is because here three pieces of information are collected, instead of just one.

The following code asks for your credit card type, number, and expiration date. It then uses the four properties of the returned result, credit_card_type, credit_card_number, credit_card_date_month, and credit_card_date_year, to query the result. Everything is simple and straightforward, just as it should be when you have a well-designed SpeechObject.

```
<?xml version="1.0"?>
<vxml version="1.0">

<form id="getCreditInfo">
  <block>
    <prompt>Please have your credit card ready.</prompt>
  </block>
  <object classid="speechobject://nuance.so.SOCreditCardInfo" name="ccInfo">
    <filled>
      <prompt>
         Credit card type is <value expr="ccInfo.credit_card_type"/>
         Credit card Number is <value expr="ccInfo.credit_card_number"/>
         Credit card Expiration Date is
         <value expr="ccInfo.credit_card_date_month"/>
         <value expr="ccInfo.credit_card_date_year"/>
      </prompt>
    </filled>
  </object>
</form>
</vxml>
```

To learn how to use other Foundation SpeechObjects in VoiceXML, you can go to the BeVocal quick reference URL shown earlier in this section. The quick reference also shows how to use BeVocal's own SpeechObjects, such as SOAirline, SOPickStock, SOCityState, SOStreet, and SOStreetNumber. To gain a complete understanding of each Foundation SpeechObject, I would recommend the Nuance *SpeechObjects Developer's Guide*, available from:

http://extranet.nuance.com/developers/documentation/speechobjects_1_1/pdf/so.pdf

Now you have a starting point and can expand your knowledge of the Foundation SpeechObjects and other available SpeechObjects, so as to be in a position to utilize their power and flexibility in your VoiceXML applications. However, if you're more ambitious and want to build your own SpeechObjects instead of just using other people's, read on.

Your Own SpeechObjects

To create your own SpeechObject, you must first install the Nuance core software, because SpeechObjects is a high-level Java API built on the core Nuance ASR to speed up application development. At the time of writing, the current version of SpeechObjects is 1.1, and it requires Nuance 7.0.2 or above. To get hold of these, you need to sign up for the free Nuance developer membership at http://extranet.nuance.com/developer. After that, you can download both Nuance version 7.0.4 and SpeechObjects version 1.1 as two zip files from:

http://extranet.nuance.com/support/downloads.html

Unzip each file and run both `setup.exe` files to complete the installation process. If you haven't already, you will also need to install the Java Software Development Kit 1.2, which can be downloaded from http://java.sun.com.

The Spelling Problem

In the e-mail/calendar application of Chapter 9, we used a feature to allow users to spell subject and text bodies when scheduling a new appointment. If you have tried that application using a real phone, instead of just the BeVocal Café Vocal Scripter tool that can always recognize your typed input 100% accurately, you'll probably be aware of the difficulty in getting your spelling correctly recognized. There are a few ways we can improve on our solution:

- Use a more finely-tuned grammar. For example, instead of just a simple grammar allowing for single letters, you can make it more natural and more easily recognized by adding "a as in Amanda", "B as in Bob", "c as in charlie", etc. A single letter or number is very easily mismatched during recognition.
- Use the N-Best result list that the ASR engine returns to have the user confirm which possible interpretation is correct. VoiceXML 1.0 only ever returns the single best result to the application, but with SpeechObjects, we can get hold of all the best possible results. This gives an effective and natural way to resolve ambiguities. For example, when the user says "b", a few possible results may be generated, perhaps "b", "p", and "v".
- With SpeechObjects, you can also implement a dynamic filtering mechanism: if the user tells you "p" is not what's spelled, then next time you can have "p" filtered out from possible results.

Now let's see how we can accomplish these three enhancements with a new SpeechObject, appropriately named `SOSpell`.

Creating SOSpell

To fine-tune the grammar for our SpeechObject, we can modify the grammar that comes with the Foundation SpeechObject `SOAlphaDigitString`. Here's the content of our modified grammar file `sospell.grammar`:

```
SOSpell_CORE [
  SOAlphaDS_AllAlpha:s {<spelling $s>}
  SOAlphaDS_Digit:n {<spelling $n>}
  space {<spelling space>}
  dash {<spelling dash>}
  underscore {<spelling underscore>}
  at {<spelling at>}
  dot {<spelling dot>}
  finished {<spelling finished>}
]

SOAlphaDS_AllAlpha [
  SOAlphaDS_LETTER_A:a
  SOAlphaDS_LETTER_B:a
  SOAlphaDS_LETTER_C:a
  SOAlphaDS_LETTER_D:a
  SOAlphaDS_LETTER_E:a
  SOAlphaDS_LETTER_F:a
  SOAlphaDS_LETTER_G:a
  SOAlphaDS_LETTER_H:a
  SOAlphaDS_LETTER_I:a
  SOAlphaDS_LETTER_J:a
  SOAlphaDS_LETTER_K:a
  SOAlphaDS_LETTER_L:a
  SOAlphaDS_LETTER_M:a
  SOAlphaDS_LETTER_N:a
  SOAlphaDS_LETTER_O:a
  SOAlphaDS_LETTER_P:a
  SOAlphaDS_LETTER_Q:a
  SOAlphaDS_LETTER_R:a
  SOAlphaDS_LETTER_S:a
  SOAlphaDS_LETTER_T:a
  SOAlphaDS_LETTER_U:a
  SOAlphaDS_LETTER_V:a
  SOAlphaDS_LETTER_W:a
  SOAlphaDS_LETTER_X:a
  SOAlphaDS_LETTER_Y:a
  SOAlphaDS_LETTER_Z:a
] {return($a)}

SOAlphaDS_AS_IN [
  (as in)
  (as)
  (like)
  (like in)
  (for)
]

SOAlphaDS_LETTER_A [a (?(a SOAlphaDS_AS_IN) [alpha adam amanda apple])~0.01]
  {return(A)}
SOAlphaDS_LETTER_B [b (?(b SOAlphaDS_AS_IN) [bravo baker boy bob])~0.01]
{return(B)}
SOAlphaDS_LETTER_C [c (?(c SOAlphaDS_AS_IN) [charlie cat charles])~0.01]
{return(C)}
SOAlphaDS_LETTER_D [d (?(d SOAlphaDS_AS_IN) [delta david dog doctor daniel])~0.01]
  {return(D)}
SOAlphaDS_LETTER_E [e (?(e SOAlphaDS_AS_IN) [echo edward edgar])~0.01]
  {return(E)}
SOAlphaDS_LETTER_F [f (?(f SOAlphaDS_AS_IN) [foxtrot fox frank])~0.01]
  {return(F)}
```

```
SOAlphaDS_LETTER_G [g (?(g SOAlphaDS_AS_IN) [golf george girl])~0.01] {return(G)}
SOAlphaDS_LETTER_H [h (?(h SOAlphaDS_AS_IN) [hotel harry henry])~0.01] {return(H)}
SOAlphaDS_LETTER_I [i (?(i SOAlphaDS_AS_IN) [india idea])~0.01] {return(I)}
SOAlphaDS_LETTER_J [j (?(j SOAlphaDS_AS_IN) [jeff juliet jack john])~0.01]
{return(J)}
SOAlphaDS_LETTER_K [k (?(k SOAlphaDS_AS_IN) [kilo karen king])~0.01]
{return(K)}
SOAlphaDS_LETTER_L [l (?(l SOAlphaDS_AS_IN) [lima larry linda louis lisa])~0.01]
  {return(L)}
SOAlphaDS_LETTER_M [m (?(m SOAlphaDS_AS_IN) [mike mary michael mother])~0.01]
  {return(M)}
SOAlphaDS_LETTER_N [n (?(n SOAlphaDS_AS_IN) [november nancy])~0.01] {return(N)}
SOAlphaDS_LETTER_O [o (?(o SOAlphaDS_AS_IN) [oscar])~0.01]    {return(O)}
SOAlphaDS_LETTER_P [p (?(p SOAlphaDS_AS_IN) [papa paul peter])~0.01]
{return(P)}
SOAlphaDS_LETTER_Q [q (?(q SOAlphaDS_AS_IN) [quebec queen])~0.01]    {return(Q)}
SOAlphaDS_LETTER_R [r (?(r SOAlphaDS_AS_IN) [romeo richard robert])~0.01]
{return(R)}
SOAlphaDS_LETTER_S [s (?(s SOAlphaDS_AS_IN) [sierra sugar sam])~0.01]
{return(S)}
SOAlphaDS_LETTER_T [t (?(t SOAlphaDS_AS_IN) [tango tom thomas])~0.01]
{return(T)}
SOAlphaDS_LETTER_U [u (?(u SOAlphaDS_AS_IN) [uniform uncle union])~0.01]
{return(U)}
SOAlphaDS_LETTER_V [v (?(v SOAlphaDS_AS_IN) [victor victory])~0.01]    {return(V)}
SOAlphaDS_LETTER_W [w (?(w SOAlphaDS_AS_IN) [whiskey walter william])~0.01]
{return(W)}
SOAlphaDS_LETTER_X [x (?(x SOAlphaDS_AS_IN) [xray xylophone])~0.01]     {return(X)}
SOAlphaDS_LETTER_Y [y (?(y SOAlphaDS_AS_IN) [yankee yes yellow])~0.01]
{return(Y)}
SOAlphaDS_LETTER_Z [z (?(z SOAlphaDS_AS_IN) [zulu zebra zoo])~0.01]
{return(Z)}

SOAlphaDS_Zero [zero oh] {return("0")}
SOAlphaDS_Non_zero [one {return("1")}
          two {return("2")}
          three {return("3")}
          four {return("4")}
          five {return("5")}
          six {return("6")}
          seven {return("7")}
          eight {return("8")}
          [ nine niner ] {return("9")}
]

SOAlphaDS_Digit [ SOAlphaDS_Zero:n SOAlphaDS_Non_zero:n ] {return($n)}
```

Notice that we also add support for a few extra words: "dash", "underscore", "at", and "dot". With this grammar, a spelling such as "J O H N underscore D O E at W R O X dot C O M finished" will be recognized as "john_doe@wrox.com". If you're not familiar with the grammar format used here, have a look at Chapter 3, which covers the Nuance Grammar Specification Language (Nuance GSL).

The following is the listing of our Java program `SOSpell.java` that implements an `SOSpell` SpeechObject as an extension of `SODialog`, performs post-processing on the N-Best recognition results, and filters incorrect user spelling based on user confirmation.

First, there's a bunch of Nuance Java packages our application needs to import:

```
import vcommerce.core.util.*;
import vcommerce.util.*;
import vcommerce.util.prompt.*;
import vcommerce.util.context.*;
import vcommerce.core.sc.*;
import vcommerce.sc.*;
import vcommerce.so.*;
import vcommerce.grammar.*;
import nuance.util.grammar.*;
import nuance.core.util.*;
import nuance.util.*;
import nuance.util.prompt.*;
import nuance.core.sc.*;
import nuance.so.*;
import nuance.sc.*;
import java.util.*;
```

Next we derive `SOSpell` from `SODialog`. However you could also extend another existing Foundation SpeechObject such as `SOAlphaDigitString`. To derive from `SODialog`, we have to implement an inner `Result` class and several additional methods. To derive from `SOAlphaDigitString`, you can borrow the `Result` class and required methods that it implements already. To better demonstrate how to create a SpeechObject though, I chose to derive from `SODialog`:

```
/**
 * class that asks users to spell a word consisting of letters, digits, space,
 * dash, underscore, at sign, and dot
 * you can enhance the grammar to allow for more characters.
 */
public class SOSpell extends SODialog
{
```

Two data members are used in `SOSpell`. `m_strSpellings` contains the spelled string so far; it's updated every time a single spelling is confirmed with the user. `m_spellFilter` is of type `SpellFilter`, which is a class we created to implement the SpeechObjects' class called `ResultFilter`. Refer to Nuance SpeechObjects API Reference for the details of each class. By extending `ResultFilter`, you can call `setFilter` to hook up an instance of `SpellFilter` with `SOSpell` and later call the method `passesFilter()` to see if a recognition result should be skipped.

```
    // store the whole spelled text string
    private String m_strSpellings;
    private SpellFilter m_spellFilter;
```

In the constructor, we initialize the two data members, set up the filter, and then tell the SpeechObject to use our own grammar file: `sospell.grammar`. The `FileDynamicGrammar` constructor accepts a grammar file, a top-level rule name, and a class reference. The code expects your grammar file to be located in the subdirectory `grammars` off any directory given in your `CLASSPATH` environment variable.

```
    // Constructor
    public SOSpell() throws VCommerceException
    {
        super();

        m_strSpellings = "";
        m_spellFilter = new SpellFilter();
        setFilter(m_spellFilter);
```

```
        // set the grammar for the spelling so
        setGrammar(new FileDynamicGrammar(
            "/grammars/sospell.grammar",
            "SOSpell_CORE", this.getClass()));
    }
```

We overload the following two methods to set up our application-specific prompts. As an alternative, you could call `setInitialPrompt()` and `setHelpPrompt()`.

```
    // Prompt creation methods
    protected Playable createInitialPrompt()
    {
       return new TTSPrompt("Please spell now.");
    }

    protected Playable createHelpPrompt()
    {
       return new TTSPrompt("Please spell your phrase one letter at a time. After
you're done, say finished.");
    }
```

For simplicity, I use text-to-speech (TTS) prompts. In a real application, you'd probably replace these with professionally recorded audio files, using a line something like this:

```
return new PromptAtom("your_audio_file_name")
```

The following method must be provided to work with the inner class `Result` to return the final result to the user. Depending on the format you require for the result, you can change the constructor of your inner class `Result` and also the calling code here.

```
    protected SpeechObject.Result createResult(String strResult)
        throws VCommerceException
    {
        return new Result(strResult);
    }
```

The next method, `processRecResult()`, is the key method here. When a SpeechObject is invoked, whether by the Nuance Java class utility Launcher that we look at later, or by the hosting service's VoiceXML platform, a few things happen. First, our initial prompt is played, the grammar is loaded, and then the recognition process begins. After an utterance is picked up by the recognition engine, and one or more result items have been generated, the `invoke()` method will call `processRecResult()`, which for each possibility suggested by the engine calls `processSingleResult()`, in turn calling `processAndFilterInterpretation()` for each possible interpretation. Each single result can have more than one interpretation if the grammar is ambiguous in that one utterance can match two or more rules. For example, the grammar `[(john ?doe) (john ?stag)]` can generate two results for the utterance "John". In our spelling example, however, no such thing can happen.

Each `processAndFilterInterpretation()` invocation calls `processInterpretation()` and `passesFilter()`. `passesFilter()` uses a filter we set ourselves to skip particular incorrect results.

So how do we perform post-processing (that is, processing once recognition results are available from the ASR engine) and which methods should we override? To have the full control we want, we must take control right from the outset, meaning the method `processRecResult()`. Inside our overloaded version of this method, we can access all the returned N-Best results, and do whatever we like to them. You don't need to worry about the four parameters of the method here: they're initialized automatically when the object is invoked. If you really need control over this too, check Nuance's *SpeechObjects Developer's Guide* for how to initialize them within an application.

```
protected SpeechObject.Result processRecResult(SpeechChannel sc,
          DialogContext dc,
          CallState cs,
          RecResult recResult)
      throws VCommerceException
{
```

Inside the method, we loop through each recognition result and check to see if it should be skipped by calling `passesFilter()`, the helper method that checks if a result passes the filter. In the implementation of the SpeechObjects framework, `passesFilter()` simply calls the `pass()` method of a `SpellFilter` object – in this case,the `m_spellFilter`'s `pass()` method.

```
int n = recResult.getNumResults();

  for (int i=0; i<n; i++)
  {
    SingleResult sr = recResult.getSingleResult(i);
    int m = sr.getNumInterpretations();

    // we always use the first interpretation as our grammar is unambiguous
    Interpretation interp = sr.getInterpretation(0);

    String strSpelling = null;
    KVSet slots = interp.getSlots();
    if (slots.keyExists("spelling"))
    {
      strSpelling = (String) slots.getObject("spelling");

      // if this spelling is already confirmed by user as incorrect, skip it
      if (!passesFilter(createResult(strSpelling)))
      {
        System.out.println("spelling being skipped: " + strSpelling);
        continue;
      }
```

If the spelling has not been confirmed as incorrect, this could be a correct spelling. So we need to confirm this with the user. But first, we compose a user-friendly prompt string based on the type of the spelling, that is, whether it is a letter, digit, or some other utterance. The method `promptOf()` will be shown later.

```
    // confirm with user if  our result is correct or incorrect
    // first compose a user-friendly prompt string
    String strPrompt = strSpelling;

    // for space, '-', '_', '@', '.', or 'finished', strPrompt is already set
    if (!strSpelling.equals("space") && !strSpelling.equals("dash") &&
     !strSpelling.equals("underscore") && !strSpelling.equals("finished"))
    {
      if (strSpelling.equals("at"))
        strPrompt = "the at sign";
      else if (strSpelling.equals("dot"))
```

```
      strPrompt = "dot as in dot com";
    else if (Character.isLetter(strSpelling.charAt(0)))
      strPrompt = promptOf(strSpelling.charAt(0));
    else if (Character.isDigit(strSpelling.charAt(0)))
      strPrompt = "number " + strSpelling;
  }
```

Now we use another Foundation SpeechObject, `SOYesNo`, to ask for confirmation.

```
SOYesNo soYN = new SOYesNo();
soYN.setMaxErrorCount(500);
soYN.setInitialPrompt(new TTSPrompt(strPrompt + "?"));
soYN.setRecognitionErrorPrompt(new TTSPrompt("Did you say " + strPrompt +
 "?"));

SOYesNo.Result res = (SOYesNo.Result)soYN.invoke(sc, dc, cs);
System.out.println("You said: " + (res.saidYes() ? "yes" : "no"));
```

If the user confirms this is the correct spelling, we check to see if it's the end of the spelling by checking for the utterance "finished". If so, we return the whole string `m_strSpellings` as the final result. If on the other hand, the user is not done spelling yet, we simply update the data member `m_strSpellings` and reset the filter. If we don't reset the filter, those spellings already in the filter would prevent their being recognized when the user gives the next letter.

```
if (res.saidYes())
{
  if (strSpelling.equals("finished"))
    return createResult(m_strSpellings);
  else
  {
    // convert three special utterances to characters
    if (strSpelling.equals("space"))
      m_strSpellings += " ";
    else if (strSpelling.equals("dash"))
      m_strSpellings += "-";
    else if (strSpelling.equals("underscore"))
      m_strSpellings += "_";
    else if (strSpelling.equals("at"))
      m_strSpellings += "@";
    else if (strSpelling.equals("dot"))
      m_strSpellings += ".";
    else // this is either a letter or digit
    {
      m_strSpellings += strSpelling;
    }

     setNoResultFoundPrompt(new TTSPrompt("OK, please continue."));

     // reset the filter
     m_spellFilter.reset();
```

The null return value normally indicates to the framework that we haven't got a valid recognition result yet. In a way, this is still true, as the SpeechObject's job is not over until we've collected an entire phrase by the spelling process. If we were to return a non-null result, the framework would interpret this as meaning the recognition task is complete, and return prematurely from the SpeechObject. Note that if you uncomment the line:

```
if (i < n-1) continue
```

below, then you'll be asked to confirm the next possible recognition result in the N-Best list, instead of being asked to spell again. Another option you may want to try is to list all the possible results in one utterance and ask the user to select the correct one. For example, when you spell "t", it can possibly get three results: "c", "t", and "d". So it can ask you "c as in Charlie, t as in Tom, or d as in David?" Here you see that SpeechObjects can let you process the N-Best list in many possible ways, which is not possible using VoiceXML grammar alone.

```
                return null;
            }
        }
        else
        {
            // an alternative to reprompting is to go thru all remaining n-best
            // results until either user confirms or the end of list is reached

            // to go thru the list instead of asking the user, uncomment next line
            // if (i < n-1) continue;

            // as we return null to indicate no result if found, we set the
            // NoResultFound prompt
            setNoResultFoundPrompt(new TTSPrompt("Please spell it again."));
```

If the user informs `SOSpell` that it is incorrectly recognizing a letter, then we save that letter to a skip list by calling the filter's `addSkipWord()` method, which is a helper method we shall define in the `SpellFilter` class later.

```
            // set a filter
            m_spellFilter.addSkipWord(strSpelling);
            return null;
          }
        }
      }
      return null;
    }
```

We override the following method to prevent the framework playing a default prompt such as "Sorry, I didn't understand" before it plays, "Please spell it again" or "OK, please continue", which we set using `setNoResultFoundPrompt`. This is necessary because we are returning `null` until the spelling is complete, and because a returned `null` normally means recognition failure.

```
    protected SpeechObject.Result handleNoResultFound(SpeechChannel sc,
                DialogContext dc,
                CallState callState,
                RecResult recResult)
          throws VCommerceException
    {

      appendPrompt(getErrorPromptByKey(NO_RESULT_FOUND),sc);
      return null;
    }
```

Next is the helper method that generates more easily understandable prompts for each letter.

```
private String promptOf(char ch)
{
  switch (ch)
  {
  case 'A':
    return "a as in alpha";
  case 'B':
    return "b as in bravo";
  case 'C':
    return "c as in charlie";
  case 'D':
    return "d as in delta";
  case 'E':
    return "e as in echo";
  case 'F':
    return "f as in foxtrot";
  case 'G':
    return "g as in golf";
  case 'H':
    return "h as in hotel";
  case 'I':
    return "i as in india";
  case 'J':
    return "j as in juliet";
  case 'K':
    return "k as in kilo";
  case 'L':
    return "l as in lima";
  case 'M':
    return "m as in mike";
  case 'N':
    return "n as in november";
  case 'O':
    return "o as in oscar";
  case 'P':
    return "p as in papa";
  case 'Q':
    return "q as in quebec";
  case 'R':
    return "r as in romea";
  case 'S':
    return "s as in sierra";
  case 'T':
    return "t as in tango";
  case 'U':
    return "u as in uniform";
  case 'V':
    return "v as in victor";
  case 'W':
    return "w as in whiskey";
  case 'X':
    return "x as in x ray";
  case 'Y':
    return "y as in yankee";
  case 'Z':
    return "z as in zulu";
  }
  return "";
}
```

Below is the inner Result class that every SODialog-derived class has to implement. Each SODialog.Result class should define convenience (helper) methods providing access to the recognition result. For our spelling problem, there's only one piece of data to be accessed: the string of spelled text. So a single convenience method, named getSpelling(), is defined. Other SpeechObjects may have more than one piece of data to be accessed, so more than one convenience method will need to be defined for that SpeechObject. For example, SODate has getYear(), getMonth(), and getDay() methods. Also notice that getString() and setString() are two of the many methods you can use from a SpeechObject.Result class, defined in a superclass called KVSet that SpeechObject.Result and therefore SODialog.Result both extend. You can use them to set or get recognition results.

```
    // start of inner class Result
    public static class Result extends SpeechObject.Result
    {
       // convenience function
       public String getSpelling()
       {
             return getString("SPELLING");
       }

       // Constructor
       protected Result(String strSpelling)
       {
            setString("SPELLING", strSpelling);
       }

       // Playable that has to be implemented for a concrete class extended from
  SODialog
       public void appendTo(PromptPlayer player)
       throws VCommerceException
       {
             player.appendPrompt(getSpelling());
       }

       // this method is also required for a concrete SODialog subclass
       public String toString()
       {
             return getSpelling();
       }

       } // end of inner class Result

    }
```

Finally, here's the filter class that extends ResultFilter. The pass() method is required to test if a given value is to be filtered out or not. We use a Vector member to keep track of which spellings should be skipped.

```
  // the filter class used to skip incorrect result
  class SpellFilter implements ResultFilter
  {
    private Vector m_vecSkipWords;

    public void reset()
    {
      m_vecSkipWords = null;
    }

    public void addSkipWord(String strSpelling)
    {
      if (m_vecSkipWords == null)
```

```
        m_vecSkipWords = new Vector();

      m_vecSkipWords.addElement(strSpelling);
    }

    public boolean pass(SpeechObject.Result result)
    {
      if (m_vecSkipWords != null && m_vecSkipWords.contains
       (((SOSpell.Result)result).getSpelling()))
        return false;
      else
        return true;
    }
  }
```

The following diagram describes the application above to help you understand the flow of the spelling process.

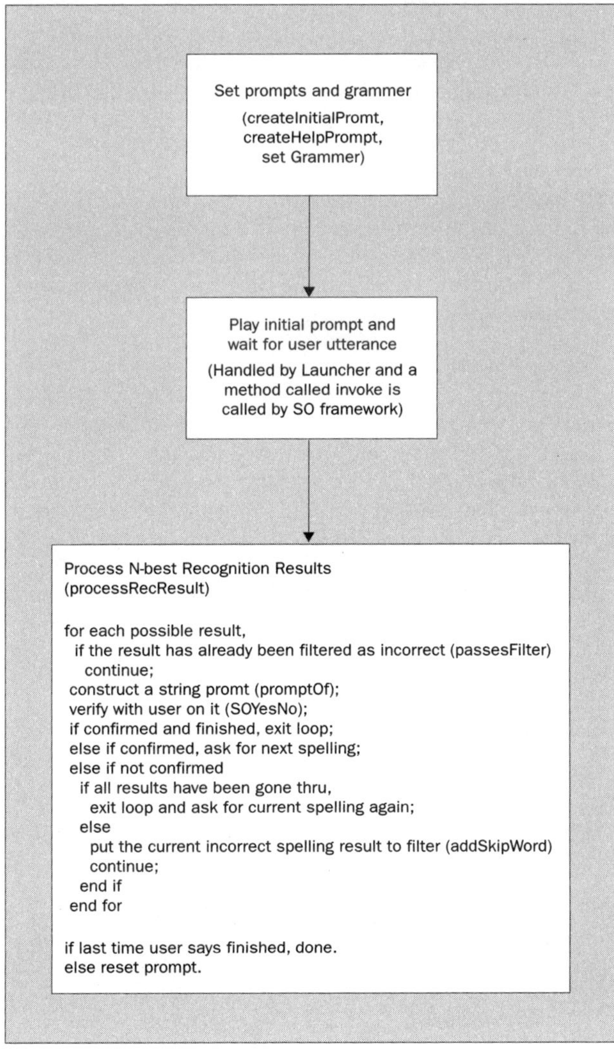

Using SOSpell

To test `SOSpell.java` with `sospell.grammar` on your local machine, you first need to compile `SOSpell.java`. I used Symantec Visual Café 4 (not to be confused with the VoiceXML platform, the BeVocal Café), a Java IDE, to build the class file. With this package, the steps to follow are:

1. Start Visual Café, create a new Project from the **File** menu, select **Empty Project** in the New Project dialog box;
2. Add the file `SOSpell.java` to the project;
3. In the **Project-Options-Directories**, add the following Nuance SpeechObjects JAR files to the Input class files: `%jnuance%\fso.jar`, `%jnuance%\jsc.jar`, `%jnuance%\nsc.jar`, `%jnuance%\swingall.jar`, `%jnuance%\vcom.jar`, `%jnuance%\vcomsc.jar`; also, change the directory for Output files to where you want your created class to be;
4. Select **Project – Build Application**; this will create three class files in your Output files directory: `SOSpell.class`, `SOSpell$Result.class`, and `SpellFilter.class`.

You can also use JDK 1.2 itself to accomplish this. Firstly, ensure that the following paths are given in your `CLASSPATH` environment variable: `%jnuance%\fso.jar`, `%jnuance%\jsc.jar`, `%jnuance%\nsc.jar`, `%jnuance%\swingall.jar`, `%jnuance%\vcom.jar`, and `%jnuance%\vcomsc.jar`. Then just navigate to the directory where `SOSpell.java` is found, and execute the following command line:

```
javac SOSpell.java
```

After you build the application, you need to start all the required Nuance recognition processes before testing `SOSpell`, including a license manager, a resource manager, a recognition server, and a compilation server. Detailed information can be found in Nuance's *Getting Started with SpeechObjects.* After all the above processes are started successfully, you can use the Nuance utility Launcher to test `SOSpell`. The process for testing other SpeechObjects with Launcher is very similar:

```
java nuance.launch.Launcher –play rm.Addresses=localhost lm.Addresses=
 localhost SOSpell
```

Here's a typical interaction with the user:

SOSpell:	"Please spell now."
User:	"J."
SOSpell:	"K as in Kilo?"
User:	"No."
SOSpell:	"Please spell again."
User:	"J."
SOSpell:	"J as in Juliet?"

User:	"Yes."
SOSpell:	"OK, please continue."
User:	"O."
SOSpell:	"Number zero?"
User:	"No."
SOSpell:	"Please spell again."
User:	"O."
SOSpell:	"O as in Oscar?"
User:	"Yes."
SOSpell:	"OK, please continue."
User:	"E."
SOSpell:	"E as in Echo."
User:	"Yes."
SOSpell:	"OK, please continue."
User:	"Underscore."
SOSpell:	"Underscore?"
User:	"Yes."
SOSpell:	"OK, please continue."
User:	"T."
SOSpell:	"T as in Tango?"
User::	"Yes."
SOSpell:	"OK, please continue."
User:	"At."
SOSpell:	"The at sign?"
User:	"Yes."
SOSpell:	"OK, please continue."
User:	*continues spelling out "wrox.com"*
...	...
User:	"Finished."
SOSpell:	"Finished?"
User:	"Yes."

After the dialog above, the final recognition result will be: joe_t@wrox.com

To make `SOSpell` available from BeVocal Café, you will need to compile your class files and grammar file into a JAR archive. You may also want to compile all the prompts into another JAR or zip archive. Select Visual Café Project | Deploy, and the JAR file called `SOSpell.jar` will be created. If you use JDK, execute jar cvf SOSpell.jar *.class in the directory where you compiled `SOSpell.java`.

Open this JAR file with a tool such as WinZip: you'll see three class files and a manifest file describing the information in the archive. You'll need to add the `sospell.grammar` file to the archive. As we pass `/grammars/sospell.grammar` to new `FileDynamicGrammar` in the `SOSpell` constructor, we need to create a directory named `grammars` on your C: or D: drive, and then copy the `sospell.grammar` to that directory. Then when you add that grammar file to `SOSpell.jar` by dragging-and-dropping the file into the WinZip window, you'll see a dialog box similar to the following:

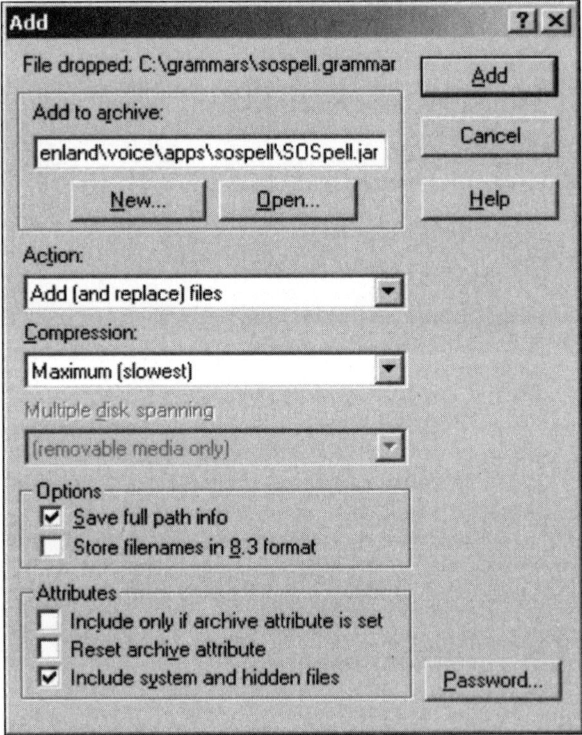

Check Save extra folder info for WinZip 7.0, or Save full path info for WinZip 8.0 so that when BeVocal Café loads your remote `SOSpell.jar` file, it will know where to look for your grammar file. Then click Add to add the `sospell.grammar` file to the JAR file.

> *To make your life easier, you can simply pass `/sospell.grammar` to the new `FileDynamicGrammar` and uncheck Save full path info or Save extra folder info when you add the grammar file to the `SOSpell.jar` archive.*

After you have the JAR file, simply copy it to your web server directory. Now we can use the SpeechObject from within our own VoiceXML applications, so we can replace the spelling code in the e-mail/calendar application of Chapter 9 with something similar to the following:

```
<object classid="speechobject://SOSpell" name="spellings"
 archive="http://www.yourserver.com/voicexml/SOSpell.jar">
  <filled>
    <prompt>
      you said <value expr=" spellings"/>
    </prompt>
  </filled>
</object>
```

Alternatively, to test the SpeechObject by itself, just add the <object> element to a form:

```
<?xml version="1.0"?>
<vxml version="1.0">

  <form id="form1">
    <block>
      <prompt>Before loading your object</prompt>
    </block>
    <object classid="speechobject://SOSpell" name="spelling"
     archive="http://www.yourserver.com/voicexml/SOSpell.jar">
      <filled>
        <prompt>
          you said <value expr="spelling"/>
        </prompt>
      </filled>
    </object>

  </form>
</vxml>
```

After calling your BeVocal developer phone number, you'll enter a dialog just as when running SOSpell on your local machine. After all the dry theory and hard coding, doesn't the voice on the other end of the phone sound sweet? Don't worry, as you gain experience of using SpeechObjects, the process that may seem long-winded now will become a quite natural procedure.

If you want to use audio prompts instead of TTS prompts in your SpeechObject, add all the audio files to a separate zip or JAR file, then in the <object> element, add a data attribute like this:

```
<object classid="speechobject://SOSpell" name="spellings"
  data="http://www.yourserver.com/voicexml/SOSpellPrompts.zip"
  archive="http://www.yourserver.com/voicexml/SOSpell.jar">
```

One thing you should be aware of is that although BeVocal Café supports the SpeechObjects API, for security reasons it doesn't allow direct Java JDK access from your SpeechObjects to the local file system, nor to JDBC or the local network. This is because after loading your remote SpeechObjects, BeVocal Café runs your code on their own server. The main purpose for using remote SpeechObjects is to allow you to access your own library of reusable complex dialogs and grammars. A tip – try not to add non-speech-related tasks, such as sending e-mails or accessing a database, to your SpeechObjects. Instead, use standard web server technologies such as ASP or JSP in tandem with the VoiceXML <submit>, <goto>, or, best of all, <subdialog> elements to accomplish such tasks.

Future Upgrades

Although we've gone through a lot of trouble to use SpeechObjects to implement a better solution for spelling out a phrase, there are still enhancements possible for `SOSpell`. Some of its failings are caused by the limitations of current ASR engines, which are simply no match for the human ear and brain. Other problems are related to the spelling itself: although it seems simple at first, recognizing words spelt out loud is in reality a pretty awkward task. Many letters are easily confusable, principally due to their short length. But with the N-Best post-processing approach, we have the chance to resolve this difficult acoustic ambiguity problem in a plausible and natural way. A further enhancement to the spelling algorithm would be to specify the probability of each letter being spoken, to favor common letters such as 'e' and 't' over less common ones like 'v' and 'z'.

Because spelling words like this can be useful in many situations, you may decide to continue the work started here. Some improvements might be to use a spell-matcher library when you know most likely words in advance, thus anticipating the most likely next letter among the N-Best results, or even suggesting words after the initial few characters have been given. For free-form spelling, you may also consider using some semantic cues to sort the N-Best results, now that you know how to deal with the N-Best result format, and have seen how filtering can be used as a mechanism for interacting with users more intelligently. Another area where you could focus attention is improving the overall performance of the spelling process – as you may have noticed, spelling anything but the shortest message can be long-winded and tedious.

Summary

In this chapter, we've talked about how to use Nuance SpeechObjects and Foundation SpeechObjects in VoiceXML applications to overcome some of limitations of the VoiceXML language, and open the way to more sophisticated voice applications. There are already many SpeechObjects available from Nuance and other third parties that you can use directly. Usually, a developer license will be provided for testing and evaluation; to deploy them in a commercial environment, the license fee will typically be from several hundred dollars to over $1,000 per port. However, SpeechObjects can save you a lot of time and effort by reducing the need to develop your own grammars, and by simplifying the design of user-friendly dialogs, and the processing that they require. They can speed up the whole development process, allowing you to get applications to market faster. With a little additional effort, you can even create your own SpeechObjects, which give you great control over the raw recognition results of a speech engine. Your own SpeechObjects are capable of processing a list of possible results, and by helping resolve the important and difficult question of acoustic ambiguity, can make your applications much more user-friendly. You can deploy SpeechObjects easily on current VoiceXML platforms, and reuse them in a variety of problem domains. They are full of potential, and the returns they offer more than compensate for the investment of time and effort required to become familiar with their modes of operation.

```
<?xml version="1.0"?>
<vxml version="1.0">
<form id="foo">
<block>
<prompt>
Hi. My name is Bob
</prompt>
</block>
</form>
</vxml>
```

11

The Future

VoiceXML is a technology of the future. As it stands now, its use is really restricted to pure voice browsers. This doesn't provide anything altogether new: automated speech response has been around in this form for quite a while. However, VoiceXML does have a serious leg-up on standard dedicated telephony platforms – with its voice recognition engines and grammars built into the core of the language, quite sophisticated applications can be rapidly developed, especially given its foundation on XML syntax. It also has the backing of several major corporations, but it is still really limited to a single mode: voice. This is not to say that being the best in the telephony field is a bad thing; it's what VoiceXML was designed for, but the language's full potential will not be realized with the current paradigm. As the technologies evolve, we will see a continued convergence with existing Internet technologies. The Voice Internet, the wireless Web, and the standard Internet are already being harmonized on paper by various standards bodies, and in the minds of more imaginative developers. When these ideas take off in practice, VoiceXML will really shine. It is a web language, just like HTML, cHTML (Compact HTML), and WML, placing it at the forefront when people start expecting voice interactivity from their palmtops and other wireless devices. It may be a few years off, but it is likely that VoiceXML expertise will become as commonplace among web developers as HTML knowledge is today.

WAP and VoiceXML – Joint Initiative?

With the arrival of the 3G wireless world imminent, it is easy to envision a major role for voice technologies in the future of the wireless web. Convergence of wireless technologies is inevitable; there is no doubt about it. Nevertheless, the technologies involved, especially the protocols for voice and data, are largely isolated from each other. Currently, the voice side and the display side of hybrid voice/visual applications have no clear means of communication, and cannot know what the other is doing.

Even taking this into account, voice and wireless still go hand in hand. Given the limited and variable display capabilities of most mobile devices, audio rendering would make a welcome addition, not to mention that speech navigation and input is much more natural than typing on a tiny keypad or using a stylus. Voice is also more convenient in situations where a data display would be a hindrance, or even dangerous (like when driving, for instance).

The Old Way: Multiple Channels, Multiple Authoring

Today, we can browse the Internet on our desktops or palmtops, and we are even seeing the beginnings of the new-fangled Voice Internet. To a user exploiting these different browsing platforms, or *channels*, everything operates wonderfully – the channels appear separate but functional and consistent. Users have an array of media they can use to access Internet content, but the problem with the current situation is simple: it is Developer Hell.

The M x N Problem

Presently, if we plan to create a site or web application to be accessed via multiple channels, including desktop PC, palmtop, and phone, we can be sure it will not be a simple process. Each channel we implement will have to be hand authored from the ground up, using different languages and processes as appropriate: HTML for the standard Internet, WML for the wireless side, and VoiceXML to provide the telephone access we desire. This is less than efficient, considering the only component of the system these implementations can currently share is the back-end database, and even then, there are cases where even the database needs to be tailored for different media. Let's see if we can come up with some figures to indicate the complexity of this problem. Say we have a site with 20 core pages (M) to produce the site content, and that we want to these pages to be accessible over, say, five channels (N). To achieve this, we are going to have to author $M \times N = 100$ pages of mirrored subject matter. If this is doesn't seem too bad, try factoring in the maintenance that these pages are going to require, and you'll be able to see what a huge task we have on our hands, draining resources and time. As the range of devices grows and the number of available channels increases, this situation is in danger of becoming even worse. Imagine a large change in site functionality that might take days to implement on a single channel, and then imagine having to follow a similar procedure ten or twenty times more for every channel.

The New Way: Common Interaction Design

With all the work it takes right now to create and maintain a dynamic web application that supports multiple channels, it is hardly worth the effort. What developers need is some method of tying all of these channels together at some base level to make application creation and modification a simpler and faster process. At least, that was the consensus reached at the W3C's convention on Wireless convergence held in Hong Kong in September 2000.

Single Authoring for Multiple Channels

At the Hong Kong convention, major players like IBM recommended research into a single language that would control the user's progression through a general online application, no matter what the channel. This recommendation was widely accepted by most interested parties as the next step to think about: far from actualization, but necessary. This single language would mean that every channel in an application or site would share certain interconnected components.

In order to make sure that our implementations for each channel are appropriately interlinked, we need to find the highest level of commonality. Given that all of the implementations will serve the same core function – for example a webmail program on wireless will provide the same core features as that program's implementation on the regular web – we can design a generic diagram of the user's path through an application: the user's interaction. Consider another example, of a web stock-quoting application: no matter what the channel, at some point we will want to request user input for a company or its associated stock symbol to quote for. If we had a general description of where in our application this input was to present itself, and how we should deal with the results of that input, we could use this description to map that interaction through every channel (using XSL stylesheets), eliminating the M x N problem. If you're thinking that this is merely a reformulation of the M x N problem as we now require a separate stylesheet for each document for each channel, you may be right for specialized pages at least. But even then, if extreme specialization is required, changing presentation for M x N pages is much simpler (and safer) than changing content.

There are several other additional benefits that this new language would bring. For one, it continues the trend of separating content from presentation. All critical input and output components would be written in this versatile language, while separate stylesheets would apply transformations to present XML-based content on the supported channels, by incorporating these shared components as appropriate. By doing so, much easier manipulation and modification of content is possible, allowing for one-time writing, and one-step changes.

At this point, no one really knows what form this Common Interaction Design Language will eventually appear as, or when. Nevertheless, it, or a derivative technology, will make developing for multiple channels a much more efficient procedure. Developers will still have the task of creating independent stylesheets for each channel to specialize the presentation of the interaction, but if the stylesheets are as generic as possible, cross-channel modifications will be accomplished in one fell swoop. The diagram overleaf clearly illustrates this concept. Contrast this with the steps it takes to create a multi-channel application using traditional multiple authoring.

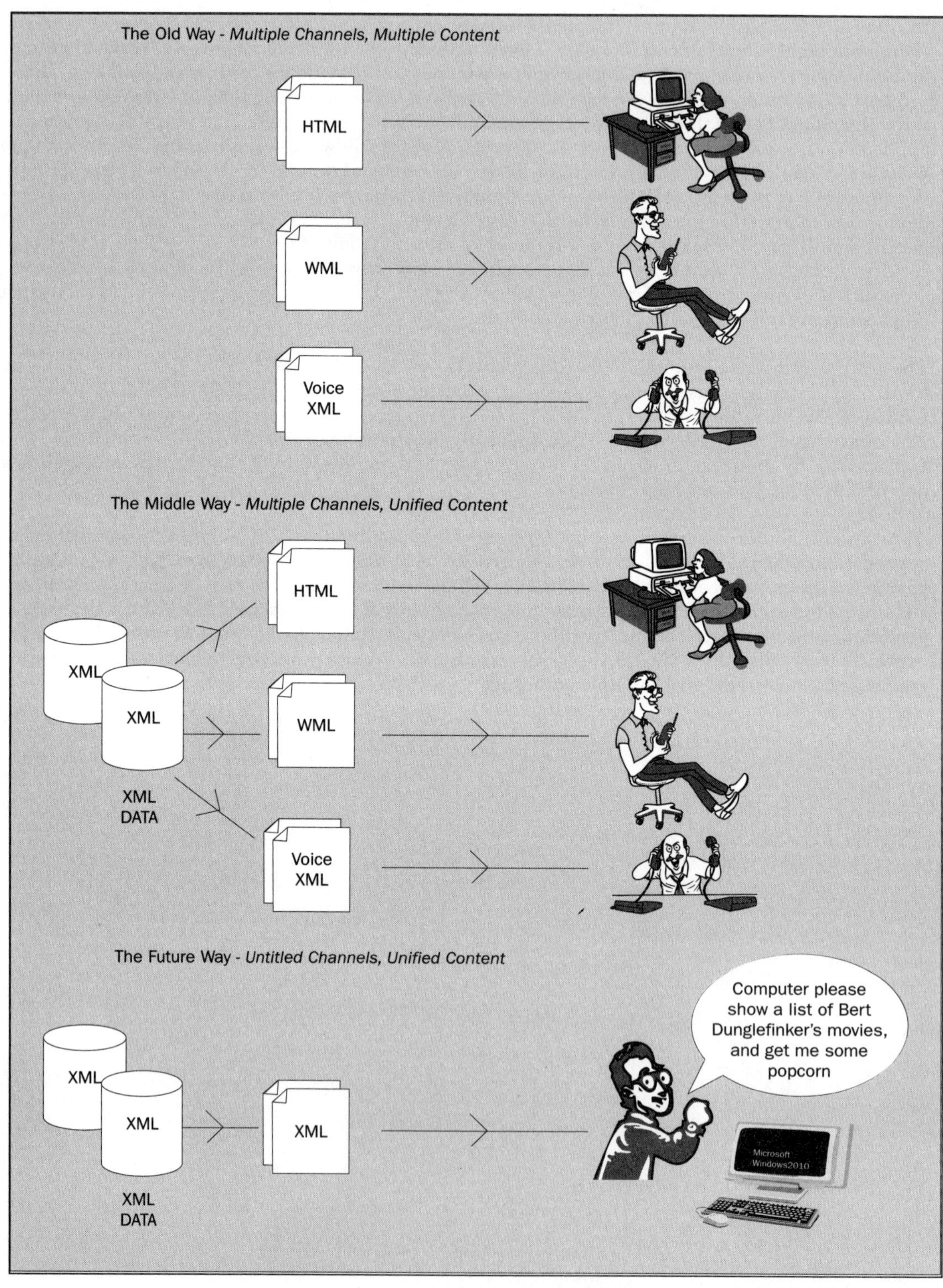
The Old Way - *Multiple Channels, Multiple Content*
HTML
WML
Voice XML
The Middle Way - *Multiple Channels, Unified Content*
XML
XML
XML DATA
HTML
WML
Voice XML
The Future Way - *Untitled Channels, Unified Content*
XML
XML
XML DATA
XML
Computer please show a list of Bert Dunglefinker's movies, and get me some popcorn
Microsoft Windows2010

Issues for the Convergence of VoiceXML and WML

Various issues have surfaced during the initial stages of talks geared towards assisting and encouraging the convergence of VoiceXML and WML. Principally:

- VoiceXML was created as a telephony language to be used over a traditional switched connection, while WML is used over a different packet-based data connection. Right now, voice and data cannot be 'beamed out' simultaneously. Indeed they may never be, but in order for the technologies to converge, this needs to be harmonized and accounted for.
- Today, VoiceXML is not processed as standard on the client, because normal phones do not yet come equipped with a local processing engine, whereas WML markup *is* rendered by the client to produce the displayed content.

Because the two languages have these fundamental incompatibilities, getting them to operate simultaneously during a single session is pretty much an impossible mission. Should you choose to accept it, you will probably find the best solution that is currently feasible is switching between voice and data by terminating the connection, and redialing in the appropriate mode. The consequence of doing this of course is to lose the user's current context in your application or site. It is unlikely we will see phones available for some time that are capable of simultaneous voice and data calls.

Clearly, because WAP and VoiceXML have not been designed to work together from the bottom up, neither technology is in a position to be integrated through a common interaction language.

Multi-Modal Applications

Seamless multi-channel protocols and technologies are something that will emerge sometime in the future, but the continued innovation in this field will soon lead to what every telephony, wireless, and XML firm is already busy hyping now: **multi-modal applications**. In this context, a *mode* denotes a mechanism for input or output; keypads are a mode of input, as is speech. Multi-modal applications therefore incorporate any number of modes seamlessly, so a user could speak their name, type in their address, and send their phone number direct from the handset; all within the same session, form, and application context.

The dream is to extend the model represented by the mouse and keyboard of a present-day desktop computer: both devices interface with the system simultaneously and interchangeably. In the early 1980s, home computers were typically operated solely with a keyboard. Today, we can operate these systems much more efficiently with the aid of multiple modes, generally a keyboard and pointing device, but there are also many other diverse modes we could potentially use, like touch screen, or voice. How useable would the Internet be if users had to browse using the keyboard only, tabbing through every button and form field until reaching the one required point? For many modern applications, multiple modes have already become necessity.

Such multi-modal applications will eventually be found everywhere. The markup languages now being considered by the W3C aim to enable both specialized and generic forms to be rendered by any compatible device, aiming primarily at voice browsers, standard browsers, and wireless devices. The real killer apps are to be found in the wireless arena, however, given the limited visual output and keyed input facilities that limit most mobile devices. Given enough time, we can expect to see the voice mode of interaction become as essential to wireless users as the pointing device has become to desktop users. The PC, already having ample display and input capabilities, will probably find these new modes a secondary convenience.

Considering that the technologies that multi-modal applications will be based on are still at a very early stage in their evolutionary process, it will be a long while before we see any device that will allow us to browse in voice and text modes at the same time. Voice browsers are likely to remain located on remote gateways for the immediate future, as recognition engines are too complex for current wireless devices. We will probably have to wait for technologies beyond the deployment 3G for cost, and especially technology, to catch up with the ideas. Everything involved is in its infancy, and there are many transitory phases yet to come in the evolution of this technology before we see anything useful.

I Want It Now! (Well, Bits of It)

Despite all the hurdles that the present-day developer must overcome to create multi-modal applications or orchestrate unsynchronized multi-channel applications, a brave few have ventured into the lion's den, finding workarounds and loopholes in existing technologies that they can turn to their advantage. To illustrate this, I'd like to introduce you to the efforts of one such company, **UltiVerse Technologies**, which has developed the wireless messaging solution known as **FreeVerse**.

FreeVerse

Among FreeVerse's features is the ability to allow the user to utilize their wireless device's voice mode to record `.wav` files to send as e-mail attachments, instead of inefficiently having to tap at a baby-sized keypad. It manages this by terminating the user's data session when voice recording begins, and initiating a voice call. The recording is performed on the server, after which the user must manually re-initiate a data session. UltiVerse overcomes the problem of losing data session information and context for the duration of the voice call by keeping hold of the user's current state on the server – normally all application and session data is lost on closing a data session. This means that once the user redials a data connection, they can be returned to the point in the web application at which they made the recording. The catch is that FreeVerse must wait the excruciatingly long times required for cellular connections to complete, and the user must manually reload their browser to effect the new session. Nevertheless, by being able to speak the content of an e-mail, sending long messages on the move becomes a much more practical option, even taking into account the cellular connect times and having to press the "back" button after the voice interaction is completed (and the data connection re-established) to refresh the site's content to reflect the interaction. Go to http://www.ultiverse.com for a neat demonstration on everything that FreeVerse can do.

Microsoft MiPad

Microsoft too has its own implementation of multiple modes, although not in the telephony arena. Its is an entire platform dedicated to synchronized voice and pointer input: the **MiPad** (pronounced "my pad"). This device contains an onboard voice recognition engine to implement the speech/text interface, but due to technical limitations and restricted storage, this engine can often make errors. To compensate for the low accuracy level, Microsoft introduced a series of innovations that allow the user to cut down on mistakes. The first of these is a basic point-and-correct concept that allows the user to tap words that are recognized incorrectly and restate just those words until a match is correctly distinguished.

This concept makes a more lightweight speech engine acceptable, although this approach requires the user to take a more active role in making sure their words are recognized correctly. Even so, this still beats having to highlight and retype the incorrect word or sentence. The second innovation borrows a concept related to the grammars of VoiceXML. When the user is at a field that specifies a name input, the system intelligently prioritizes the recognition options: likely names are given the highest priority, while unlikely names are considered as a last resort, so that "John Brown" would be prioritized above "lawn gown" and similar sounding utterances. VoiceXML grammars perform a similar function, filtering input based on confidence levels and a pre-determined set of criteria. Microsoft goes slightly father and proceeds to other possibilities after the pre-determined criteria fail. This is due to differences in context, however, so although this staggered recognition methodology works well on a device/OS platform, it would probably be less useful in a telephony context. Check it out at http://research.microsoft.com/srg/mipad.asp.

Very few other platforms or applications exist today with true multi-modal capabilities. We are seeing more and more multi-channel applications arising, but the technology and resources for supporting multiple modes in a single application either do not exist as yet, or require very creative but limiting partial solutions.

The Synchronization Issue

One of the biggest problems in the way of multi-modal progression is synchronization. Synchronization is necessary to prevent collisions between modes, to resolve protocol conflicts, and unite server- and client-side languages. The Common Interaction Design Language concept discussed earlier under the heading *Single Authoring for Multiple Channels* addresses such issues, but for now, there are no easy answers. Only after the Hong Kong Convention was it decided that a W3C Working Group needed to be established to focus on multi-modal requirements, and right now, that's all that's out there: just a bunch of requirements and ideas. The first drafts from the working group outline in detail the need for a limited, unified event model, in which markup languages working in tandem are synchronized at certain points in a user's interaction, such as on entering a form or specific input element, or when a field is filled. This means that the markup language for each channel receives notification of actions in other modes, and it can thus make sure that its own interface is updated accordingly.

Of course, there are numerous issues to deal with before synchronization can become a reality. For one, every mode has a different notion of context, so that a "back" button makes perfect sense for visual modes, but sometimes won't be appropriate for voice applications. Additionally, the event models for today's markup languages are different enough to make a unified model very difficult to implement. The interface design skills and technical knowledge alone required for a synchronized application, orchestrating several different languages' scripting engines and individual limitations, is daunting at the least. Imagine a complex script function in a normal web application that alters the way a form is presented and how it accepts input: how would this be interpreted and implemented on the voice side, assuming any input mode could be used to interact with the form? With standard displays, the page can change dynamically according to the user's actions, but in voice, what's been said has been said, so it is difficult to re-structure an entire interaction in a corresponding way.

VoiceXML 2.0 – Likely Changes and Modifications

At the time of writing, the VoiceXML 2.0 working draft is close to public release, and this section examines the changes to the language that are likely to be introduced. As VoiceXML 1.0 is the culmination of the evolution of previous dialog description languages, it is already very complete and comprehensive, despite being such an early version. However, many areas of the 1.0 document are vague and unclear, which could lead to possible inconsistencies in interpretation. This, of course, has resulted in voice browsers being developed that interpret the standard slightly differently. Currently, only VoiceGenie's gateway claims to have full compliance with the specification, largely due to the fact that its designers worked very closely with the specification's authors. Because of the complications and ambiguities in the draft, companies had to develop unique solutions and proprietary implementations to deploy platforms quickly; a situation that must be addressed to avoid a repetition of events that followed the release of the Dynamic HTML recommendation. When DHTML first hit web browsers, similar vagaries led vendors to write incompatible software, to the dismay of web developers everywhere, who found they now had to write separate code for every browser on the market. The VoiceXML 2.0 draft aims to forestall such divergence of platforms by clarifying ambiguous areas, and providing commonly sought-after extensions of the language where appropriate.

Most changes to the specification, other than those addressing readability and organization issues, are minor and incremental. In fact, VoiceGenie's view is that the 2.0 Specification could in fact be designated 1.1, because the updates that will actually be included are so few. The bottom line is that maintaining backward-compatibility is a top priority, as too many modifications to the established model would complicate things for existing applications. It is unlikely that any core features will be added, as VoiceXML is already a very complete language, at least until convergence with other technologies throws up a slew of additions and clarifications.

Probable Areas for Change

Given that modifications are few, they will probably center on clearing up any unnecessary complexities and inconsistencies in the 1.0 specification. For example, the currency data type currently includes a locale indicator that is used to specify dollars, pounds sterling, and other forms of currency. Under 1.0, this indicator stores a null-value string if not given by the user, but when spoken, the default locale is used. So even though a currency may have a null value, it will be presented to the user as the default, which will not always be appropriate. A more consistent approach would be to assign a currency data item with the default currency indicator for the current locale, rather than using a null-value string. Then, when a user in America does not specify a currency, the default dollar indicator would be assigned to the data item, as opposed to null.

There are unlikely to be many changes more substantial than this. A few tags and attributes will most likely be added to the language to extend its features and replace vendor-specific implementations that have arisen. For instance, some browsers currently support a `<debug>` tag, which allows run-time writing to a specified log, but is not officially a part of the VoiceXML language. This tag will be replaced by the specification-compliant `<log>` tag, which in fact is already supported by BeVocal. As stated before, such changes are to encourage compliance with the specification and improve browser interoperability. The `<transcribe>` element, currently included in the W3C Note on VoiceXML 1.0 as a proposed extension, is also a natural candidate for full inclusion in the language. This element allows an arbitrary user message to be captured as text, but is not intended to be practicalble for all browser contexts at this time, and none of the voice gateways currently have plans to support this element.

The other key change will be the inclusion of an XML-based grammar format. Currently, developers can author grammars using existing non-XML formats such as JSGF (the Java Speech Grammar Format), and Nuance's GSL (Grammar Specification Language), both covered by Chapter 3. It is an unnecessary hassle for developers to have to learn the syntax of independent formats, and it would be great to see grammars that fit naturally into the XML environment of VoiceXML. Dynamically evaluating generated or unknown grammars should then become a simple task, as you can leverage existing XML technologies to break complicated grammars down into a hierarchy of individual elements that represent the grammar as a whole.

As for security, very little will change, as VoiceXML security is based upon security already established for the HTTP protocol. However, listed in the W3C's working draft is a recommendation for a type of speaker verification that would allow developers to create dialogs that compare spoken input with pre-recorded speech samples for authentication purposes. The comparison would be both knowledge-based (using passwords) and acoustic, so someone who spoke the correct password but whose voice did not match with the stored sample still would not be authenticated, and vice-versa. This feature is well within the realms of currently available technology, but is not guaranteed though, as it appears in the "should have" category of the draft (another section, "must have", lists additions that are required).

Finally, VoiceXML 2.0 may include and/or support some related sub-languages. The Speech Synthesis Markup Language, for instance, is currently in development within the W3C's Voice Browser Working Group. This is a language designed to work in tandem with VoiceXML, specifically the text-to-speech component of the technology. The language aims to provide a means for developers to specify in detail the way generated speech should sound, and even the way its text should be animated in future multi-modal applications.

ETA to Real World

When the 2.0 Specification is released, there will inevitably be a hiatus before interpreters become available that take advantage of the new version. However, many developers are eager to see the improvements of 2.0, so there is pressure for browser developers to produce VoiceXML 2.0-compliant products in as short an amount of time as possible. In fact, there is a common misconception among many companies considering deploying VoiceXML applications that version 1.0 is incomplete, not secure, or unreliable, and they should wait until the release of 2.0 before creating commercial applications. This has not been helped by the continued postponement of the specification by the W3C standards body, which originally planned the release for February 2001. VoiceGenie and other corporations are hoping to be able to release VoiceXML 2.0-compliant browsers in Q3 2001, with accompanying development kits and debugging tools, so expect to hear the new voice of telephony very soon. As for 1.0 developers, you need not worry about having to re-code current applications to be compatible with these new environments and interpreters – 1.0 code will still run successfully on 2.0 browsers.

A Look Far into the Future

The ultimate goal of any telephony-related voice technology is to create flawless and completely natural interactions, so the end user cannot distinguish a system from a highly intelligent human operator. That technology may still be far off, but the industry is moving at break-neck speed and evolving rapidly. How many revolutions do the next ten years hold? It may well be that near-human speech output and near-natural speech recognition is just around the corner. Maybe in a couple of years' time, I could be logging on to amazon.com's voice portal, and mumbling the words, "yeah...umm... can I hear a clip of that jazz band who did that song about chips". Without further ado, I am then swiftly linked up to an MP3 recording of Slim Gailard's "Potato Chips", while information about the album and artist scrolls across my PDA's screen. The synthetic operator asks me in natural tones if I would like to include that song on the CD album I'm creating. This is how I envision the future: a world where writing telephony applications becomes the art of directing dialogs, a world where voice is used as the primary interface for applications as commonly as the mouse and VDU screen are today. We're getting there, and VoiceXML is definitely one big step in the right direction.

```
<?xml version="1.0"?>
<vxml version="1.0">
<form id="foo">
<block>
<prompt>
Hi. My name is Bob
</prompt>
</block>
</form>
</vxml>
```

VoiceXML Syntax Reference

This appendix contains a description of each element in the VoiceXML 1.0 language, accompanied by a table that lists attributes available for that element. This table shows attributes that are required in bold face. In some circumstances, exactly one out of several different attributes is required. When this is the case, the description of the element or its attributes indicates this.

It is not envisaged that VoiceXML 2.0 will introduce any significant changes to the elements or attributes as described in this appendix. However, some VoiceXML platforms may not implement VoiceXML 1.0 in its entirety, or they may implement their own proprietary elements or attributes. Such variations are not documented here, as they are subject to rapid change.

<assign>

Assigns a value to a variable.

Attributes

name	The identifier to use for the variable.
expr	ECMAScript expression supplying the value for the variable.

Legal Parents

<block>, <catch>, <error>, <filled>, <help>, <if>, <noinput>, <nomatch>

Legal Children

–

<audio>

Plays the specified sound file.

Attributes

`src`	The URI of the sound file to playback.
`caching`	Indicates what caching to use: `safe` means content is always refreshed, `fast` means a cached copy may be used if it has not expired.
`fetchtimeout`	The period to wait before throwing an `error.badfetch` event.
`fetchhint`	Tells the interpreter how to retrieve a file: `prefetch` means it can fetch the resource in advance when the page first loads; `safe` means the resource should only be fetched when needed; `stream` is used for very large files or streaming media, to tell the interpreter that processing may commence before the file has completed downloading.

Legal Parents

`<audio>`, `<block>`, `<catch>`, `<choice>`, `<div>`, `<emp>`, `<enumerate>`, `<error>`, `<field>`, `<filled>`, `<help>`, `<if>`, `<initial>`, `<menu>`, `<noinput>`, `<nomatch>`, `<object>`, `<prompt>`, `<pros>`, `<record>`, `<subdialog>`, `<transfer>`

Legal Children

`<audio>`, `<break>`, `<div>`, `<emp>`, `<enumerate>`, `<pros>`, `<sayas>`, `<value>`

<block>

A form item to contain other markup elements.

Attributes

`name`	The name of the form item variable that determines whether the block is to be executed. A `<block>` will only be entered if this variable is `undefined`. Defaults to an inaccessible internal variable.
`expr`	The initial value for the variable; ECMAScript `undefined` by default. When an initial value is supplied, the block will not be entered until the variable is subsequently cleared.
`cond`	A Boolean condition that must be satisfied for the element to be entered.

Legal Parents

`<form>`

Legal Children

<assign>, <audio>, <clear>, <disconnect>, <enumerate>, <exit>, <goto>, <if>, <prompt>, <reprompt>, <return>, <script>, <submit>, <throw>, <value>, <var>

<break>

Inserts a pause of a given length in output. Only one of the attributes below may be used at one time.

Attributes

`msecs`	The duration in milliseconds of the pause.
`size`	A named pause that can be either `none`, `small`, `medium`, or `large`.

Legal Parents

<audio>, <choice>, <div>, <emp>, <enumerate>, <prompt>, <pros>

Legal Children

–

<catch>

Contains the markup to execute when the specified event is thrown.

Attributes

`event`	The events that will trigger this <catch> block. Multiple event names can be given, separated by whitespace.
`count`	The interpreter automatically tracks how many times an event has occurred, and a <catch> block with a `count` attribute will not be entered unless the event has occurred at least the number of times specified. The count is reset on re-entering the <menu> or <form>.
`cond`	A Boolean condition that must be satisfied for the <catch> element to be entered.

Legal Parents

`<field>, <form>, <initial>, <menu>, <object>, <record>, <subdialog>, <transfer>, <vxml>`

Legal Children

<assign>, <audio>, <clear>, <disconnect>, <enumerate>, <exit>, <goto>, <if>, <prompt>, <reprompt>, <return>, <script>, <submit>, <throw>, <value>, <var>

<choice>

Defines an item in a menu selection. Text contained by the <choice> elements in a menu can be output by TTS using the <enumerate> element, and forms an implicit grammar for that menu. One and only one of `next`, `expr`, or `event` must be specified.

Attributes

next	The URI of the next dialog or document to transition to for this choice.
expr	An expression to evaluate when the user selects this choice.
event	An event to be thrown when the user selects this choice.
dtmf	A touch tone sequence to select this choice.
caching	Indicates what caching to use: safe means content is always refreshed, fast means a cached copy may be used if it has not expired.
fetchaudio	Specifies the URI of an audio file to play while waiting for the server to respond. If not given, the fetchaudio property is used if defined.
fetchhint	Tells the interpreter how to retrieve a file: prefetch means it can fetch the resource in advance when the page first loads; safe means the resource should only be fetched when needed; stream is used for very large files or streaming media, to tell the interpreter that processing may commence before the file has completed downloading. Defaults to the documentfetchhint property.
fetchtimeout	The period to wait before throwing an error.badfetch event.

Legal Parents

<menu>

Legal Children

<audio>, <break>, <div>, <emp>, <enumerate>, <grammar>, <pros>, <sayas>, <value>

<clear>

Clears one or more variables to ECMAScript undefined.

Attributes

namelist	A comma-separated list of the identifiers to reset. If this is not given, all variables in the current form are cleared.

Legal Parents

<block>, <catch>, <error>, <filled>, <help>, <if>, <noinput>, <nomatch>

Legal Children

–

<disconnect>

Terminates the session by relinquishing the phone line.

Legal Parents

<block>, <catch>, <error>, <filled>, <help>, <if>, <noinput>, <nomatch>

Legal Children

–

<div>

Classifies a section of text as a particular type.

Attribute

`type`	Can be either `sentence` or `paragraph`.

Legal Parents

<audio>, <choice>, <div>, <emp>, <enumerate>, <prompt>, <pros>

Legal Children

<audio>, <break>, <div>, <emp>, <enumerate>, <pros>, <sayas>, <value>

<dtmf>

Declares a touch-tone key grammar. Note that this *may* be deprecated in the VoiceXML 2.0 specification.

Attributes

`src`	This attribute gives the URI if the grammar is external.
`scope`	Defines the extent of the validity of the grammar. `document` makes the grammar active in all dialogs of the current document and relevant sub-documents. `dialog` makes the grammar active throughout the current form. In the absence of this attribute, scoping is determined by the parent element.
`type`	The MIME type of the grammar. The interpreter will attempt to determine the type dynamically if omitted.
`caching`	Indicates what caching to use: `safe` means content is always refreshed, `fast` means a cached copy may be used if it has not expired.
`fetchhint`	Tells the interpreter how to retrieve a file: `prefetch` means it can fetch the resource in advance when the page first loads; `safe` means the resource should only be fetched when needed; `stream` is used for very large files or streaming media, to tell the interpreter that processing may commence before the file has completed downloading. Defaults to the `grammarfetchhint` property.
`fetchtimeout`	The period to wait before throwing an `error.badfetch` event.

Legal Parents

`<field>`, `<form>`, `<link>`, `<transfer>`

Legal Children

–

<else>

Used as an empty element to mark the start of an alternative to execute when the containing <if> element's test condition fails.

Legal Parents

<if>

Legal Children

–

<elseif>

Used as an empty element to mark the start of a conditional alternative for when the containing <if> element's test condition fails.

Attribute

cond	A Boolean test to determine whether to execute the code following the empty <elseif> element.

Legal Parents

<if>

Legal Children

–

<emp>

Changes the level of emphasis for spoken output.

Attribute

level	The emphasis to apply when vocalizing the contained text. One of strong, moderate (the default), none, or reduced.

Legal Parents

<audio>, <choice>, <div>, <emp>, <enumerate>, <prompt>, <pros>

Legal Children

<audio>, <break>, <div>, <emp>, <enumerate>, <pros>, <sayas>, <value>

<enumerate>

Vocalizes the choices of a menu in sequence.

Legal Parents

<audio>, <block>, <catch>, <choice>, <div>, <emp>, <enumerate>, <error>, <field>, <filled>, <help>, <if>, <initial>, <menu>, <noinput>, <nomatch>, <object>, <prompt>, <pros>, <record>, <subdialog>, <transfer>

Legal Children

<audio>, <break>, <div>, <emp>, <enumerate>, <pros>, <sayas>, <value>

<error>

Contains code to handle error events.

Attributes

count	The interpreter automatically tracks how many times an event has occurred, and a <error> block with a count attribute will not be entered unless the event has occurred at least the number of times specified. The count is reset on re-entering the <menu> or <form>.
cond	A Boolean condition that must be satisfied for the <error> element to be entered.

Legal Parents

Legal Children

<assign>, <audio>, <clear>, <disconnect>, <enumerate>, <exit>, <goto>, <if>, <prompt>, <reprompt>, <return>, <script>, <submit>, <throw>, <value>, <var>

<exit>

Ends a session, terminating all loaded documents.

Attributes

expr	A return expression.
namelist	Variable names to be returned on exit. The default is to return no variables, represented by an empty ECMAScript object.

Legal Parents

<block>, <catch>, <error>, <filled>, <help>, <if>, <noinput>, <nomatch>

Legal Children

–

<field>

Contains the grammars, prompts and transitions for a single data item in a form.

Attributes

name	The dialog-scope variable that will hold the input for this field.
expr	The initial value for the field variable; ECMAScript undefined by default. When an initial value is supplied, the field will not be entered until the variable is subsequently cleared.
cond	A Boolean condition that must be satisfied for the field to be entered.
type	The name of a standard internal grammar for the field. In the absence of this attribute, a grammar must be defined by a <grammar> or <dtmf> element.
slot	The grammar slot name to assign to the variable. If not specified, the variable name is used. This attribute is really intended for grammar formats that return sets of slot/value pairs. When the grammar returns only one slot, then the variable is assigned the value of that slot regardless of the slot name.
modal	Affects which grammars are active in the field. The default false means all active grammars are enabled for the duration of the field. Setting to true temporarily disables all grammars except the field's own grammars.

Legal Parents

<form>

Legal Children

<audio>, <catch>, <dtmf>, <enumerate>, <error>, <filled>, <grammar>, <help>, <link>, <noinput>, <nomatch>, <option>, <prompt>, <property>, <value>

<filled>

Contains markup that is executed when the specified fields have been assigned valid values.

Attributes

namelist	Lists the fields that will trigger the <filled> element. Hence, a <filled> element inside a <field> cannot specify namelist or mode, and is fired when that field's variable is filled. For a <filled> in a form, namelist defaults to all that form's field items.
mode	If set to all, the default, the element is entered when all of the specified fields are filled. The alternative is any, meaning the <filled> element is executed when any of the specified fields is filled by the last user input. A <filled> element in a field-level item cannot specify the mode attribute.

Legal Parents

`<field>`, `<form>`, `<object>`, `<record>`, `<subdialog>`, `<transfer>`

Legal Children

<assign>, <audio>, <clear>, <disconnect>, <enumerate>, <exit>, <goto>, <if>, <prompt>, <reprompt>, <return>, <script>, <submit>, <throw>, <value>, <var>

<form>

Contains elements that represent a single dialog, be it two-way or one-way.

Attributes

`id`	A unique identifier for the form.
`scope`	Defines the extent for which grammars defined in this form are valid: either the default `dialog`, limiting the grammar to that form, or `document`.

Legal Parents

<vxml>

Legal Children

<block>, <catch>, <dtmf>, <error>, <field>, <filled>, <grammar>, <help>, <initial>, <link>, <noinput>, <nomatch>, <object>, <property>, <record>, <subdialog>, <transfer>, <var>

<goto>

Invokes a new dialog in either the current document, or an external file. One and only one of `next`, `expr`, `nextitem`, or `expritem` must be specified.

Attributes

`next`	The URI of the dialog to transition to. The `id` of a form can be supplied, preceded by a hash character, `#`.
`expr`	An ECMAScript expression to generate the URI.
`nextitem`	The `id` of the form item in the current form to transition to.
`expritem`	An ECMAScript expression to generate the `id` for the next form item to visit.
`caching`	Indicates what caching to use: `safe` means content is always refreshed; `fast` means a cached copy may be used if it has not expired.
`fetchaudio`	Specifies the URI of an audio file to play while waiting for the server to respond. If not given, the `fetchaudio` property is used if defined.

fetchhint	Tells the interpreter how to retrieve a file: prefetch means it can fetch the resource in advance when the page first loads; safe means the resource should only be fetched when needed; stream is used for very large files or streaming media, to tell the interpreter that processing may commence before the file has completed downloading. Defaults to the documentfetchhint property.
fetchtimeout	The period to wait before throwing an error.badfetch event.

Legal Parents

<block>, <catch>, <error>, <filled>, <help>, <if>, <noinput>, <nomatch>

Legal Children

–

<grammar>

Lists utterances that the speech engine should listen for.

Attributes

src	The URI specifying the location for external grammars.
scope	Defines the extent of the validity of the grammar. document makes the grammar active in all dialogs of the current document and relevant sub-documents. dialog makes the grammar active throughout the current form. In the absence of this attribute, scoping is determined from the parent element.
type	The MIME type of the grammar. If this is omitted, the interpreter context will attempt to determine the type dynamically.
caching	Indicates what caching to use: safe means content is always refreshed; fast means a cached copy may be used if it has not expired.
fetchhint	Tells the interpreter how to retrieve a file: prefetch means it can fetch the resource in advance when the page first loads; safe means the resource should only be fetched when needed; stream is used for very large files or streaming media, to tell the interpreter that processing may commence before the file has completed downloading. Defaults to the grammarfetchhint property.
fetchtimeout	The period to wait before throwing an error.badfetch event.

Legal Parents

<choice>, <field>, <form>, <link>, <record>, <transfer>

Legal Children

–

<help>

Provides markup to execute when an utterance in the standard help grammar is matched.

Attributes

`count`	The interpreter automatically tracks how many times an event has occurred, and a `<help>` block with a `count` attribute will not be entered unless the event has occurred at least the number of times specified. The count is reset on re-entering the `<menu>` or `<form>`.
`cond`	A Boolean condition that must be satisfied for the `<help>` element to be entered.

Legal Parents

`<field>`, `<form>`, `<initial>`, `<menu>`, `<object>`, `<record>`, `<subdialog>`, `<transfer>`, `<vxml>`

Legal Children

`<assign>`, `<audio>`, `<clear>`, `<disconnect>`, `<enumerate>`, `<exit>`, `<goto>`, `<if>`, `<prompt>`, `<reprompt>`, `<return>`, `<script>`, `<submit>`, `<throw>`, `<value>`, `<var>`

<if>

Contains markup that is conditionally processed according to the specified condition.

Attributes

`cond`	A Boolean test that, when `true`, causes the execution of the section starting at the `<if>` tag, and extending up to either the closing tag or any `<else>` or `<elseif>` element.

Legal Parents

`<block>`, `<catch>`, `<error>`, `<filled>`, `<help>`, `<if>`, `<noinput>`, `<nomatch>`

Legal Children

`<assign>`, `<audio>`, `<clear>`, `<disconnect>`, `<else>`, `<else>if>`, `<enumerate>`, `<exit>`, `<goto>`, `<if>`, `<prompt>`, `<reprompt>`, `<return>`, `<script>`, `<submit>`, `<throw>`, `<value>`, `<var>`

<initial>

Contains the elements for a mixed-initiative dialog. It is followed by `<field>` elements to be filled by the initial user response, and to subsequently gather any data that was skipped.

Attributes

name	The name of the form item variable that determines whether the element is to be executed. The <initial> element will only be entered if this variable is undefined. Defaults to an inaccessible internal variable.
expr	The initial value for the variable; ECMAScript undefined by default. When an initial value is supplied, the element will not be entered until the variable is subsequently cleared.
cond	A Boolean condition that must be satisfied for the element to be entered.

Legal Parents

<form>

Legal Children

<audio>, <catch>, <enumerate>, <error>, <help>, <link>, <noinput>, <nomatch>, <prompt>, <property>, <value>

<link>

Defines a transition common to all dialogs in the link's scope, branching control as determined by the attribute next, expr, or event. Every <link> must have one and only one of these attributes.

Attributes

next	The URI of the dialog to transition to. The id of a form can be supplied, preceded by a hash character, #.
expr	An ECMAScript expression to dynamically generate the URI to transition to.
event	An event to be invoked when an utterance matches the link's grammar.
caching	Indicates what caching to use: safe means content is always refreshed, fast means a cached copy may be used if it has not expired.
fetchaudio	Specifies the URI of an audio file to play while waiting for the server to respond. If not given, the fetchaudio property is used if defined.
fetchhint	Tells the interpreter how to retrieve a file: prefetch means it can fetch the resource in advance when the page first loads; safe means the resource should only be fetched when needed; stream is used for very large files or streaming media, to tell the interpreter that processing may commence before the file has completed downloading. Defaults to the documentfetchhint property.
fetchtimeout	The period to wait before throwing an error.badfetch event.

Legal Parents

`<field>`, `<form>`, `<initial>`, `<vxml>`

Legal Children

<dtmf>, <grammar>

<menu>

Contains a dialog that performs an action according to which of the child <choice> elements is matched.

Attributes

id	A unique identifier for the menu.
scope	Defines the extent of the validity of the menu grammar. The default of dialog makes the grammar active in the <menu> alone. document makes the grammar active in all dialogs of the current document and relevant sub-documents.
dtmf	This is false by default. Set it to true to associate an implicit DTMF grammar with any choice without an explicit one, based on the position of that choice within the menu.

Legal Parents

<vxml>

Legal Children

<audio>, <catch>, <choice>, <enumerate>, <error>, <help>, <noinput>, <nomatch>, <prompt>, <property>, <value>

<meta>

Supplies meta data for an application as a name/value pair.

Attributes

name	The name for this meta data property.
http-equiv	The name of an HTTP response header used as an alternative to name. <meta> elements must have either a name or an http-equiv attribute.
content	The value of the meta data.

Legal Parents

<vxml>

Legal Children

–

<noinput>

Contains markup to execute when the interpreter fails to register input for an item.

Attributes

count	The interpreter automatically tracks how many times an event has occurred, and a <noinput> block with a count attribute will not be entered unless the event has occurred at least the number of times specified. The count is reset on re-entering the <menu> or <form>.
cond	A Boolean condition that must be satisfied for the <noinput> element to be entered.

Legal Parents

<field>, <form>, <initial>, <menu>, <object>, <record>,
<subdialog>, <transfer>, <vxml>

Legal Children

<assign>, <audio>, <clear>, <disconnect>, <enumerate>, <exit>, <goto>, <if>, <prompt>, <reprompt>, <return>, <script>, <submit>, <throw>, <value>, <var>

<nomatch>

Contains the markup for when the interpreter fails to match an utterance to any applicable grammar.

Attributes

count	The interpreter automatically tracks how many times an event has occurred, and a <nomatch> block with a count attribute will not be entered unless the event has occurred at least the number of times specified. The count is reset on re-entering the <menu> or <form>.
cond	A Boolean condition that must be satisfied for the <nomatch> element to be entered.

Legal Parents

<field>, <form>, <initial>, <menu>, <object>, <record>,
<subdialog>, <transfer>, <vxml>

Legal Children

<assign>, <audio>, <clear>, <disconnect>, <enumerate>, <exit>, <goto>, <if>, <prompt>, re<prompt>, <return>, <script>, <submit>, <throw>, <value>, <var>

<object>

Provides an interface for non-VoiceXML components.

Attributes

`name`	The name of a variable that takes an ECMAScript value as defined by the object.
`expr`	The initial value for the variable; ECMAScript `undefined` by default. When an initial value is supplied, the object will not be invoked unless the variable is subsequently cleared.
`cond`	A Boolean condition that must be satisfied for the field to be entered.
`classid`	The URI specifying the location of the object. URI conventions are platform-dependent.
`codebase`	Provides a base path to resolve relative URIs in `classid`, `data`, or `archive`. By default, this is derived from the URI of the current document.
`codetype`	The content type of the object that is downloaded from the `classid` URI. By default, this is the same as the `type` attribute's value.
`data`	A URI indicating the location of the object's data.
`type`	The content type of the data indicated by the `data` attribute.
`archive`	A space-separated list of URIs for resources relevant to the object, which may include the URIs of the `classid` and `data` attributes.
`caching`	Indicates what caching to use: `safe` means content is always refreshed, `fast` means a cached copy may be used if it has not expired.
`fetchaudio`	Specifies the URI of an audio file to play while waiting for the server to respond. If not given, the `fetchaudio` property is used if defined.
`fetchhint`	Tells the interpreter how to retrieve a file: `prefetch` means it can fetch the resource in advance when the page first loads; `safe` means the resource should only be fetched when needed; `stream` is used for very large files or streaming media, to tell the interpreter that processing may commence before the file has completed downloading. Defaults to the `objectfetchhint` property.
`fetchtimeout`	The period to wait before throwing an `error.badfetch` event.

Legal Parents

`<form>`

Legal Children

`<audio>`, `<catch>`, `<enumerate>`, `<error>`, `<filled>`, `<help>`, `<noinput>`, `<nomatch>`, `<param>`, `<prompt>`, `<property>`, `<value>`

<option>

Specifies an allowable input for a `<field>` element.

Attributes

<dtmf>	The touch-tone sequence that selects this option.
<value>	The string to assign to the field variable when the option is selected. If not given, the content of the <option> element, with leading and trailing whitespace removed, will be used.

Legal Parents

`<field>`

Legal Children

–

<param>

Parameter to pass to an <object> or <subdialog>.

Attributes

name	The identifier to refer to this parameter from within the object or subdialog.
value	A string literal to assign to the parameter.
expr	An expression that can be used in place of value to compute a value for parameter. One of value or expr is required.
valuetype	For <object> elements only, this indicates whether the parameter value is data (data) or a URI (ref). The default is data.
type	Only applies to <param> used with <object> when valuetype is ref. Indicates the MIME type of the information retrieved from the URI.

Legal Parents

<object>, <subdialog>

Legal Children

–

<prompt>

Specifies a TTS or prerecorded message requesting input from the user.

Attributes

bargein	Controls whether a user can interrupt a prompt. Default is true.
cond	An expression that must be satisfied for the prompt to be spoken.
count	A number indicating the minimum number of times the prompt for this item must already have been spoken before this particular prompt is used.
timeout	The time that the interpreter will wait for input before throwing a noinput event. The default timeout is platform-specific.

Legal Parents

<block>, <catch>, <error>, <field>, <filled>, <help>, <if>, <initial>, <menu>, <noinput>, <nomatch>, <object>, <record>, <subdialog>, <transfer>

Legal Children

<audio>, <break>, <div>, <emp>, <enumerate>, <pros>, <sayas>, <value>

<property>

Provides a means of control over platform-specific settings.

Attributes

name	One of a set of predefined properties.
value	The value to give the named property.

Legal Parents

`<field>, <form>, <initial>, <menu>, <object>, <record>, <subdialog>, <transfer>, <vxml>`

Legal Children

–

<pros>

Alters certain characteristics of TTS output such as intonation. Derived from the word prosody.

Attributes

rate	Speaking rate.
vol	Output volume.
pitch	Pitch.
range	Specifies the pitch range.

Legal Parents

<audio>, <choice>, <div>, <emp>, <enumerate>, <prompt>, <pros>

Legal Children

<audio>, <break>, <div>, <emp>, <enumerate>, <pros>, <sayas>, <value>

<record>

Records a message spoken by the user as an audio file.

Attributes

name	The field-item variable that will hold the recording.
expr	The initial value for the variable; ECMAScript undefined by default. When an initial value is supplied, the recording will not be initiated until the variable is subsequently cleared.
cond	A Boolean condition that must be satisfied for the element to be entered.
modal	Affects which grammars are active. The default true means all active grammars are temporarily disabled for the duration of the recording. Setting to false will enable grammars active at the time. However, most platforms do not support simultaneous recognition and recording.
beep	Set to true to emit a tone just before recording starts. The default is false.
maxtime	The maximum length of the recording.
finalsilence	The interval of silence that marks the end of speech.
dtmfterm	The default true allows DTMF key presses to terminate recording. The DTMF tones themselves are not recorded.
type	The MIME format of the resulting recording. The default is platform-specific.

Legal Parents

<form>

Legal Children

<audio>, <catch>, <enumerate>, <error>, <filled>, <grammar>, <help>, <noinput>, <nomatch>, <prompt>, <property>, <value>

<reprompt>

Restates the currently active prompt.

Legal Parents

<block>, <catch>, <error>, <filled>, <help>, <if>, <noinput>, <nomatch>

Legal Children

–

<return>

Ends the current subdialog, returning control to the calling dialog.

Attributes

`event`	An event to throw on returning to the calling dialog.
`namelist`	Variables to be returned to calling dialog as an ECMAScript object. The default is to return none.

Legal Parents

`<block>`, `<catch>`, `<error>`, `<filled>`, `<help>`, `<if>`, `<noinput>`, `<nomatch>`

Legal Children

–

<sayas>

Allows certain properties to be set to affect how a word or phrase is spoken. This is likely to become `<say-as>` in VoiceXML 2.0.

Attributes

`phon`	A Unicode International Phonetic Alphabet (IPA) representation to be spoken in place of the contained text.
`sub`	Text to be spoken in place of that contained by the `<sayas>` element.
`class`	One of `phone`, `date`, `digits`, `literal`, `currency`, `number`, or `time`.

Legal Parents

`<audio>`, `<choice>`, `<div>`, `<emp>`, `<enumerate>`, `<prompt>`, `<pros>`

Legal Children

–

<script>

Contains a sequence of ECMAScript client-side code to execute.

Attributes

`src`	The URI specifying the location of external scripts.
`charset`	The character encoding for external code specified by `src`.
`caching`	Indicates what caching to use: `safe` means content is always refreshed, `fast` means a cached copy may be used if it has not expired.
`fetchhint`	Tells the interpreter how to retrieve a file: `prefetch` means it can fetch the resource in advance when the page first loads; `safe` means the resource should only be fetched when needed; `stream` is used for very large files or streaming media, to tell the interpreter that processing may commence before the file has completed downloading. Defaults to the `scriptfetchhint` property.
`fetchtimeout`	The period to wait before throwing an `error.badfetch` event.

Legal Parents

<block>, <catch>, <error>, <filled>, <help>, <if>, <noinput>, <nomatch>, <vxml>

Legal Children

–

<subdialog>

Temporarily transfers the interpreter to another dialog, returning to the point of invocation on completion.

Attributes

src	The URI for the <form> or <menu> to call, using the hash character to precede the form identifier: documentURI#formid.
name	A variable to hold the ECMAScript object returned by the subdialog, which will have the properties defined in the namelist attribute of the <return> element.
expr	The initial value for the variable; ECMAScript undefined by default. When an initial value is supplied, the subdialog will not be initiated until the variable is subsequently cleared.
cond	A Boolean condition that must be satisfied for the element to be entered.
modal	Controls which grammars are active during the subdialog. By default, true meaning all grammars active in the calling dialog are disabled. Set to false for them to remain active.
namelist	A list of variables to submit to the server when fetching an external document, by default none.
method	The HTTP request method, either get by default, or post.
enctype	The MIME type for the submitted document. The default is application/x-www-form-urlencoded. Additional types available vary from platform to platform.
caching	Indicates what caching to use: safe means content is always refreshed, fast means a cached copy may be used if it has not expired.
fetchaudio	Specifies the URI of an audio file to play while waiting for the server to respond. If not given, the fetchaudio property is used if defined.
fetchtimeout	The period to wait before throwing an error.badfetch event.
fetchhint	Tells the interpreter how to retrieve a file: prefetch means it can fetch the resource in advance when the page first loads; safe means the resource should only be fetched when needed; stream is used for very large files or streaming media, to tell the interpreter that processing may commence before the file has completed downloading.

Legal Parents

<form>

Legal Children

<audio>, <catch>, <enumerate>, <error>, <filled>, <help>, <noinput>, <nomatch>, <param>, <prompt>, <property>, <value>

<submit>

Sends the information collected by a form to the server.

Attributes

`next`	The URI to which the query is submitted.
`expr`	An ECMAScript expression that can be provided instead of `next` to dynamically determine the URI. Either `next` or `expr` is required.
`namelist`	The list of variables to submit. All field item variables are submitted by default.
`method`	The HTTP request method, either `get` by default, or `post`.
`enctype`	The MIME type for the submitted document. The default is `application/x-www-form-urlencoded`. Additional types available vary from platform to platform.
`caching`	Indicates what caching to use: `safe` means content is always refreshed, `fast` means a cached copy may be used if it has not expired.
`fetchaudio`	Specifies the URI of an audio file to play while waiting for the server to respond. If not given, the `fetchaudio` property is used if defined.
`fetchhint`	Tells the interpreter how to retrieve a file: `prefetch` means it can fetch the resource in advance when the page first loads; `safe` means the resource should only be fetched when needed; `stream` is used for very large files or streaming media, to tell the interpreter that processing may commence before the file has completed downloading. Defaults to the `documentfetchhint` property.
`fetchtimeout`	The period to wait before throwing an `error.badfetch` event.

Legal Parents

<block>, <catch>, <error>, <filled>, <help>, <if>, <noinput>, <nomatch>

Legal Children

–

<throw>

Throws either a predefined event or an application-defined event.

Attribute

event	The name of the event being thrown.

Legal Parents

<block>, <catch>, <error>, <filled>, <help>, <if>, <noinput>, <nomatch>

Legal Children

–

<transfer>

Transfers the user to a new destination.

Attributes

name	A variable to hold the outcome of the transfer attempt.
expr	The initial value for the variable; ECMAScript undefined by default. When an initial value is supplied, the element will not be entered until the variable is subsequently cleared.
cond	A Boolean condition that must be satisfied for the element to be entered.
dest	The URI to transfer to: either telephone or IP telephony address.
destexpr	An ECMAScript expression that can be provided instead of next to dynamically determine the URI. Either destexpr or expr is required.
bridge	Decides the behavior of the interpreter once the call is connected. The default false causes a telephone.disconnect.transfer to be thrown as soon as the call connects. A value of true suspends document interpretation until the transferred call is completed.
connecttimeout	How long to attempt connection before returning the noanswer condition. The default time is platform-specific.
maxtime	The maximum length of the call for when bridge is true. The default 0 indicates the call can continue indefinitely.

Legal Parents

<form>

Legal Children

<audio>, <catch>, <dtmf>, <enumerate>, <error>, <filled>, <grammar>, <help>, <noinput>, <nomatch>, <prompt>, <property>, <value>

<value>

Inserts the value of an ECMAScript expression in spoken output.

Attributes

expr	The expression to evaluate.
class	One of currency, date, digits, literal, number, phone, or time.
mode	Either tts (text-to-speech), or recorded. The default is tts.
recsrc	When mode is recorded, this provides the URI of the audio file to play. Multiple URIs can be supplied, which are then replayed in series.

Legal Parents

<audio>, <block>, <catch>, <choice>, <div>, <emp>, <enumerate>, <error>, <field>, <filled>, <help>, <if>, <initial>, <menu>, <noinput>, <nomatch>, <object>, <prompt>, <pros>, <record>, <subdialog>, <transfer>

Legal Children

–

<var>

Declares a variable.

Attributes

name	The identifier for the variable.
expr	An expression to initialize the variable. If none is provided, variables retain any existing value or are set to undefined.

Legal Parents

<block>, <catch>, <error>, <filled>, <form>, <help>, <if>, <noinput>, <nomatch>, <vxml>

Legal Children

–

<vxml>

Top-level element of any compliant VoiceXML document.

Attributes

version	The version of VoiceXML used in the document. The initial version is 1.0.
base	The base URI for the application.
lang	The language and locale that apply to the document.
application	For multiple-document applications, this provides the URI of the application root document.

Legal Parents

–

Legal Children

<catch>, <error>, <form>, <help>, <link>, <menu>, <meta>, <noinput>, <nomatch>, <property>, <script>, <var>

<?xml version="1.0"?>
<vxml version="1.0">
<form id="foo">
<block>
<prompt>
Hi. My name is Bob
</prompt>
</block>
</form>
</vxml>

Useful Resources

Wrox Resources

Web Sites:

http://www.wrox.com

http://p2p.wrox.com

Books:

Outlook 2000 VBA Programmer's Reference, ISBN 1-861002-53-X

Professional Active Server Pages 3.0, ISBN 1-861002-61-0

Professional ADSI CDO Programming with ASP, ISBN 1-861001-90-8

Professional JSP, ISBN 1-861003-62-5

Professional Outlook 2000 Programming, ISBN 1-861003-31-5

Professional PHP, ISBN 1-861002-96-3

Professional WAP, ISBN 1-861004-04-4

Professional XML 2nd Edition, ISBN 1-861005-05-9

Professional XSL, ISBN 1-861003-57-9

XSLT Programmer's Reference 2nd edition, ISBN 1-861005-06-7

Organizations

VoiceXML Forum Homepage, originators of the VoiceXML specification:
http://www.voicexml.org

W3C Voice Working Group homepage:
http://www.w3.org/Voice

Wireless Application Protocol (WAP) Forum:
http://www.wapforum.org

Specifications

W3C

Voice Extensible Markup Language (VoiceXML) version 1.0, W3C Note, 5 May 2000:
http://www.w3.org/TR/2000/NOTE-voicexml-20000505

Extensible Stylesheet Language (XSL) homepage:
http://www.w3.org/Style/XSL

XML Schema homepage:
http://www.w3.org/XML/Schema

Miscellaneous

ECMAScript scripting language specification:
http://www.ecma.ch/ecma1/stand/ecma-262.htm

Java Speech Grammar Format (JSGF) specification:
http://www.javasoft.com/products/java-media/speech/forDevelopers/JSGF

Java Speech Markup Language (JSML) specification:
http://java.sun.com/products/java-media/speech/forDevelopers/JSML

Software and Tools

Web-based VoiceXML Development Environments and Gateways

BeVocal:
http://cafe.bevocal.com

HeyAnita:
http://freespeech.heyanita.com

Tellme:
http://studio.tellme.com

VoiceGenie:
http://developer.voicegenie.com

Voxeo:
http://community.voxeo.com

VoiceXML Tools

IBM Reusable Dialog Components (RDC):
http://www-4.ibm.com/software/speech/enterprise/wvs-rdc.html

IBM WebSphere Voice Server SDK:
http://www.ibm.com/software/speech/enterprise/ep_12.html

Motorola Mobile Application Development Kit (MADK) version 2.0:
http://developers.motorola.com/developers/wireless

Nuance tools, including SpeechObjects and V-Builder:
http://extranet.nuance.com/developer

Emacs major mode for VoiceXML:
http://studio.tellme.com/downloads/code-emacsmode.html

SpeechWorks ASR software:
http://www.speechworks.com

SpeechWorks' open source VoiceXML interpreter, Open VXI:
http://www.speech.cs.cmu.edu/openvxi

Audio Editors and Tools

CoolEdit audio software:
http://www.cooledit.com

LAME audio encoder:
http://www.sulaco.org/mp3

mpg123 real-time MPEG audio player:
http://www.mpg123.de

Shoutcast Winamp-based distributed streaming audio system:
http://www.shoutcast.com

Other Web Tools

Apache Web Server:
http://www.apache.org

Saxon XSLT processor:
http://users.iclway.co.uk/mhkay/saxon

JavaMail e-mail API:
http://java.sun.com/products/javamail

Curl file transfer tool:
http://curl.haxx.se

IBM WebSphere Studio:
http://www.ibm.com/software/webservers/studio/download.html

Nokia 7110 mobile phone emulator:
http://www.nokia.com/corporate/wap/sdk.html

Online XML Schema validation (XSV) tool:
http://www.w3.org/2001/03/webdata/xsv

Wordnet online lexical reference system:
http://www.cogsci.princeton.edu/~wn

PHP embedded server-side scripting language:
http://www.php.net

APC caching add-on for PHP:
http://apc.communityconnect.com

Zend Cache add-on for PHP:
http://www.zend.com

Geeklog web discussion system:
http://www.geeklog.org

Phorum web-based discussion software written in PHP:
http://www.phorum.org

Books and Articles

How to Solve It, by George Polya (Gyorgy Polya), 1971, Princeton Univ Press; ISBN 0-691023-56-5

Inside Distributed COM, by Guy Eddon and Henry Eddon, published by Microsoft Press; ISBN 1-572318-49-X

Datacomm Research Report:
http://www.datacommresearch.com/voicepr.html

Outlook Object Model and CDO :
http://support.microsoft.com/support/kb/articles/Q237/9/13.asp

Microsoft MiPad multi-modal PDA:
http://research.microsoft.com/srg/mipad.asp

Computer Telephony Labs "Voice Portals Using VoiceXML" Report, Jan 31 2001:
http://www.commweb.com/article/COM20010129S0003

```
<?xml version="1.0"?>
<vxml version="1.0">
<form id="foo">
<block>
<prompt>
Hi. My name is Bob
</prompt>
</block>
</form>
</vxml>
```

Index

A Guide to the Index

The index covers all numbered chapters and the appendices. It is arranged alphabetically, word-by-word, with symbols and numerals preceding the letter A. Angle-bracket element delimiters and hyphens have both been ignored in alphabetizing. Acronyms, rather than their expansions, have been preferred as main entries, on the grounds that unfamiliar acronyms are easier to construct than to expand. Plural forms have been preferred for all concrete terms, although alphabetization may separate them from the singular form in compound phrases. Finally, to avoid repetition, some variant endings are indicated with an asterisk as a truncation symbol.

Symbols

A

B

D

E

F

G

H

I

M

N

O

P

Q

R

S

T

U

V

W

X

```
<?xml version="1.0"?>
<vxml version="1.0">
<form id="foo">
<block>
<prompt>
Hi. My name is Bob
</prompt>
</block>
</form>
</vxml>
```